A Journey into Russia

First published as *Mein russisches Abenteuer* by DuMont Buchverlag, Köln, Germany, in 2012
Copyright © DuMont Buchverlag, 2012

First published in Great Britain in 2014 by The Armchair Traveller at the bookHaus
70 Cadogan Place, London SW1X 9AH
www.thearmchairtraveller.com

English language translation copyright © Eugene H. Hayworth, 2014

A CIP catalogue record for this book is available from the British Library

Print ISBN: 978-1-907973-94-9
Ebook ISBN: 978-1-907973-97-0

Typeset in Minion by MacGuru Ltd
info@macguru.org.uk

Printed and bound by TJ International Ltd, Padstow, Cornwall

A Journey into Russia

Jens Mühling

Translated from the German by
Eugene H. Hayworth

Armchair Traveller
at the bookHaus

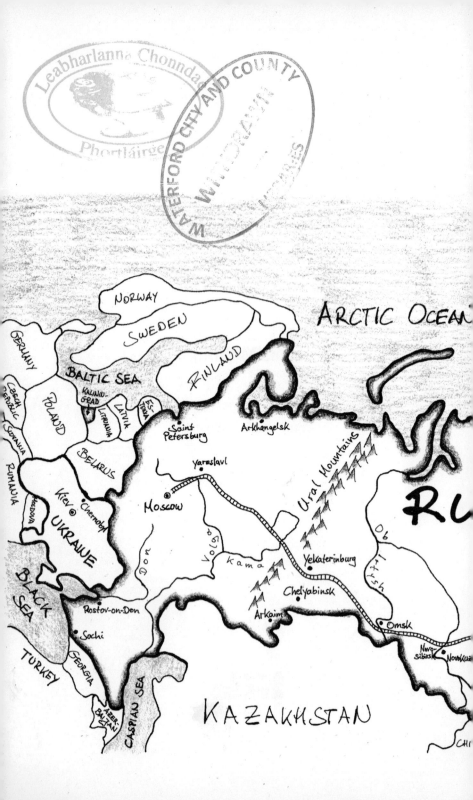

NORWAY

SWEDEN

FINLAND

ARCTIC OCEAN

GERMANY

BALTIC SEA

KALININ-GRAD

POLAND

CZECH REPUBLIC

LATVIA

ESTONIA

LITHUANIA

Saint Petersburg

Arkhangelsk

Ural Mountains

RU

SLOVAKIA

BELARUS

Yaroslavl

RUMANIA

MOLDOVA

Kíev

Chernobyl

Moscow

Don

Volga

Kama

Ob

Yekaterinburg

Irtysh

UKRAINE

BLACK SEA

Rostov-on-Don

Chelyabinsk

Arkaim

Sochi

GEORGIA

TURKEY

AZER-BAIJAN

CASPIAN SEA

Omsk

Novo-sibirsk

Novokuz

KAZAKHSTAN

CHI

Contents

ICE (Kiev)

Higher up the country becomes an utter desert; not a single tribe, so far as we know, inhabits it. It always snows – less, of course, in the summer than in the wintertime. These northern regions, therefore, are uninhabitable, by reason of the severity of the winter.

Herodotus, 5th century BC

Loe thus I make an ende: none other news to thee
But that the country is too cold, the people beastly bee.

Ambassador George Turberville reporting to Elizabeth I of England, 1568

It will be very disadvantageous for us if our neighbours look more closely and carefully at us. The fact that until now they understood nothing about us was a great source of our strength.

Fyodor Dostoyevsky, 1873

The Puzzle

It was the year 2010. For most people. For some it was 7518, for others it was 50, for others still, 1010. On that winter's evening in Moscow, however, all of this temporal dissidence was still in my future. It was to cross my path during the course of a long year which had only just begun, and for the time being, it was 2010 to me.

It was one of those Moscow nights where it is afterwards no longer possible to say when the line was crossed between casual drinking and complete inebriation. From their fourth trip to the kiosk, Sasha and Vanya had brought back a bottle purchased entirely for its name: *Tri Starika* said the label – 'Three Old Men'. The three of us clinked glasses to the joys of old age. After the first sip we decided on no account to grow old in Russia.

Sasha was on top form. His toasts grew longer with each glass, more eccentric, more philosophical. When we had emptied about two of the three old men he looked at me, suddenly serious.

'This book,' he said. 'If you really want to write about Russia, you have to remember one thing. Get something to write with.'

'Sasha, I'm not that drunk, I'll memorise it ...'

'Get something to write with!'

Something in his eyes made me obey. As I came back into the kitchen with a notepad and pencil, Sasha bent over the table and began to dictate: 'The inscrutable Russian soul ...'

I groaned. Sasha aimed a stern index finger at the notepad. 'Write!' Shrugging, I picked up the pencil.

'The inscrutable Russian soul ...' he repeated, while I dutifully scrawled his words onto the page, '... does not exist.'

I looked up. Sasha kept a straight face. 'Write! There's more.'

When I discovered the notepad the next morning under a mountain of dirty dishes, Sasha and Vanya were still sleeping. I made myself coffee to get rid of my hangover, and with difficulty deciphered my scribbles:

The inscrutable Russian soul does not exist.
The Russian soul is no more inscrutable
than the headache after a night of drinking.

Russia entered my life as a lie.

It was the year 2000 (for most people). One summer day a friend, Kristina, called me; we knew each other from university. Kristina was nearing the end of her degree. She wanted to be a journalist. A notice at the university had caught her eye:

TV producer looking for interns!

A man with a heavy Slavic accent had answered the phone and invited Kristina to his apartment. He said he worked from home. Kristina sensed an opportunity but was wary of the circumstances – would I mind coming along just to be on the safe side?

A few days later we were sitting in Yuri's living room. He was in his late twenties, good-looking in an eccentric kind of way, a lanky, haphazardly dressed type, who served us tea and Russian sweets. Yuri's German was good but he spoke slowly, with a strong accent and long, reflective pauses, making his sentences sound unintentionally serious. We had been talking for about five minutes when he asked us to come over to his computer. He wanted to show us a film that he had produced for a German TV station.

'Russia's millionaires have everything money can buy,' the sonorous voice of a speaker said, while on the TV screen business men in big cars drove past landmarks that I could vaguely connect to Moscow. 'There is only one thing they cannot buy,' the voice continued. 'The unexpected!'

The camera zoomed in on a man in a necktie, mid-forties, with cold facial features. 'Igor S., Millionaire,' a subtitle stated, while the speaker's voice dubbed over the man's Russian sentences. 'I came into money in the Nineties. It wasn't always easy – you know what I mean.' Igor fired an invisible gun in the direction of the camera. 'But those times are over. And you know what? I miss the thrill of that time. The unpredictable, the adventure. I'm rich, but my life has turned grey.'

For people like Igor, the speaker continued, an exclusive club had now been launched in Moscow whose members, for an exorbitant membership fee, were guaranteed three unexpected experiences per year. The employees of the 'Agency of Controlled Coincidence', all of them former KGB agents, explored the everyday lives of their clients in detail; men with hard, grey faces appeared on the screen, bent over maps, whispering, playing with binoculars and cameras. At the appropriate time, they had seemingly random attractive women cross the paths of their victims – in the elevator, at the petrol station, in a beach café, on the golf course. Using the shaky perspective of a secret service film, the movie let the viewers witness some of these staged encounters, their erotic dénouement left to the imagination the minute the camera discreetly swivelled sideways.

Towards the end of the film Igor S. came back to speak again. The club had changed his life, he said. Because he never knew when a controlled chance encounter would pop up in his life, he basically regarded every woman he encountered as a potential agent of the club – and, therefore, experienced not three adventures a year, but dozens. Grinning, he lit a cigar. Cut. Commercial.

Yuri looked at us expectantly.

'That's incredible,' I said. 'This club – who would come up with something like that?'

Kristina didn't say anything. She just stared mutely at the TV screen.

'*I* would come up with something like that,' Yuri said. 'There is no club. The story is invented. The actors are friends of mine.'

Kristina remained silent. I smiled uncertainly.

'You know,' said Yuri, 'the real stories in Russia are more incredible than anything I could invent. It's just that no one in Germany will buy them from me. So I tell the stories about Russia that people here want to listen to.'

I felt as if I had been caught red-handed. The film had indeed confirmed the vague image I had of Yuri's homeland.

Kristina cleared her throat. It had just occurred to her, she said, that she was supposed to be at an appointment that she had completely forgotten about. She urgently needed to leave.

I stayed a bit longer. Together, Yuri and I finished off the sweets. He talked about Russia, about his studies, his career in private television. It had gone well for him, but at some point he just couldn't take Moscow anymore and had gone to Berlin. He didn't know anyone in Germany, but he had managed to build a small studio that sold television films reasonably successfully.

I asked what had been so bad about Moscow. Yuri thought about it for a moment. 'Russia is a pretty interesting country,' he said. 'And that's really the problem. It's *too* interesting. Too much happens. You don't know in the morning how the day will end.'

He elaborated on this thought for a while. I listened in silence, while somewhere in the back of my mind a seed was planted. I tried to imagine a country where too much happened. A country where the real stories were more incredible than the invented ones.

The next day Kristina called me. She did not want to begin her journalistic career with fake television films. She had called off the internship with Yuri.

I called Yuri and accepted.

Before I met Yuri, Russia was a white speck on my internal map. More precisely: a hole.

As a child I had a large puzzle. Assembled, it revealed a map of the world. Each country had its own colour. Some colours filled many puzzle pieces, others only a few. Some countries – Liechtenstein, Malta, Andorra – were so small that they shared their puzzle piece with other countries. These were the simple countries. You knew immediately where they belonged.

There were very many olive-coloured puzzle pieces. That was the Soviet Union. It was larger than every other country, much larger. The Soviet Union was the most difficult country of all. It was more difficult than the oceans, which were of course even larger, but for those you could follow the longitude and latitude, whose helpful grid spanned all the light-blue pieces of the puzzle. There were no lines in the Soviet Union, only uniform olive-coloured puzzle pieces that all looked alike. Every time I put the puzzle together, I left the Soviet Union until the end. And at this unfinished stage the map of the world has forever etched itself onto my mind: a colourful puzzle with a big, frustrating hole on the top right.

By the time my internship began in the autumn of 2000, Yuri had lost interest in inventing stories. He was now occupied with scientific topics.

He was working on a piece about a Russian mathematician for a German TV show. On my first day at work he explained to me what I needed to know.

'The man's name is Anatoly Fomenko, and he has figured out that we actually live in the year AD 1000, not 2000.'

'Right,' I said. 'Good.'

Yuri had met Fomenko in Moscow. He showed me filmed excerpts from the interview: in a small cubicle sat a lean man in his sixties, whose face was hard to make out behind a pair of giant glasses. On the walls hung pictures that Fomenko, Yuri explained, had painted himself. I could vaguely make out black and white surrealist landscapes, with mountains made of skulls, melting watches, dancing columns of numbers.

We got to work. Yuri translated Fomenko's Russian sentences into German; I revised them and wrote a synchronised text. Sentence by sentence we went through the interview. Only towards the end did I begin to understand the mathematician's weird theory.

Fomenko's world consisted of numbers. They were everywhere, you only had to ferret them out. Sometimes they hid behind other, incorrect numbers, but Fomenko would not let himself be fooled. He treated historical numbers with particular suspicion – almost all conventional dating of historical events he deemed incorrect. To discover the real numbers, he had developed a method which he used to evaluate historical chronicles. He freed such texts first from their non-mathematical ballast. In essence, for Fomenko a documented history was just a succession of political rulers: King A is replaced after four years by King B, who is followed after thirteen years by C, C after two years by D, after whose seven-year reign the chronicle ends. Thus Fomenko reduced texts that filled hundreds of pages to short formulas:

He had done this with a great many texts. Herodotus, Tacitus, Cicero, Thucydides, the Bible, the Torah, the Vedas, the Quran; the entire treasure chest of historical narratives of the world melted away under Fomenko's hands into short sequences of numbers. The amazing thing was this: it was always the same sequences of numbers. In chronicles that described historically widely separated events, Fomenko discovered identical patterns in the successions of rulers:

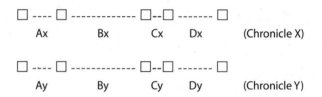

Fomenko drew a bold conclusion from these similarities: in reality the chronicles described the same events, the same rulers, the same era. It was only later that they had been reinterpreted as descriptions of different eras. 'The complete historical chronology that we are taught in school,' Fomenko said in the interview with Yuri, 'is based on errors, falsifications, lies and manipulations.'

When I had jotted down this last sentence, I looked doubtfully at Yuri. 'Do you believe this stuff?'

He focused on the question and thought about it for some time. 'I don't consider it to be a question of faith,' he then said. 'From a logical point of view, I can't find any error in the theory.'

I nodded silently. As I remembered at that moment, Yuri had mentioned at our first meeting that he had studied cybernetics in Moscow. I didn't even know exactly what cyberneticists do. What did I know about logic?

In order to illustrate Fomenko's methods, Yuri had designed a computer animation. A timeline appeared on the screen, divided into fields of different length, which were labelled with the names of great dynasties. Initially the timeline was motionless; then the great Fomenkodance began: individual fields broke away from their historical mooring and wandered homelessly up and down the timeline until they found fields with an identical structure, with which they then merged in an uncanny fashion. The Habsburgs joined with the Holy Roman Empire of the German Nation; the Romanov dynasty turned into the Carolingians; Charlemagne became Ivan the Terrible. Watches melted, columns of numbers danced, 2000 years of history cast off their malignant tumours, 1000 years remained.

Hesitantly I looked at Yuri. He grinned. It was at that moment that I began to grasp the meaning of his assertions about fiction and reality. Russia being populated by crazy millionaires appeared pretty plausible to me. Anatoly Fomenko, on the other hand, seemed like a character from a contrived science fiction film.

The day ended again with tea and sticky sweets. While Yuri talked about Russia, my eyes wandered back and forth between him and the screen, where the history of the world was still performing its confusing dance in an endless loop. I caught myself adding a new puzzle piece to my image of Yuri's homeland. I tried to imagine a country where history could be chopped into pieces and reassembled anew.

Years of puzzles followed. Shortly after my internship with Yuri I went to Russia for the first time. I wanted to get to know the country. On one of my first nights in Moscow I got caught in a fist fight between an Orthodox monk and his clandestine lover. I decided to come back at all costs.

I learned the language. Over the course of one long, ice-cold winter I took a class at Moscow's Pushkin Institute, where an ageing Pushkin enthusiast let loose the six-headed monster of Russian declension on me: *'Puuushkin! Puuushkin-a! Puuushkin-u! Puuushkin-a! Puuushkin-ym! Puuushkin-e!'*

I read. Cities and rulers added themselves to my puzzle: Kiev, Moscow, Saint Petersburg. Yaroslav the Wise, Dmitry the False, Ivan the Terrible, Peter the Great. *Tsar, tsarya, tsaryu, tsarya, tsarem, tsare.* Nicholas I, Alexander II, Alexander III, Nicholas II. *Revolutsiya, revolutsiyi, revolutsiyi, revolutsiyu, revolutsiey, revolutsiyi.* Lenin, Stalin, Khrushchev. *Sotsializm, sotsializma, sotsializmu, sotsializm, sotsializmom, sotsializme.* General Secretary D is replaced after 18 years by General Secretary E, who is followed after 15 months by F, F after 13 months by G, after whose six-year reign the Soviet Union ends. *Perestroika, perestroiki, perestroike, perestroiku, perestroikoy, perestroike.*

I travelled. From one jigsaw puzzle piece to the next. I saw the peaks of the Caucasus, the forests of Siberia, the volcanoes of Kamchatka. I swam in the Moscva and the Volga rivers, in the Black Sea and in Lake Baikal. I experienced the chaos in Chechnya, the revolution in Kiev, the war in Ossetia.

Ten years after my encounter with Yuri I was working as a journalist for a daily newspaper in Berlin. My main focus was Russia. When anything happened there, the editor-in-chief called me into the morning conference and said: 'Now Mühling will explain the Russian soul to us.' I would explain. With a little guilt. Because at heart I still considered this Russia to be the old riddle from my childhood: a stack of olive-green jigsaw puzzle pieces next to a large, frustrating hole. The stack grew, but the pieces did not come together as a whole. The country was too large, too contradictory; you hardly knew where to begin. And what the newspapers said, including what I wrote myself, all too often resembled my tables of declension: *Putin, Putina, Putinu, Putina, Putinym, Putinye.*

In a large, unsorted drawer of my desk I kept excerpts from the Russian press. Whenever I noticed something in the newspapers or on the Internet I cut it out and put it with the other slips of paper, so I could come back to it later. On rainy days when there was nothing else to do I sometimes skimmed through the drawer, looking for something other than the usual news stories.

SCIENTISTS DECIPHER RUSSIAN GENE

REMAINS OF ANCIENT SETTLEMENT DISCOVERED
IN THE SOUTHERN URALS

DON COSSACKS DEMAND NATIONAL INDEPENDENCE

PETERSBURG PRIEST CONSECRATES STALIN ICON

Over the years the drawer, with its inscription 'Russia, Ideas', grew fuller and fuller. I lost track of some stories long before I got my hands on them again. Such discoveries were the most profitable, because with the passing of time they sometimes appeared to me in a completely different light. So it was with the story of Agafya Lykova, which I pulled out of the clutter of newspaper clippings one rainy day.

OLD BELIEVER HERMIT REFUSES TO LEAVE THE TAIGA

It was a short account about a religious hermit. Agafya Lykova lived alone in the forests of southern Siberia, more than 200 kilometres away from the nearest settlement. She was one of the so-called 'Old Believers', a splinter group of the Russian Orthodox Church. Her parents had fled to the Taiga shortly before the Second World War, to escape the Red Terror of the Bolsheviks. They had started their journey with two small children; another two, including Agafya, were born in the wilderness. For more than 40 years the family had lived there without any contact with the outside world. It was only in 1978 that Soviet geologists had accidentally encountered the Old Believer hermits.

Agafya, the youngest daughter, was by now the only survivor of the family. People had repeatedly urged her to abandon her hut in the Taiga and move to civilisation. She refused.

A few years must have passed since I had cut out the article. I could still remember that I had thought of Yuri while I tucked the slip of paper into the drawer – it was one of those Russian stories that sound so unbelievable they can only be true. At that time, however, I had no idea what Old Believers were. Now I knew. And that gave a whole new meaning to Agafya Lykova's story.

In the not exactly bloodless history of Russia, the 17th century was one of the bloodiest. A bizarre religious controversy divided the country: people argued over the question of whether to make the sign of the cross with two fingers or with three. The Moscow Patriarch, who advocated for the three-finger cross, persecuted the followers of the two-finger cross viciously; he had unruly believers' hands chopped off, and their priests' tongues ripped out. Many rendered the mutilations unnecessary by simply chopping off their own thumbs in order not to have to blaspheme God with three fingers. Whole communities barricaded themselves in their churches, set their altars on fire and watched as the flames ate away at their hands, two fingers outstretched to the very end.

The conflict had been sparked by one man who exerted all of his dubious ambition to rectify the course of history. Around the middle of the century Patriarch Nikon, head of the Russian Orthodoxy, introduced a church reform. He invoked the origins of the Orthodox faith: the Russians had adopted Christianity from Byzantium in 988, when the Grand Duke of Kiev baptised his subjects according to the Greek rites. Over the centuries the inevitable happened: little by little, the Russian Orthodoxy developed its own, non-Greek traits, arising partly as a result of incorrect translations of Greek liturgical texts, but more often through the everyday practice of the faith. No Russians considered

11

these characteristics to be a betrayal of their Orthodox roots. Patriarch Nikon alone was embarrassed when he received Greek dignitaries in the Kremlin, whose astonishment at the customs of the Russians did not escape him.

With his reforms, Nikon attempted to rectify the most obvious deviations of the Russian liturgy from the Greek. At first glance, they were trifles: the Trinity was no longer praised with two hallelujahs but with three; one letter was to be added to the name of the Lord, 'Iisus' instead of 'Isus'; there should be not seven loaves but only one on the altar during the Eucharist; finally, the sign of the cross would no longer be made with two fingers but with three, the way the Greeks did it.

These interventions might have been accepted without complaint if at the same time much more drastic changes had not been overtaking Russia. The long isolated country was opening up to the West. Things appeared that had never been in Russia before; tobacco, tea and coffee; trimmed beards; sacred images with saints barely recognisable, so outlandishly were they depicted; foreigners, summoned by the Tsar to modernise the country, brought foreign manners to Russia, foreign languages and foreign gadgets. On the main tower of the Kremlin wall a huge mechanical clock from England appeared, the first in all of Russia. Its message was unmistakable: the times were changing.

All of these upheavals had one thing in common with Nikon's reforms: they made Russia look bad. Many Russians did not want to admit that the traditions of their fathers should suddenly be worth less than the inventions of foreigners, be it English clocks, Dutch paintings, German books or Greek church rules. The Old Believers, as the opponents of reform were soon called, rejected Nikon's heresies as vehemently as the ever-advancing West. Their two-fingered cross became a gesture of resistance against a Russia that was betraying its roots in every respect.

The times were changing. And perhaps, as the Old Believers in fact suspected, the world was actually approaching its prophesied end. There was evidence. As the religious controversy reached its bloody climax, people in Russia wrote the year as 7174 – their calendar started with the creation of the world. But in the West, where the years were numbered from the birth of Christ, a different number appeared on the calendar, a terrible one: 1666. There could be no doubt: the foreigners were messengers of the apocalypse.

While Russia drifted towards the west, the Old Believers fled towards the east. Persecuted by the Patriarch's henchmen, they withdrew to the sparsely populated, peripheral regions of the Russian Empire. They founded communities where time stood still, where nothing diluted the spirit of old Russia, no tobacco and no coffee, no razor and no clockworks, not one hallelujah too many, not one altar loaf too few.

Centuries passed. Whenever the Old Believers came under pressure they simply withdrew a bit deeper into the Siberian forests. The strategy succeeded until 1917, when revolution broke out in distant Saint Petersburg, plunging Russia into a new bloodbath. The missionaries who now appeared in the villages of the Old Believers neither made the cross with two fingers, nor with three; they did not cross themselves at all. Instead, they preached truths that a German philosopher had put into their heads: religion is an opiate; there is no God.

The Old Believers did what they had always done: they fled deeper into the wilderness. In the Thirties, however, as Soviet agriculture was forcibly collectivised, planning squads invaded even the most remote settlements. In one small community in Southern Siberia they encountered resistance. A shot was fired; an Old Believer died. Horrified, the brother of the murdered man decided to turn his back on the world for good. Taking his wife and two small children, Karp Lykov wandered into the wilderness. When his youngest daughter Agafya was born a few years later, the old Russia had withdrawn to a tiny corner of the Taiga.

I read the newspaper clipping over and over. Outside, drops of rain beat against the windowpane. Inside, my puzzle started moving.

It seemed to me that chance had dealt me a tiny, at first glance incidental, detail, on which in some cryptic way half the puzzle hung. At the crucial crossroads of Russian history, the Lykovs and their ancestors had consistently taken a step in the opposite direction. Along historical side-paths Agafya Lykova had ended up in the Taiga, and according to the newspaper article she was still living there. She was the last inhabitant of a Russia that would cease to exist after her death.

I read through the notes that I had scribbled on the edges of the newspaper article: Kiev 988, Moscow 1666, Petersburg 1917, Siberia 1978. It read like stations along a journey.

I asked my editor-in-chief for a year's leave and said goodbye to my friends. One winter's morning I boarded an overheated night train at Berlin's Zoo station. In the next compartment sat a young Polish couple whose sweet nothings whispered through the deserted corridor while the train car began to move in ghostly silence. It wasn't until the Tiergarten flashed past the windows that the sounds of their romance were drowned out by the beating wheels.

Russia is not a Country

Poland started with the shimmering purple ice floes of the Oder and culminated in a crescendo of barbed wire and uniforms. A sign with the inscription 'Dorohusk' pushed against the windows of my compartment as the train slowed. Military boots had left dance-step patterns in the snow. A few hastily renovated administrative buildings seemed overwhelmed by the historic task that was expected of them in their old age: suddenly, the horizon of a continent had moved to under their windows. Taken by surprise, they kept watch over it.

On my journey, the Polish-Ukrainian border was the first of many more or less arbitrary dividing lines between Europe and that nameless, unstructured hinterland that did not, or no longer, or not yet, or not entirely, belong to Europe, or did not want to, or was not permitted to, or should, or could, or must belong to Europe – God only knows. The only thing that can be said with clarity about such borders is that behind them is where the ambiguities begin.

The train was more carefully prepared for the changeover than the passengers. When we reached the no-man's land between the barriers, workers in overalls decoupled the train cars and rolled them onto hydraulic lifts. In turn, the wheel frames were replaced, to prepare the train for the wider rail tracks which begin behind the border and extend to the Pacific Coast. The distance between the Russian tracks, as one of the workers explained to me, is 85 millimetres wider than the European ones; replacing the chassis can take up to three hours, depending on the train. I wrote down the numbers with the feeling that the complicated differences between Europe and Russia had to be hidden somewhere in this simple formula.

On the Ukrainian side of the border a young female customs officer examined our passports. She was barely out of earshot when the Russian fellow traveller in my compartment burst into laughter. 'Did you hear that?' He chuckled with delight.

'What?'

'That language!' Chuckling, he raised his voice two octaves and imitated the customs officer: '*Dokumenty, bud lasko!*' For a moment he let the soft twitter of the Ukrainian sounds reverberate, before he changed back to his native Russian language. 'They speak like children! Ah, these sweet Ukrainians!' His fat cheeks quivered with laughter.

Oleg came from Moscow; he worked as a sales representative for a former state-owned company and had been travelling the Moscow-Warsaw train route for almost three decades. He had crossed the Ukraine almost as often as his living room, but it had only become evident to him at a late stage that the residents of this neighbouring republic had their own language. It was the year Oleg's firm and the Ukraine decided, at the same time, to no longer be Soviet state property. Oleg had never grown accustomed to either. The privatisation of his company had cut deep lines of stress across his forehead. The independence of the Ukraine, however, amused him no end.

'In the beginning, they were still ashamed. On the train they just quietly whispered to each other, like children who have gotten into some kind of mischief. It was only when the customs officers started to speak Ukrainian that the passengers also slowly dared to. And today … today …' A fit of laughter left him momentarily speechless. '… Today they sometimes act as if they don't understand my Russian! Like children who have invented a secret language!'

With my right foot I discreetly pushed the compartment door shut. Oleg spoke so loudly that the entire carriage had to listen to his chauvinistic giggling, and when it comes to their national honour, Ukrainians understand Russian very well.

'Forget all this talk about independence,' Oleg continued. 'Ukraine was never independent – never! The eastern part was always Russian, the west Polish, Lithuanian, Austrian. Now they have their own country and come up with nothing but sheer nonsense: a Ukrainian language, a Ukrainian history, their own government. Their language is a peasant dialect, their history a fairy tale, their state a circus.' Amused, he shook his head. 'It is not really a country at all.'

Even so, the next morning I disembarked in Kiev, the capital of a non-country.

Ice blanketed the city. In glassy streaks it covered the sidewalks and slowed the movement of pedestrians to a tentative dance step. Everyone was cursing – the roads had not been cleared for weeks; no one knew why. Red and white streamers of barrier tape ran through the city centre like the web of a huge plastic spider. I ducked under the barriers like everyone else. I understood what they meant only when a giant icicle shattered into a thousand fragments close by my feet. I carefully raised my head. Under the eaves of the roof a reptile's glass teeth grinned at me.

The Dnieper River, which divides the city into two distant halves, was completely frozen. Little black points stood out against the white of the snow-covered river. As I grew closer, they became human silhouettes. They were ice fishermen. Hundreds of them crouched motionless beside their boreholes.

Again I found myself at one of those illusory dividing lines that separate Europe into an inside and an outside. West of the Dnieper, the country that is now called Ukraine had been ruled for centuries by European powers, while the East, Kiev included, had belonged mostly to Russia. Only after the Second World War were both regions combined into a Soviet Republic. Collectively they had declared their independence after 46 years of socialist marriage. Only later did the two unequal spouses begin to argue about their provenance, about their relationship to Europe and Russia. Now that the first threats of divorce hung in the air, the Dnieper roughly marked the border on which the Ukraine based its marital quarrel.

But that was not the reason I had to begin my travels here. I was seeking the vestiges of a much older border. Russia's narrative had started in Kiev. Here, on the banks of the Dnieper, the country had emerged from the foggy realm of myth, to join the more clearly contoured paths of history.

I tried to imagine it: a day in the year 988, perhaps a spring day, but perhaps also a bitingly cold winter's day like today; it's possible the men had to break holes in the ice of the Dnieper. The season is not documented, only the fact that prince Vladimir of Kiev personally supervised the baptism of his subjects.

As the ruler of the young empire named Kievan Rus, Vladimir had recently decided to replace the pagan polytheism of his subjects with a more contemporary state religion. He sent out scouts to learn more about the fashionable monotheisms which had sprung up throughout the surrounding kingdoms. He rejected Islam immediately when he learned about the Muslim Bulgars' abstinence from alcohol: 'Drinking is the joy of the Rus,' declared Vladimir. 'We cannot go without it.' The Judaism of the nomadic Khazars seemed unfit for state purposes, and in the churches of the Catholic Germans the Prince's scouts had 'beheld no glory.' What Vladimir's emissaries reported about the churches of Byzantium, however, sounded quite different: 'We knew not whether we were in heaven or on earth. For on earth there is no such splendour or such beauty, and we are at a loss how to describe it. We know only that God dwells there among men, and their service is better than the ceremonies of other nations.'

So it was the Christian God in His Greek Orthodox manifestation that Vladimir decided upon. The King had the old pagan wooden idols, whose bellies must have still been glistening with the fat of the last sacrificial offerings, unearthed and cast into the Dnieper. I wondered if he had watched with pride or with qualms as the pantheon of fallen Slavic gods passed by, Perun and Khors, Dazhbog and Stribog, Semargl and Mokosh, with their wooden bodies and silver heads and golden moustaches.

Then came the day on which, it is said, the devil groaned in despair, for he lost the people of Rus. Vladimir had his subjects gather at the shore of the Dnieper. No one understood the Greek Baptism prayers that accompanied the sacrament given by the priests, who had come especially from Byzantium. Had they, I wondered, only sprinkled the people on the banks with river water drop by drop, or had the entire people waded into the Dnieper, jubilant and unclothed, as it was later depicted on the icons?

I scanned the riverbank and tried to bring the story to life. But I was cold, my concentration was dwindling, and I felt the first steps in Russia's 1000-year history retreat right before my eyes. High above the river bank Prince Vladimir stood on the hills, larger than life, a neon cross in his extended copper hand; but his pose seemed lifeless, a pompous embodiment dating from the 19th century, later illuminated. It has been a long time since this statue stood on Russian ground. Russia's borders have shifted eastward, and it seemed to me now that all that was left of the founding myth of the country was the sputtering answer of Russian students, given when they are asked to date the beginning of their homeland's history: 988, the Baptism of Rus. Was I looking for more than a number in a textbook?

Just as I was about to leave, one of the ice fishermen stood up and looked up into the hills above the shore. Church domes lined the snowy slopes, gold on white, a wintry bed of onions. The fisherman raised his fingertips to his forehead, to his chest, to the right, then to the left shoulder before he touched the ice at his feet with the palm of his hand. He repeated the gestures a second and a third time before he lifted the ice drill to his shoulder and went on his way.

Sluggishly, the fallen wooden gods floated along the Dnieper River. They left Kiev behind them; they crossed the southern steppes and were finally washed into the Black Sea. And with them a chapter of Russia's past disappeared. Because what happened prior to the Baptism is now largely unknown.

Herodotus, the Greek historian who travelled the Black Sea coast in the 5th century BC, struggled in vain to gather reliable information about the world north of the Scythian steppes. 'No one can give any exact account,' Herodotus complained. Once he was told of barren deserts, once of impenetrable forests or marshes, populated by the most incredible tribes: bald-headed, goat-footed and even one-eyed. Even farther north, the Greek learned, the sun only shined when it rained elsewhere, while in the summer one storm followed the next. Herodotus noted the rumours sceptically. There was only one he trusted: unbearable cold prevailed to the edges of the known world. The air to the north, the Scythians assured him, was 'full of feathers', and what was behind the feathers, nobody knew. In any case, people could not possibly live in those frozen wastelands.

It must have been a shock for Herodotus' Greek readers when, a few centuries later, the first Nordic longboats emerged from the flurry of feathers, manned with warriors, their hair and beards as pale as the snowy landscapes from which they came. The Norman Varangians, relatives of the Vikings, reached the Byzantine world over the branching river system that connects the European north with the Black Sea.

Along the way, on the banks of the Rivers Neva, Daugava and Dnieper, they met a people who had rarely been seen until then: the Slavs.

If one believes the single source that reports the meeting of these two feathered peoples, their encounter was more than unusual. The tightly run expeditions of the Varangians, their streamlined boats, their success as traders and as warriors, must have made a great impression on the Slavic people living along the rivers. Tired of the incessant feuds that devastated their own domain, some of the Slavic tribes decided in 862 to approach the 'Rus', one of the ruling clans among the Varangians.

'Our land is great and rich,' they explained to the astonished Normans. 'But there is no order in it. Come reign as princes, rule over us.'

Supposedly, it was three Varangian brothers who journeyed eastwards together to fulfil the Slavs' desire. Rurik, the firstborn, founded a principality; Kiev became its power centre. Two ice-dwelling cultures merged, and from then on the Slavs and their Varangian rulers were referred to by the same tribal name: Rus.

The Greeks must have followed the birth of this northern hybrid state with a few shivers. They would feel reconciled only a good century later, when Rurik's great-grandson Vladimir brought Byzantine Christianity to Kiev. Mysteriously, by that time every trace of the Varangians had disappeared from Russian history – within a century, Igors and Olgas had displaced the Ingvars and Helgas in the dynastic family trees. Did the Varangians abandon their Norse names and adapt themselves to their subjects, did they become Slavs? Or is the entire history of their takeover a legend? Only a single Russian chronicle refers to it. Nevertheless, until the 17th century Russia's princes and tsars considered themselves heirs of a Norman race, as descendants of Rurik. It was only later, after the extinction of the Rurik dynasty, that a strange kind of national shame arose – suddenly no one wanted to admit that Russia allegedly owed its name and its statehood to a foreign people. Generations of patriotic historians tried to expel the Varangians from the national history. None of them succeeded entirely.

From the shores of the Dnieper a narrow path leads to the wooded hills above the city. When I arrived at the top I stopped and traced the course of the river with my eyes. It curved before it disappeared into the haze – a huge, ice-grey question mark.

The man who had documented Russia's beginnings stares out of coal-black eyes into the darkness. His hands rest on a desk surrounded by the instruments of his guild: the quill to the right, the inkwell to the left, between them an open book. But all these attributes descend into the dark edges of the painting, outshone by a dazzling halo that glows behind the strangely disembodied head of the chronicler. Nestor, the historian of the Rus who was canonised as a saint by the Russian Orthodox Church, was born a good century after the mass baptism in Kiev; he reconstructed the takeover of the Varangians and the introduction of Christianity from earlier, now lost chronicles. His *Tale of Bygone Years* is the oldest extant chronicle of the Eastern Slavs. Nestor put it down on paper in a monk's cell at the Kiev Cave Monastery, which was founded shortly after the arrival of Christianity. The labyrinthine passages wind through the hills west of the Dnieper shore to this day. With one candle in hand I followed the narrow tunnels until Nestor's icon appeared before me.

I continued to stand in front of the holy image for a while. In the confines of the dark passage pilgrims and tourists pushed their way in front of me, some crossing themselves as they passed, others stopping and pressing their lips to Nestor's hands, his monk's robe, the wooden frame of the icon. Motionless, the chronicler listened to the prayer of one young woman who whispered to him for several minutes.

I thought about the words of the chronicle, which Vladimir's scouts had used to praise the Byzantine churches: 'On earth there is no such splendour or such beauty.' In particular, it must have been the Orthodox icons, which had so overwhelmed the emissaries, that made the German churches seem colourless and empty in comparison. I looked down the corridor. An army of saints guarded the walls. Their faces were difficult to keep apart in the darkness, but that only intensified their effect. In the candlelight only their eyes were recognisable. They were so eerily animated that I involuntarily realised what the Slavic scouts must have felt in their presence: 'That God dwells there among men.'

Nestor's gaze inspected the pilgrims who passed his icon in an endless procession. Many people stopped to kiss the glass lid of a coffin that stood in a niche under the holy image. It took me a moment to comprehend that coffin and icon belonged together, that the body bulging through the convex shroud was Nestor's mummy. Nature's sleight of hand preserves him from decay, like all the other saints in glass coffins who line the corridors of the monastery. A trick of nature – or God's Will, whichever. Some of the shrouds contain small, gaping holes from which protrude holy hands, shrivelled claws, their fingers curved as if in fivefold proof of God's existence. Nestor's corpse is completely covered, but the knowledge that under this cloth rests the hand that documented Russia's beginnings surrounds the coffin like a historical halo.

After the October Revolution the Bolsheviks transformed the monastery into a 'museum of atheism'. They stuck scornful messages on the icon's wooden frameworks, explaining that the items on exhibit illustrated the lunacy of a lost world. At least they left them hanging there. After the Revolution other icons ended up in the Dnieper. Just like the Slavic gods 1000 years earlier, it was now Christian saints floating down the river, under a heaven in which, as it was said, God no longer lived.

'You are not allowed to take photographs here!'

A monk blocks the path of a tour group in one of the monastery churches. 'No photographs! This is a house of God!'

The tour guide confronts the man. 'Get out! You have no business here! Stay in the monastery, where you belong!' She turns to the tourists. 'Take your photographs! This is a museum; you paid an admission fee.'

'Money!' the monk exclaims. 'God is not for sale!'

'Get out! I'll call the security guards!'

The man reluctantly clears the way. Frightened, the tourists push past him.

'Don't listen to him,' the tour guide hisses. 'He's crazy.'

I intercepted Natalya during her lunch break, after she had said goodbye to her tour group. She was about 60, an energetic woman in an enormous mink coat. Her voice was the volume of a Red Army choir. Even when she whispered, her Russian was brutal and piercing. That is the way someone speaks, I thought, who has spent decades drowning out the sound of school groups.

I no longer remember how we started talking about God. Natalya assured me that she had never believed. At the same time, she spoke so emotionally about the wonders of the caves that I had difficulty accepting she was an atheist. 'Have you seen the mummies? 118 saints! Thousands of monks were buried in the caves, and even now no scientist can explain why some have decomposed and others have not. One-hun-dred-and-eight-teen! Where else is that possible?'

She talked about the miracles of icons, about mysterious healings. I could not shake the feeling that at the bottom of her heart she had changed sides long ago. That she did not admit it, not even to herself, seemed to have complicated reasons. She had considered the monastery a museum for her entire life. She was suspicious of the fact that monks had started living here again. Monks might know something about miracles, but what did they understand about fire prevention, about the restoration of icons, about tour groups? Did monks know how to drown out the sound of a school class?

Hence the argument I had observed that morning. 'The abbot sends his people into the museum to scare the tourists,' Natalya said. 'They would love to take over the entire monastery.'

So far, only half of it belonged to them. The caves had been given back to the Orthodox in the symbolic year 1988, 1000 years after the Slavs' baptism. The lower part of the monastery now belonged to the Russian Orthodox Church, the upper part to the Ukrainian state. In the caves, the Patriarch ruled. In the museum, Natalya.

'Come,' she said. 'I'll show you something.'

We crossed the central courtyard. Natalya unlocked the side entrance of a small church and pushed me into the dimly lit interior. She waved her arm around the nave. The complete interior was painted with frescoes.

'Look at these pictures,' she said. Her eyes glistened. 'These are *our* icons. *Ukrainian* icons.'

I scoured the walls, but I discovered nothing Ukrainian. The pictures looked like baroque European frescoes. Saints gesticulated in despair, frightened merchants fled the temple, their faces distorted by fear before an angry Christ. I thought about the Russian icons in the caves, about their stoic glances, their rigid facial expressions, the petrified gestures of blessing formed by their hands. The contrast to the emotional drama of the mural paintings could not have been greater.

'They look a bit Italian,' I said carefully. 'Or Dutch.'

'But they are Ukrainian! Ukrainian!' Natalia cried. 'The European style is just precisely what accounts for our icons! You talk like the abbot! Not Orthodox, he says, not canonical! He would prefer to have everything here painted over with Russian icons.'

Natalya's voice grew louder, until her rage filled the entire nave. 'Do you know what the Russians call us Ukrainians? Little Russians! And yet *we* are the true Russians! *We* are the descendants of Kiev Rus! The Muscovites didn't start calling themselves Russians until the 18th century – they stole our name! They are not even rightfully Slavs; the scientists have found that their genes are 70 per cent Tatar, Finnish, Estonian ...'

Natalya was now gesturing as fiercely as the saints on the walls. It looked as if she was standing in the centre of a large, patriotic choir who, under her direction, were singing the hymn of the Ukraine. I listened silently until she concluded with a sentence I had heard not long ago in a train compartment, although the other way around.

'That Russia – it is not really a country at all!'

It took me a long time to find the oldest part of the caves. The entrance was supposed to be on a hill south of the monastery, away from the stream of pilgrims and tourists. I found the hill quickly, but what was waiting for me at the top was so strange that I forgot what I was looking for. Mythical stone creatures blocked my path. One behind the other, they lined the slopes above the riverbank: huge, eccentric villas, some still unfinished with just bare brickwork – the district had to be as new as the wealth of its inhabitants. Directly in front of me a centauric daydream jutted into the heavens: the head of the Neuschwanstein Castle on the body of the Chrysler Building. In one icy fountain Greek goddesses picked grapes. When a steel gate opened beside me, I got a look into the nave of a cathedral-like garage. Three black jeeps rolled out in solemn procession, the bonnet mascots emerging first like the icons in a priest's outstretched arms.

Opposite this capitalist sanctuary, on the other bank of the Dnieper, stand the prefabricated housing units of the Soviet Era. Their battered gray fills the horizon, a monument to Soviet brotherliness, or to brotherly indigence, depending on your perspective. I wondered if the residents of the villas had deliberately settled within sighting distance of these Socialist slums, if the view gave them the feeling of being on the winning side of history. Once again the gods in Kiev had changed. Now it's the oligarchs who triumphantly look out over the river, just as the Communists had done 100 years before them, and the Christians 1000 years before that. The Dnieper flows patiently toward the south. No wooden gods and icons float along its water now, just the reflections of a crumbling utopia.

In the shade of one of the villas I finally discovered the entrance to the caves. It was closed. But I was lucky. Not far away a group of people were crowded around a priest. The priest had a full black beard and a thunderous bass voice. As I soon realised, his audience was listening to the bass without seeing the beard. Some wore dark glasses; others squinted with unfocused eyes at the winter sky.

'Those of you who see nothing at all,' the priest roared, 'please keep close to those who see a little bit better. And watch out for the candles, my lovelies!'

I mixed in with the blind people inconspicuously. When the priest looked in my direction I fixed my eyes vacantly on a point near his left ear. He smiled benevolently. Then he unlocked the chapel door, distributed thin yellow candles, and showed us the way to the underworld.

Hesitant feet probed their way down the steps. I at first dodged the burning candles, a reflex in the narrow confines of the corridor, but a sixth sense seemed to show the blind ones the way; they moved almost more confidently in the dark than I did. When an old woman grabbed my arm she seemed more in search of company than support; her quiet chatter did not cease.

'You're not from the home, are you? Isn't it wonderful here? Each Sunday we make these trips. The last time we were in the Vladimir Cathedral, where a wonderful deacon prayed with us. Wonderful, completely wonderful …'

She only grew silent when the priest's bass voice began to roll through the aisles. He talked about the Mongols. In the 13th century they had overrun Kiev and in the general chaos that swept the city, the entrance to the caves had been blocked. By the time the Mongols withdrew a century later, the subterranean monastery had been forgotten. It was only at the end of the 19th century that a rainbow appeared in a Kiev woman's dream, its luminous end pointing up a hill on the southern bank of the Dnieper. The woman followed the directions and stumbled upon the covered mouth of a tunnel.

A strange image presented itself to the archaeologists who entered the caves a little later. In the cloister's burial niches they found 96 skeletons, systematically laid to rest. Another 35 skeletons were scattered around the cave floor, in contorted positions. These were the remains of the monks who had been trapped alive in the caves during the Mongols' onslaught. Six centuries had since passed, too much time to determine whether they had starved, died of thirst, or suffocated. The Church canonised them as martyrs and their bones were laid out beside the older skeletons in the burial niches.

The priest's voice swelled like a roll of thunder as he invoked the suffering of the martyrs. His bass voice dashed across the centuries: first the Mongols had attacked the caves, then the Bolsheviks. The last abbot of the Soviet era had been shot in 1937; his predecessor had starved to death in a labour camp four years earlier. Since then both had been canonised. The bones of new martyrs filled the burial niches.

'Pray with me now, my lovelies,' the priest concluded. 'Pray with me to the Holy Martyrs.' He let the long-drawn syllables of the chant echo through the corridors. The blind people joined in.

'Oh Holy Fathers, revered martyrs and passion-sufferers of the Sverinets Caves, pray to God, the All-Merciful, for our sins …'

Singing, the procession continued on their way through the corridors until we reached the burial niches. Gray bones lay in the chambers, behind metal gratings, which the priest dismissed as 'purely symbolic.' 'Touch the relics, my lovelies! Hold them, it will do you good.'

His lovelies did it. Groping hands pushed through the metal bars. The blind people smiled, enraptured, when their fingers divined the outlines of a skull, a tibia, a curved rib. The old woman at my side groped, searching the walls. 'Where? Where?' I took her hand and led it, hesitant at first, then with purpose, over the curves of a pelvic bone. Her dead eyes gleamed like the flames of a candle. 'Yes …' she whispered. 'Yes …' Her fingers seemed to sense something that escaped my eyes. Suddenly I felt out of place and inferior – a sighted sceptic among blind believers.

This was not the first time that I experienced the miracle of the Orthodox revival. All over Russia I had seen the full churches and the holy images on buses and taxis, and I had often wondered how all of that was possible in a country where hardly any church had been open for 70 years. Half of Russia seemed to be grasping blindly for a faith of which little remained – little except bones.

Lenin's Nose

Everything about him is pushing forward. The striding leg, the extended chin, even the nose. The nose hangs ten metres above the Bessarabian Square in Kiev's city centre. It is made of granite and it belongs to Vladimir Ilyich Lenin. The revolutionary olfactory organ protrudes boldly into the wind.

The longer you look, the less you understand which way the wind is blowing. Lenin's granite body braces himself against an invisible resistance, his eyes searching the horizon as if he is longing for an opponent. You wonder what this man is still fighting for, where it urges him to go after all these years; you follow his eyes – but there is nothing. Time has taken away the meaning from this pose. Now it only illustrates the saddest of all historical fates: the man on the pedestal stares forever into a future that has passed without ever becoming the present.

A red tent stands at the foot of the monument. In front of the tent stands Vera Yefimovna, and Vera Yefimovna is now completely in character.

'You wonder what is going on here? I can tell you, young man. I can tell you precisely!' She must be about 70, but her eyes sparkle like those of a young pioneer. 'Ukrainian fascists have chopped off the nose of the leader of the world proletariat!'

My eyes wander up and down the monument, from the base to the apex. Lenin's nose is there, where it belongs.

'We had to replace the entire head! And the left hand! They assaulted him with a hammer! Fascists!'

Her angry monologue is erratic; it takes me a while to sort out the events. Last summer, it must have been about eight months ago, Lenin's nose was knocked off. I do not find out who has done this; Vera Yefimovna only talks about 'fascists'. In the meantime the monument has been restored, at the expense of the Kiev Communists, who have also set up the tent next to Lenin. Since then, Vera Yefimovna and her comrades have guarded the statue around the clock, in shifts, the men at night and the women during the day. They do this on an honorary basis, usually in threes; there are two more women standing beside the tent.

We chat. The women show me photos of Lenin monuments from all over the world: Havana, Calcutta, Copenhagen. Lenin is worshipped everywhere, it is only in the Ukraine that people want to cast him off. There is even a Berlin Lenin, but the photo is old and I don't have the heart to tell the women that the statue was demolished years ago. I feel sorry for them. The two who are showing me the pictures are even older than Vera Yefimovna. They seem happy to have found a mission late in life in a world that otherwise has little use for communists.

'Are you one of us?' they ask. 'Are you our man?'

I don't understand. They giggle. 'GDR or FRG? East or West?'

I understand. 'I grew up in West Germany.'

'But you're in favour of Soviet power?'

The question is so unexpected that an answer does not occur to me right away. 'I never lived under Soviet power,' I say cautiously. 'I cannot imagine socialism.'

They nod silently. Now they are the ones who feel sorry.

Vera Yefimovna reaches for my arm. 'Two, nine, five, eight, eight, seven, zero. My telephone number. Call me. We will meet and I will explain socialism to you.'

Then she disappears. Her replacements are there. Three men take the night shift, two of them retirees, the third recognisably younger; he wears a threadbare officer's jacket. I hear them whisper with the women – a German, interested in Lenin; no, from the West. The man walks up to me, with a sarcastic smile on his lips. Before I can even greet him, let alone attack, he opens with a counter-attack.

'So you are one of those who think that the Soviet Union is the ultimate evil.'

'I ...'

But it is pointless. I cannot stop him. This war started before either of us was born and it is not in my power to stop it.

'Freedom, always your talk about freedom – what kind of freedom is it that is imposed on foreign nations by force?'

He does not wait for my answers; he does not need them, he knows my answers well. I open and close my mouth like a beached fish, incapable of interrupting the flow of his words. He puts accusations in my mouth that I have never formulated, only to retaliate with counter-accusations: East Berlin 1953? Serbia 1999! Budapest 1956? Afghanistan 2001!

Prague 1968? Iraq 2003! We face each other like two empires. I am the West, I am America, I am NATO. Most of all, I am the bourgeoisie.

'Of course you would love to exterminate us communists, young man, you can't help it; it is your historical role and you play it very well. In the Ukraine, meanwhile, the bourgeoisie has managed to displace the Communists almost completely from Parliament. Don't tell me that was the will of the Ukrainian people! You are much too intelligent to fall for the manipulations of the international exploiting class ...'

Just this once I manage to interject an answer. 'I assume that people do not vote for the Communists because they never apologised.'

'Apologised?' With mock astonishment he raises an eyebrow. 'For what? Name just one crime we must apologise for.'

'I have no bills to settle with you.'

'One. Just one.'

I know that I will not change him. Yet, I say that I saw the Sverinets Caves; I mention the priests who were shot – 'Why', I ask, 'for what?'

He laughs – a dry, ugly laughter. 'Dialectic, young man. Very simple. The priests alleged: There is a God. The Bolsheviks established: There is not. Idealism against materialism. Incompatible theses. Only one can prevail. The law of history.'

His cynicism takes my breath away. 'History did not shoot bullets,' I protest.

'Oh yes, young man,' he replies, smiling. 'Oh, yes. And it will shoot again, whether you like it or not.'

After a quarter of an hour I feel like I have given up inside. My concentration is waning, and with it my Russian. I look at Lenin. His left hand, the one that has been replaced, is fixed in the gesture of an orator who forever agitates the masses. But the audience is dying out. It is only the pigeons who can still be agitated here, and sparrows, and a stray German.

The two old women from the early shift follow our discussion, smiling. I am not sure whether they understand the argument, whether they are aware of it at all. As I leave, they say goodbye to me as if I were a relative.

In the evening I searched the Internet for Lenin's nose. I found a confessional video by the attackers, filmed in the summer of the previous year.

It begins with a man who steps out of the coarse-grained night to face the camera, not young and not old, his hair cropped, his voice hoarse and tense. 'My name is Mykola Kokhanivskiy. I am a Ukrainian nationalist. I am carrying out the President's order to dismantle the monuments of the totalitarian past. Glory to the Ukraine!'

Cut. Five men put a very long ladder into place. An ugly scratching and scraping, until its upper end rests on Lenin's chest. Kokhanivskiy tosses a bag over his shoulder. After 28 steps, he stands at eye-level with Lenin; the Communist's head is twice as large as that of the nationalist. Kokhanivskiy pulls a hammer out of the bag.

The recording is very grainy; the work of destruction can only be imagined. Sparks fly, pounding echoes through the night, iron on granite, again and again. Cars drive by, passers-by turn their heads, on the surrounding balconies an audience gathers. No one asks questions, no one intervenes. Finally two militiamen appear at the foot of the ladder. Cut. End.

'Hello? Hellooo?'
  'Vera Yefimovna, hello, this is …'
  'My little German!'
  'Exactly. You wanted to explain socialism to me, you remember?'
  'I will explain everything to you! When should we meet?'

We met a few days later on the left bank of the river, in one of the prefabricated housing districts I had seen from the monastery caves. Someone had described the area to me as a quarter for Soviet bigwigs, built for the privileged of the old system. It was difficult to imagine. Endless rows of concrete blocks pushed their way past the window of my bus, and I did not understand how anyone could consider it a privilege to live here. It wasn't until I got out and began to walk to the meeting place that I noticed that the neighbourhood was not half as depressing as it had appeared from the opposite bank of the river. The prefabricated buildings only seemed interchangeable at first glance. Generations of residents had cobbled together glass and wood remnants to expand the balconies into winter gardens, which adorned the facades like a mosaic of scarce resources. Poplars and birch trees lined the river, and even now, in the winter, it was easy to foresee how green the waterfront must be in the summer. With a bit more imagination I could now even picture how, 50 years ago, a young lecturer of Marxism-Leninism must have proudly accepted the keys to his new apartment, how he had sat on the balcony drinking his first end-of-the-work-day beer, and how, patting the belly of his pregnant wife, he had silently thanked the great Lenin.

The real residents of the neighbourhood now looked at a completely different urban backdrop. On the opposite bank of the Dnieper the onion domes of restored churches gleamed, flanked by the fancy villas of the nouveau riche. Vera Yefimovna hated God, and she hated money. Now, both spoiled her view side by side.

'Have you seen Brezhnev's dacha? The mightiest man in the Soviet Union lived in a tiny wooden building! And now look at these palaces – who do these people think they are? They haven't lifted a finger in their entire lives! They push money back and forth, and nothing else!'

We sat in the foyer of an old Intourist Hotel. At first I did not understand why we had arranged to meet here, of all places, but after a while it dawned on me: the hotel lobby had to be one of the few public places where pensioners could sit in the warmth without paying any money. The hotel staff ignored us. They did not even take notice when Vera Yefimovna unpacked the cookies she had brought with her, which we crumbled all over the leather sofa.

She had prepared herself. Along with the cookies she pulled a file out of her handbag. She spread articles clipped from Party newspapers in front of me: 'The Truth About the Bourgeoisie'; 'Twenty Years of Economic Genocide'; 'Why They Lie to Us'. In addition, she put down six handwritten pages. These were her theses on socialism. She read them to me out loud, with a resolute voice. This is how I remember our conversation: a life story interrupted by loudspeaker announcements.

'First! The Slavs have a stronger public spirit than other peoples, a more pronounced awareness of the collective. It wasn't by chance that the USSR – the Union of Socialist Soviet Republics – was founded by the Slavs.'

She was born in the late Thirties. In a small settlement in the eastern Ukraine, surrounded by the steel mills and coal pits of the Donets Basin. In her childhood memories a grandmother loomed; her parents, in contrast, remained vague, as if they had never been the main characters in the drama of her life.

'Second! The Germans gave the world Marx and Engels, who formulated the laws of the development of human society. The Slavs gave the world Lenin and Stalin, who implemented the idea of Socialism into reality.'

Her childhood ended early. When the Germans came, the men from the settlement were sent to war; the women and the children were evacuated to Kazakhstan. After the war she returned home, but her house was no longer standing. Vera Yefimovna never saw her father again. Only one single man from the street where she had spent her childhood returned from the front. The man's wife was overjoyed; she spent all of her money at the shop and baked a cake. Then she summoned all the street's fatherless children: 'Children', she called, 'look, I will show you something! This here, this is called a cake! This is how we ate before the war!'

'Third! In the Thirties, capitalism needed a war. All of Europe kneeled in the dust before Hitler. It was only the USSR who annihilated fascist Germany.'

A few years after the war a neighbour showed her a book with pictures of old paintings. They were the Russian classics: Repin, Levitan, Kuindzhi, Surikov. Vera Yefimovna looked at the paintings. She was 11, her childhood over, but she had discovered the love of her life: pictures.

A few years later Stalin died. Vera Yefimovna took the next train to Moscow. She was too late for the mourning parades, but she saw Stalin laid out in the mausoleum, right next to Lenin. She cried as she had never cried before.

'Fourth! Until the October Revolution Russia was an illiterate, agrarian state. My grandmother was a simple woman from the country; she could neither read nor write. I, her granddaughter, have two university degrees.'

At a provincial Ukrainian university she enrolled in Chemistry, out of common sense, not out of passion. During the day she stared wearily at the periodic table of elements; her nights belonged to the pictures. She read everything available at the local library; after paintings she discovered photography, and after photographs, the cinema. When she had completed her degree in Chemistry, she applied to the Moscow Film School. Hundreds of candidates competed for a place. During the entrance examination they pulled pictures out of a stack; those who could not name the painting right away were out. Without hesitation,

Vera Yefimovna replied: Repin, Levitan, Kuindzhi, Surikov. She was accepted. She became a cinematographer.

'Fifth! Out of all the arts, the cinema is the most important – Lenin said that. Charlie Chaplin brought the little man to the screen, but only the USSR gave the world directors who made the proletarians heroes: Eisenstein! Pudovkin! Dovzhenko!'

After her studies they sent her back to the Ukraine, to Kiev. They gave her work in the Dovzhenko Film Studios, named after one of the greatest directors of the Soviet pioneer years. On the premises was an apple tree that Alexander Dovzhenko had personally planted. When Vera Yefimovna sat under the tree, her heart sometimes ached with pride. There she sat, the granddaughter of an uneducated peasant woman, and reaped the fruits of the Revolution.

'Sixth! It was not the capitalist countries, but the USSR that sent the first cosmonaut into space: Yuri Gagarin, the son of a peasant family.'

The years passed. Vera Yefimovna was no longer young, but not yet old, when one day the people in Kiev began to whisper. One claimed to have seen smoke, yellow clouds high above the edge of town. Another had heard about firefighters who lay dying in the hospitals. The relatives of a third had already fled to the south; a fourth said: I know people in the Party, they deny everything, and if they deny it, then it must be true. Nonsense, said Vera Yefimovna, who was herself in the Party and knew of nothing – if that were true, they would have cancelled the May Day parade!

But the parade was held. On 1 May 1986, just like every year, Vera Yefimovna carried a big poster of Lenin through Kiev, while no more than 100 kilometres away a power plant was burning: the V. I. Lenin Nuclear Power Station at Chernobyl.

'Seventh! When the power plant exploded we all stuck together, like in the war. Immediately, there were heroes who voluntarily went into the burning reactor, to prevent something even worse from happening. The Soviet Union saved the world from disaster.'

Two years after the accident Vera Yefimovna drove to Chernobyl. For four months she dragged her camera through the restricted zone that surrounded the burned-out reactor; she made a documentary film. Two decades had passed since then, but the images were still stuck in her head. While she talked about shooting the film, she cupped her right hand again and again over an invisible lens that she panned across an imaginary landscape.

'Close-up. Barbed wire. On the barbs – raindrops. They dissolve, falling down like tears. Pan out on the wide shot. Behind the barbed wire – the abandoned city of the nuclear workers. A painting! Everyone in the cinema cries!'

After Chernobyl, many things were no longer as they had been before Chernobyl, so they called the documentary 'The Brink'. When it opened in the cinemas, the title suddenly sounded as if it meant a completely different brink – the one faced by a whole country who stood before it with bated breath. What lay behind this brink was, for Vera Yefimovna, even more terrible than Chernobyl. It was the biggest conceivable accident in world history: the Soviet Union exploded, its core melted, and in one uncontrolled chain reaction the country began to split.

Powerless, Vera Yefimovna looked on as her world crumbled. The Soviet empire dissolved; one Soviet republic after another went its own way, including, in the end, the Ukraine. Moscow's European satellites swung into other orbits, even the Germans suddenly turned against Marx. A little later war broke out in Yugoslavia and during the NATO bombing of Belgrade the Serbian ambassador in Kiev held a shambolic press conference. Vera Yefimovna filmed the man for television. She had memorised his warnings.

'Eighth! Today a new fascism is emerging in Europe under the leadership of the USA and the European Union. After Yugoslavia, the next war of the bourgeoisie will be against the Ukraine. NATO's first bomb will fall on the Kiev hydroelectric power station; half the city will drown.'

A dark, chaotic storm shattered Vera Yefimovna's world. In a short time everything Lenin had built was lost. Only Lenin himself still stood on Bessarabian Square, but even that was no longer a matter of course. Many other Lenin monuments had been dismantled after independence. Recently, about a year ago, a politician had proposed placing any remaining Lenins on an island in the Dnieper and building a 'Park of the Soviet Era' around them, as a tourist attraction. Vera Yefimovna found the proposal outrageous. When shortly afterwards the nationalists came with their hammer, she was almost grateful that she was now able to stand beside her red tent every day and explain to people why Lenin belonged in their midst and not in an amusement park.

'Ninth! I hate the bourgeoisie. I do not want to live under the bourgeoisie; it is like stepping back in time. As if tomorrow feudalism were to be reinstated.'

One day a television crew appeared at the Lenin monument. They interviewed Vera Yefimovna on camera. 'What is your greatest dream?' the journalists asked.

'I dream,' she answered, 'about going to the train station and buying a ticket to the Soviet Union.'

The next day she was approached by an unknown woman on the bus. 'Weren't you on television yesterday?' Vera Yefimovna nodded proudly. What had happened then angered her so much that to this very day she couldn't even find words to describe it; instead she mutely handed me a photo. It showed her face. I didn't recognise it immediately, because between so many bruises there was little face left. The woman on the bus was not a supporter of the Soviet Union.

'Tenth! Of course there were errors, there were mistakes. Only someone who does not act does not make mistakes – Lenin said that. We had to construct Communism from nothing. Nobody showed us the way; we were the first who had taken it. We were like Gagarin in space.'

Vera Yefimovna snapped her file shut. She looked at me silently for a few seconds.

'Any questions?'

I had listened to her account mostly without saying a word, and the many questions that had gone through my head seemed in the unexpected silence of the hotel lobby suddenly meaningless. Two young receptionists cast amused glances at me. During Vera Yefimovna's lecture I had seen them raise their eyebrows a few times, but after a while they had become accustomed to the unusual rhetoric and continued filing their fingernails. Now their glances seemed to say: poor fellow, how did you fall into the hands of this madwoman? I looked away. Vera Yefimovna and I might be living in different worlds, but as much as her world view alienated me, I could not deny my sympathy for this woman.

'You talked about errors, Vera Yefimovna, about mistakes,' I finally said. 'What were those mistakes?'

It wasn't clear to me until after the conversation that Vera Yefimovna had understood my question differently than I had intended. I was thinking about the priests who had been shot, the camps, the show trials, the deportations. She asked herself, however, why her world had been lost.

'The Soviet government was too good to the people,' she said. 'It was too soft, too mild.' Her eyes narrowed in anger; she spoke the words now with a hardness that was meant to rectify all the softness of the past. 'We were not strict enough with our enemies. That was our error.'

The man who had Lenin's nose on his conscience almost crushed my fingers with his huge hands. I met Mykola Kokhanivskiy in a cafe downtown; a Kiev journalist had given me his phone number. On the telephone we had not found a common language – I hardly understood his Ukrainian, and he did not want to speak any Russian. Nevertheless, we managed somehow to arrange to meet. He brought his lawyer to the meeting, as a translator. At first I took his refusal to speak Russian as a political whim – the two languages are very similar, and almost every Ukrainian understands Russian, most grow up bilingual. But when Kokhanivskiy finally changed to Russian after all, because the cumbersome back and forth of the translation slowed the fury of his speech, I realised that he actually did have a poor command of the language. He rarely spoke it; he did not like it. For him it was 'the tongue of the occupiers.'

Nevertheless he did not come, as the political geography of the country would have suggested, from the western Ukraine. He had grown up in a small town in the southeast, not far from the Black Sea. 'Cossack soil,' he said. He pronounced the words with a tenderness which transformed his choleric face for a moment into that of another, gentler man.

Every trace of this man disappeared as Kokhanivskiy spoke about his family history. He talked about his grandparents, who had fought against the Bolsheviks after the October Revolution, like so many here, where the new regime had managed to consolidate its power only with difficulty and violence. Even in the Thirties Stalin distrusted the peace in the Ukraine. When he again sensed resistance during the forced collectivisation of agriculture, he broke the indignation of the peasants with an artificially induced famine. This also happened in other parts of the Soviet Union, but nowhere did it hit the peasants as hard as in the Ukraine. Millions died; some say dozens of millions. No one knows the exact number, because in many regions there was simply nobody left to count the dead.

No one could estimate the number of victims in Kokhanivskiy's family either. One uncle starved in early infancy, four of his grandfather's brothers had been sent to Siberian camps. These were the cases Kokhanivskiy had found documented in archives. Other family members had survived only in the memories of relatives, their stories passed along in whispers from generation to generation – just like a sentence from Lenin that Kokhanivskiy had heard from his father: 'In the hands of the workers' state, the bread monopoly is a weapon more potent than the guillotine.'

Kokhanivskiy let the sentence linger, then he suddenly leaned forward; I felt his breath on my face. 'It was Lenin's idea to starve the Ukrainians. It was implemented only after his death, by Stalin, but the plan was Lenin's. And they want to put *me* on trial! Me! *Lenin* should be on trial!'

For half a year now Kokhanivskiy had been waiting for his trial. The investigation dragged on. The prosecutor was still considering the evidence, specifically: the fragments of Lenin's nose. Kokhanivskiy was accused of hooliganism, defined in the Ukrainian criminal code as 'unmotivated violence'. Kokhanivskiy did not admit guilt. He hammered his arguments on the table top with the palm of his hand: 'My violence (*wham!*) is extremely (*wham!*) motivated (*wham!*).'

He did not consider his assault a crime. He referred to an 'Ordinance for the Dismantling of Monuments from the Totalitarian Past,' enacted by Viktor Yushchenko, the president who rose to power in 2005 after the Orange Revolution. There were many things that Yushchenko had wanted to change in the Ukraine, among them the country's relationship with Lenin. But his ordinance was so vaguely formulated that it was easy for the responsible authorities to ignore. Not much had come of Yushchenko's other revolutionary promises, which is why the Ukrainians had quickly voted him out of office again.

'But his ordinance is still in force!' Kokhanivskiy cried, followed by a *wham!* from the palm of his hand. 'And if nobody else will implement it, then I will implement it myself!'

He had been planning the assault for a long time. First he had practiced on smaller monuments, to know what to look out for. 'Granite is hard to destroy. You have to know where the sensitive areas are. You need to strike the nose!'

A grin spread across his face, and not for the first time in the course of our conversation did I feel something like affection for the angry man. In his better moments Kokhanivskiy simply seemed to be a driven man who could not let injustice rest – and as long as he only took out his revenge on monuments, at least he would not take it out on people, which he was certainly capable of.

In his worse moments Kokhanivskiy was a hostage of a past he wanted to shatter. For two hours I listened to sentences that began with justified anger, before they grew hopelessly mired in conspiracy theories. All of the pain and suffering of the Ukraine, in Kokhanivskiy's eyes, had come out of Russia, and could only be rectified with further suffering. You had to strike the Russians where it hurt the most; you had to destroy their history. Monument by monument, nose by nose.

'Now they want to build a park for Lenin!' Kokhanivskiy moaned, shortly before we said goodbye. 'Build a park, for all I care. But not in Kiev! In all of the Ukraine there is only one single place where Lenin would be rid of me.'

I looked at him questioningly. He raised his hand.

'Chernobyl!'

Wham!

The Saviour of Chernobyl

Early in the morning I set out and drove through the snow and the dawn until a checkpoint barrier blocked my way. My papers were in order; the barrier lifted like a finger. It pointed at a cloudless sky.

Once, someone had stuck a compass in a map. Circling, they lopped off 4,300 square kilometres of the world from the world. Concentric rings of barbed wire define the structure of that no-man's-land until today: the 30-kilometre zone, the ten-kilometre zone, the reactor zone. In the centre stands a coffin. Buried under 300,000 cubic metres of reinforced concrete lies Block IV of the V. I. Lenin Nuclear Power Station of Chernobyl, stricken 26 April 1986 at 1:23 am, cause of the accident: human failure.

The red and white striped ventilation pipe juts out of the concrete-embedded power station like a poisoned candy cane. I had seen photos from 1986, of a firefighter hoisting the red Soviet flag to the top of the ventilation pipe, a last heroic deed for a country destined for death. In Kiev I had tried to find the man, but a colleague from his crew tiredly dismissed this idea. 'He's dead. There were five of us men; all are dead. I'm almost dead too.'

I followed the river Pripyat, which had once supplied the reactor with cooling water. After four kilometres I reached the ghost town of the same name, Pripyat, built in 1970 for the employees of the nuclear plant. In one single April night its population plummeted from 50,000 to zero.

Continuous snow covered the roads. A panicked deer dashed through the central town square as I approached. Its hooves hammered a few irregular beats on the asphalt, and then the silence returned. Snow and concrete and silence – other than that, there was nothing.

I walked through an abandoned school building for a long time. I entered classrooms and felt like I was being stared at, even though there had not been anyone sitting on the school benches in decades. Wind drove the snow through the broken windowpanes. Weeds had taken root in the floor cracks, the shoots of young birch and poplar trees had pried away single wooden panels with patient pressure. Between them, open textbooks told a random story:

If a friend from another country wants to learn something about Vladimir Ilyich Lenin, what do you tell him? – Peace for the world! – During the eight years Friedrich Schiller spent in military school, he learned to hate despotism. – All the best to the children; that is the law in our country.

In one of the rooms the entire floor was covered with discarded gas masks. Their fish eyes stared blindly into the emptiness. Their snouts crunched under my feet.

Lenin was everywhere. His roguish goatee adorned wall posters, busts, portraits, book covers. Twice I read his name on street signs, once on the façade of a hospital, countless times on the administrative buildings of the reactor named after him. I almost walked into a snow-white Lenin monument that I did not see until I was standing directly in front of it. It was hidden in the snow like a stone chameleon.

It was only after a couple of hours of wide-eyed wandering that I realised what accounted for the true fascination of this abandoned landscape. Its emptiness is twofold: it wasn't just the people who were missing; everything that had happened after 1986 was also absent. History had ended here with one sudden bang, not with the gradual alterations that had taken place beyond the barbed wire. Tentatively, I invoked the image of Kiev and stripped away everything in my mind's eye that would vanish after a nuclear disaster. It was nothing like Pripyat. There would still be garbage in Kiev, advertisements, luminous yogurt containers, the clamour of posters; there would still be contradictions, banalities, a meaningless surplus of things and images which is only produced by consumerist societies. The 'Zone' is different. It is an integrated entirety. Everything in it belongs together; even its most mundane debris is part of a socialist whole. Although its concrete façades are crumbling, it seems in an eerie way more intact than the country that surrounds it. I had found it, the 'Park of the Soviet Era' that they wanted to build in Kiev.

Fifteen kilometres away from the reactor, between the second and third ring of barbed wire, is the city of Chernobyl. It would be unremarkable if it weren't for the church. Its freshly whitewashed walls outshine the grey ruins all around.

'Don't you have a Geiger counter with you?'

Father Nicholas, a bearded man of 60 years, looked at me quizzically.

'No.'

'Good. You don't need it. It would not work in the church.'

Now I looked at him questioningly.

'It is the House of God. The radiation can't penetrate here.'

And that was, as it turned out, only one of many wonders.

Father Nicholas pulled a rattling bunch of keys from the folds of his robe and unlocked the church door. We entered a zone within the Zone. In disbelief, I let my eyes wander around the ceiling frescoes, the gold metal fittings of the altar wall. Just above our heads hovered a giant chandelier, which awakened with a flicker when Father Nicholas turned on the light. Its beam flooded the room and chased away every shadow of the catastrophe. Somewhere out there, there had to be a reactor, but suddenly it seemed light years away.

'Well,' Father Nicholas began. He spoke abruptly, his sentences often beginning at the end, like those of someone who has discovered speaking late in life. Outside the window dusk was falling as he started his narration. It was only later, as Father Nicholas drove me back to the perimeter of the Zone in his car, that he slowly approached the beginning of his story.

'Well. It was like this.'

When it happened, Father Nicholas was not yet called Father Nicholas. Just as the Zone was not called the Zone. Chernobyl was called Chernobyl, but that meant a city, not a disaster. God was called God, but you had better not call Him by name.

Nuclear power plants create fissions; that is why they are there. But this one, in whose shadows Father Nicholas grew up, this one fissured everything: ways of life, families, names. And time. Only afterwards did people realise that there had been a before.

When it happened, Father Nicholas was called Nicholas Yakushin. He worked in an agricultural machinery complex; he was an engineer. An engineer knows how a nuclear power plant works. A priest knows how a soul works. Father Nicholas knew both. He also knew that the nuclear power plant had no soul. 'How can it have one, when it was built without soul?'

With the palm of his hand Father Nicholas slapped the steering wheel of his 1994 Opel. The Opel was old, but it could stand the beating. Why? Because the Germans had built it with soul. 'We,' Father Nicholas said, pointing out of the car window to the smokestacks and the utility poles and the steel beams and all the rest of the Soviet remnants, 'we built and built and built for 70 long years. But we did it without soul.'

The Yakushins were a family of priests. Nicholas's great-grandfather had served in the Church of Saint Ilya, Nicholas's grandfather as well. Then the Bolsheviks came. They hammered on the church door and cried: stop praying, Father; man has no soul. The grandfather did not agree: man, he said, most certainly has a soul, and it is immortal. The Bolsheviks detained the grandfather. When he was released, he was old. That was his good luck. He died early enough to escape Stalin's terror, which hardly any clerics survived. The grandfather's son, Nicholas Yakushin's father, did not become a priest. The times were not right.

Nicholas was nevertheless baptised, secretly, at home, the way most Orthodox were. Those who baptised their children in the church had to reckon with work-related harassment. When Nicholas was born, shortly after the end of the war, the church was closed anyway; the local kolkhoz used it as a grain silo. Thus Nicholas got to know his forefathers' church: filled to the dome with wheat. On the ceiling a besieged Christ faded away, his hands spread over the grain as if in self-protection, not in blessing.

The town of Chernobyl, or Chornobyl, in Ukrainian, is old, ancient, even if it does not look it anymore. None of the original buildings are left. First the Mongols razed the city; later came Lithuanians, Poles, Bolsheviks, finally the Germans. Today there are only a few wooden houses standing between the concrete blocks, none of them older than two centuries. But Chernobyl was founded at the same time as Kiev, and when prince Vladimir had his subjects baptised in the year 988, the citizens of Chernobyl were amongst the first Christians of the Slavic world.

To those for whom this past was still present – despite the futurist ecstasy of the Soviet period – it was no surprise that here, in Chernobyl, 1000 years after the Slavs' baptism, time should come to an end, just as it had been proclaimed in the Book of Revelation:

The third angel sounded his trumpet, and a great star, blazing like a torch, fell from the sky on a third of the rivers and on the springs of water. The name of the star is Wormwood. And a third of the waters turned bitter, and many people died from the waters, because they had been made bitter.

This John wrote in Chapter 8, verses 10 and 11. But in Ukrainian 'wormwood' means: Chornobyl.

It was a grey morning, the last before the holy week. Nicholas Yakushin was on the way to market; he wanted to buy fish for the last meal before Lent. From Kiev he saw motorcades heading to the power plant, soldiers, firefighters, physicians, all in respiratory masks. The people in the city were asking questions. No one answered them. An exercise, Nicholas Yakushin thought. It must be an exercise. Smoke wafted from the power station.

On Easter Monday, nine days after the accident, Chernobyl was evacuated. It is only temporary, they told the people. No one believed it. The elderly had to be carried onto the buses by force. Where is this radiation you are talking about, they asked. We don't see anything!

Soldiers closed up the houses. They sealed up the church. Silence covered Chernobyl. Christ spread his pale hands over the orphaned nave; mice rummaged between the floor planks for remnants of grain. The wind carried seeds through the broken windows; weeds grew over the altar.

One day looters came. Looking for scrap metal, they journeyed through the Zone and broke into the abandoned houses. They attached a steel cable to the sealed church door and hitched it to a tractor. The rope snapped. Its broken end sailed through the air; it looked for a target and found a sinner. One of the looters collapsed, struck in the face; the others fled. Everyone in the Zone knows the story of God's vengeance.

Nicholas Yakushin was evacuated to Kiev with his family. From time to time he returned to his hometown, then stood in front of the church and wept. The metal dome of the bell tower had come loose; it squeaked in the wind. The walls crumbled. Wild boars had churned up the church-yard; the gravestones jutted crookedly from the desecrated earth.

One day Nicholas Yakushin could not bear it anymore. He stood in front of the Bishop of Kiev's residence and would not move from the spot until the church authorities listened to him. The church of my fathers is falling apart, he said. The church needs a priest. The superiors held council. After one month they sent for Nicholas. We have searched, they said, but we have not found anyone. Nobody wants to go there. Put yourself in the position of the priests – you yourself would not want to be sent to the Zone either.

And it came to pass that Nicholas Yakushin became Father Nicholas.

That was ten years ago now. His old life had overlapped the new one for a while. An engineer knows how to build a house, even a house of God. Father Nicholas built a scaffold. Before he scaled the church roof, he crossed himself. He straightened the dome. He plastered the walls and replaced the windows; he pulled up the weeds and repainted the pale hands of Christ.

When everything was ready, Father Nicholas placed a large icon in front of the altar wall. The icon was from Kiev. One of the clean-up workers, who had crawled through the melting power plant after the accident, had let it be painted. The Saviour had appeared to the man in a dream. Christ walked on a cloud; the cloud floated above the power plant; a star named Wormwood fell from heaven; it gathered the dead and the survivors of the Zone in its light.

The man had let his dream be painted. Father Nicholas showed me the icon. It was a little unorthodox. In iconographic paintings people are not usually featured, certainly not people in firemen's uniforms, not to mention people in gas masks. Nevertheless, the icon won the blessing of the Church; the metropolitan bishop of Kiev consecrated the 'Saviour of Chernobyl' personally. He was still saying his prayers when the first miracle occurred: a pigeon flew right past the image, almost grazing its wings on the Saviour. When the image was sprinkled a little later with holy water a rainbow arched over the icon like a halo. So it went, miracles upon miracles. Father Nicholas collected dozens of testimonials. If you carried the icon through a rainy city, the sky cleared. If you placed it in a church, a rainbow formed over the dome. A paralysed woman without control of her arm since childhood days prayed kneeling in front of the portrait until her fingers moved.

Father Nicholas had wandered through half the Ukraine with the icon, from the Black Sea to Chernobyl, the same route that once the Slavs' apostle Andrew had taken. The icon worked its miracles. It helped the people, and in gratitude the people helped Father Nicholas. With the money that they threw into the pouch for him, he renovated his church at home.

When the church was finished the people came. First they came out of curiosity, Father Nicholas says, not because they believed. There were old people who had returned to the Zone in order to live in their abandoned villages, people who did not believe in radiation or were too old to fear it. There were security guards, who had been stationed on the borders of the Zone. There were the nuclear workers, who still maintained the demolished power station.

They all asked: Father, what are you doing?

I'm building a house, Father Nicholas answered. A house for God, so He can return to Chernobyl.

And behold: God did return.

'When a person enters the Zone,' says Father Nicholas, 'he finds himself at the edge of death. He is afraid. He thinks about dying, about the afterlife, about eternity. Thus God enters his life. You can tell by looking at the people in the Zone what is going on inside them.'

Soon the people who came to visit Father Nicholas in the church began to ask questions. What will become of us, Father? Why is all of this happening? Is God punishing us? Will He forgive us? And when we die, is it true that our souls live on?

'In the entire Zone,' says Father Nicholas, 'there is not one unbeliever today.'

He must know, because he knows them all, the returnees and the guards and the power plant employees, and Father Nicholas knows that in some respects they live better than the people outside the Zone. Many of the evacuees, who live in Kiev or elsewhere in the Ukraine, suffer from diseases which the scientists have no name for. Stress, the physicians say, migration-related stress, Chernobyl stress. Many have died from this stress, from heart cases, lung cases, blood cases, head cases.

'But we,' says Father Nicholas, 'we in the Zone are in good health, God the Almighty be praised. The old people in the abandoned villages are dying, but they are dying of old age, not diseases.'

They even drank the water. Father Nicholas pointed out the car window; beside the road the Pripyat's snow-covered ribbon of ice began to emerge. The river flows past the power station. Its water is bitter. 'We bless it,' says Father Nicholas, 'and then we drink it.' He made the sign of the cross over the Pripyat, 'In the name of the Father, he whispered, of the Son and of the Holy Spirit.

'We must believe. Nothing will happen to those who believe.'

Once a year, at Easter, the borders of the Zone are opened. Then the survivors come and weep for their dead. Many visit the church then. It is the greatest holiday for Father Nicholas. Every year on the Day of Resurrection he sings the Orthodox Easter liturgy:

'Christ is risen from the dead, trampling down death by death, and upon those in the tombs bestowing life.'

All night and through the dawn Father Nicholas stands in his church and cries: 'Christ is risen!'

And a weak but audible choir replies: 'Truly, He is risen!'

Shortly after Easter, or shortly before, depending on the Church calendar, the anniversary of the Day of the Disaster is remembered. Every year, on 26 April at 1:23 am, Father Nicholas rings the funeral bell in the churchyard, a chime for each year that has passed.

The scientists say that 20,000 years must pass before people will be able to return to the Zone.

Father Nicholas dropped me off at the checkpoint barrier. I rode back to Kiev in a bus full of tourists. They came from America, Australia, England; most of them were young backpackers. They had spent the day in Chernobyl: a tourist in Kiev could hardly miss this trip. A Ukrainian excursion guide sat between them and told horror stories that always had the same punch line: Chernobyl is not as contaminated as everyone believes; the really bad radiation is lurking someplace else.

'Do you know where the most dangerous place in all of Kiev is?'

Dramatic pause. Heads shake.

'The Lenin Monument.'

Dramatic pause. Inquiring glances.

'Made of granite! Nothing stores radioactivity better! The thing radiates as much as it did on the first day!'

When we arrived in Kiev that night, the whole group ran to the monument en masse. Lenin and his communist security guard were photographed extensively. The red tent appeared abandoned, but then a zipper was unzipped from the inside and a sleepy pensioner blinked with irritation at the unexpected flurry of flashbulbs. After a few seconds he withdrew, cursing.

Long after the tourists had disappeared, I still stood there and stared at the snowbound tent. An unexplainable respect for its inhabitants suddenly overcame me – for their stubbornness, for their incorrigibility, even for the megalomania of their failed social experiment. I looked around me. The road was deserted, only occasional lights burned in the windows of the surrounding houses. Many of the people who lived behind these windows must have once dreamed the same dream that still kept Vera Yefimovna and her comrades awake. What were the people behind the windows dreaming about now? Did they still have dreams at all? I did not know; I was travelling in order to find out.

Lenin was enthroned above the tent like a stone totem pole, a pagan god, the idol of a sect. There were still a few disciples who read the promise of a better world on his lips, not in the afterlife, but here, on earth. They dreamt the old dream, even if it was a nightmare, full of blood and bones and suffering. They had sacrificed too much for the dream; they had gone too far to turn back now. The further they fell into social isolation, the more stubborn their convictions became. They were like the Old Believers. One day they would flee to Siberia and take their

Lenin with them. And someday, in 300 years perhaps, a German journalist would travel through Russia in their footsteps, in order to track down the last communists in the Taiga.

On the day before my departure I returned to the Dnieper. It was a sunny day – the first since my arrival in Kiev. Light reflections danced over the splintered crust of ice which the frozen river had thrust over the banks. The beach cracked in time with my footsteps.

I heard them before I saw them. Splashing water, sensual snorting, only a bush separated me from the noise. When I circled around it, I was standing too close to the naked figures to ignore them. They were old; their tired skin hardly found support in their swimsuits and bikinis. But their eyes gleamed. Three men and four women were standing around a hole in the ice watching the black river water splash within; a fifth woman waded straight into it. When she was standing in the water up to her hips, she fell forward, snorting, and swam to the basin's rear edge of ice before she turned back and climbed to shore. Moaning, she shook herself, drops of water splashing from her reddened skin. It occurred to me that I was actually seeing the history-saturated water of the Dnieper for the first time on the body of this woman. Up until now, a layer of ice had separated me from it.

I sensed religious motives. When I inquired, they all laughed.

'Religious? Since when are ice bathers religious?'

'We're Communists! We don't believe in anything!'

'I'm not a Communist!'

'Really? Listen to this: Petrovich is not a Communist.'

'Do I have a Party book? I never had a Party book!'

'You're a Communist nevertheless, in your heart you are …'

'I believe in Russia, and nothing else.'

'To hell with Russia. Russia betrayed us!'

'I only believe in my health. An ice bath every Sunday.'

'A healthy country is invincible. Do you know who said that? That was …'

'No one defeated us! Our winter made short work of them. The Swedes, Napoleon, Hitler.'

'Hey, German, did you see the Second World War memorial in the hills? *The Motherland Calls*? We set it up for your countrymen.'

'They did not appreciate our winter at all.'

'I bet this one here doesn't like our winter either.'

'Already looks very pale.'

'Hey, German, are you cold?'

And then they all looked at me. And there was no turning back.

A thousand needles pierced my skin as I sank into the water, but it lasted for only a moment before the pain turned into euphoria. As I climbed back to land, cheered on, I was the happiest man in the whole of Kiev. Tested and baptised, I moved on to Moscow.

BLOOD (Moscow)

Satan has obtained our radiant Russia from God,
so that she may become crimson with the blood of martyrs.

Archpriest Avvakum, 1673

You will not stay among the living
You will not rise from the snow
Twenty-eight wounds from the bayonet
And five bullet holes.
A garment full of grief
For my beloved I sewed.
Oh Russian earth, it loves the taste
It loves the taste of blood.

Anna Akhmatova, 1921

And what if our seed won't sprout, Lenin.
With blood I've fertilised this country
And forged new industries with human bodies
Ground into bone meal in my grinders, I
The great Stalin, leader of nations.

Heiner Müller, 1995

We Fight, We Reconcile

'What is the purpose of your trip?'

The border guard's stamp hovers over my passport. One answer, a correct one, and I will be on Russian soil.

'Moscow.'

The border guard makes a face. 'Moscow! What is your *purpose* for travelling to Russia?'

For a moment I do not know it myself. I am seeking an Old Believer hermit, but is that a purpose?

'I'm a journalist. I work for a German newspaper.'

The stamp hesitates.

'I write about Russia.'

Impatiently the stamp hammers down on my passport: *Rossiya 2 March 2010.*

Between snow and heaven the horizon grew hazy. Then Moscow pushed itself in between, bit by bit. Dacha settlements moved past the train window, car wrecks, people in fur hats. Pale pigs, snouts buried in the snow. A power station, a furniture store, the construction frame of a church. Motorcades in cloverleaf loops of asphalt, the spider web of high-voltage lines. Then prefabricated buildings. More prefabricated buildings, a sea of prefabricated buildings.

In Kiev I had almost wistfully said goodbye to the concrete living quarters and their ailing charm, but Moscow's monotone excessiveness brutally swept these memories from my mind, like the roar of a symphony after a mild overture. Dazed, I compiled meaningless calculations: rows of windows multiplied by storeys multiplied by streets – how many of Moscow's 15 million residents raced past me in the same breath? Innumerable and invisible, they populated their concrete honeycombs, an industrial swarm of bees, a labour force portioned and stacked for state purposes.

Soviet Moscow was built as the capital of a dream empire, as the centre of a global utopia, whose aim was the happiness of all people. The Muscovites were not always entirely happy with the major renovations that began in the Thirties, but they understood that the happiness of mankind was more important than their own little happiness. Understandingly they joined in when the national anthem was sung at the Soviet parades: 'We will destroy this world of violence down to the foundations, and then we will build our new world.' Stalin put the old tsarist Moscow through the wringer, until the last remnant of force was squeezed out of it. When in the end the renewed city towered over the ruins of the ancient world, when nothing else stood in the way of the happiness of all people, because all exploiters had been enslaved, all saboteurs shot, all counterrevolutionaries drowned in their own blood, the Muscovites repeated full of comprehension the motto that Stalin had set out to praise his work: 'Life has become better! Life has become merrier!'

Then came the topping-out ceremony. The old gods had been overthrown; the new ones now adorned the roofs and gables of Moscow's freshly built palaces. A stone pantheon of muscular welders and stately milkmaids settled into the sky above the capital. I saw the proletarian statues fly past the windows of the train as I approached the city centre, weathered guardians of a discarded utopia. They looked tired. They had carried the happiness of humanity on their shoulders for too long. Relieved, they now left this burden to the billboards they had recently come to share the roofs with.

I had rented a room in advance. My landlady, a depressed chemist in her forties, spoke consistently in the plural: 'In the apartment we take our shoes off.' – 'We use the washing machine only on the weekend.' – 'We do not shop in this supermarket.' I could not shake the feeling that I had taken the place of a deserted lover who had disappeared from her life, but not from her sentences. When on the third day after my arrival I met a Muscovite friend who spontaneously offered me a room in his apartment, I accepted with relief. With a guilty conscience, I pressed two weeks rent into the chemist's hands when I left.

'Why so much?' she asked, amazed.

'To cover the cost until you guys find a new tenant.'

Confused, she looked at me. 'You guys?'

So I ended up at Vanya's. Once again.

We had known each other for eight years – just about as long as I knew Russia. In the summer of 2002 I had gone to Moscow for the first time for a longer period of time, to work as an intern in the foreign office of a German newspaper. The newsroom director had procured a room for me, at Vanya's, who was then 18 years old and shared the apartment with his mother. My Russian at that time was limited to stereotypical greetings and stammered toasts, but Vanya spoke fluent German; as a child he had lived in Cologne with his mother.

The apartment had four rooms. Vanya's mother lived in one of them; she had gone away, visiting relatives in Belarus. Next to it was the living room, where I was to sleep. Vanya steered me past a third, locked room, with a vague gesture that seemed to say: I'll explain to you later.

He himself inhabited the fourth, the tiniest room. It was stuffed to the ceiling with the paraphernalia of a Moscow boyhood: books (predominantly Russian classics), CDs (predominantly Russian guitar rock), school textbooks, clothes and several battered musical instruments, of which only an electric guitar was in use.

'My band is called *Scheiße*,' Vanya said.

'How do you say *Scheiße* in Russian?'

'*Govno*. But the band is called *Scheiße*. In German. Sounds better.'

Vanya made tea and put on a CD by a Russian band called 'DDT'. He sang the lyrics along with the music and translated the best parts for me.

Yesterday in the woods I saw the Russian idea
It walked amongst felled pine trees
With a sling around its neck.

In the evening Lena came home. She inhabited the third room, temporarily, as Vanya explained to me. Lena came from Belarus and had only just moved to Moscow. She was about my age, a pale, Slavic beauty. We did not share a common language. I stammered my greeting phrases and held out my hand, a gesture she returned reluctantly. Vanya explained to me later that in Russia you do not shake a woman's hand.

I spent the next day at the editorial office. When I came home in the evening Vanya was not there, but the door to Lena's room was open. She was sitting on the sofa and watching television with a priest. The man was wearing casual clothing, but his black beard and long hair, tied in a ponytail, told me that he must be Orthodox. He stood up and held out his hand. 'Arseny.'

'I am very pleased to meet you,' I stammered. 'My name is Jens.'

And with that our options for communication were exhausted. I was about to go directly to my room but Lena and Arseny protested with vigorous hand gestures and invited me to their couch. I sat down. In silence, we watched television. Periodically Arseny reached for a voluminous cream cake and cut off large pieces that he handed to me. '*Kushay!*' he said. '*Kushay!*' I ate. The cake was our single means of communication. It took me a long time to get to sleep that night because my belly hurt.

'Monk,' Vanya said the next morning. 'Not priest. He is my mother's confessor.'

Arseny appeared on a regular basis over the next few days. It only gradually became clear to me that he did not come over just to watch television. He brought Lena flowers, and in the evening when they said goodbye, he looked into her eyes for a long while – just a bit too long for a monk. I found him slightly creepy from the beginning. His gaze contained something probing. He was not tall, but he had the stature of a wrestler, with giant hands that looked like the claws of a mole, especially when they protruded from the sleeves of his monk's habit.

When I came home on the fourth or fifth evening, Lena was alone in the apartment. She was suddenly a different person. Until then she had shyly avoided me when our paths crossed in the apartment; now she talked to me nervously. I shrugged my shoulders in uncertainty. I understood nothing.

When Vanya came home he briefly spoke to Lena, then he took me aside. 'She had a quarrel with Arseny. He might show up here tonight. Don't open the door for him, okay?'

Later, when I was already in bed, the doorbell rang, once, then again, then incessantly. The sound gave way to hammering, then I heard a loud crash. A few seconds later Arseny tore open the door to my room. He had a long iron rod in his hand. From what he cried, I understood only a single word: 'Where?' Clueless, I shook my head. He rushed into the corridor. Next I heard Lena scream. I hurriedly got dressed. I had not yet finished when Vanya appeared in the door. 'Come quickly.'

We rushed down the corridor to Lena's room. Arseny was leaning over the bed. His massive body covered Lena. I could not see her, all I could hear was the noise of the blows – a dull clapping, like a book that is abruptly slammed shut.

We pushed ourselves in between the two of them. Alone, neither of us could have contained Arseny, but with two of us we managed to keep him at a distance. While he tried to push us aside he stared at Lena steadfastly. He looked like he was out of his head and barely seemed to notice us. When he finally realised that Lena was out of his reach he began to plead with her in a low, imploring voice. I did not understand anything, I just saw his hypnotic stare. Lena crouched behind us on the bed. Her hair was rumpled. She did not seem to be injured, but her right cheek was very red. From the corner of my eye I saw that she was staring at Arseny with an expression I could not read. There was no fear in it and no hatred, more a strange kind of triumph. Involuntarily I wondered whether this was the first time the two of them had confronted each other.

'No,' Vanya said, shaking his head. 'It's happened a few times.'

'What is Arseny saying?' I asked.

'God will punish you,' Vanya translated. 'You're a whore, I gave you everything, you took everything from me. And so on.' His voice trembled. I looked at him. He was white as chalk.

'What should we do? Should we call the police?'

Vanya shook his head vehemently. 'Absolutely not. The apartment doesn't belong to us, we're not registered here, and the police would only make trouble.'

I thought it over. 'If we can somehow manage to push Arseny out of the apartment and lock him out …'

'That won't work,' Vanya interrupted. 'He kicked in the door.' He pointed to the floor. Lying in one corner of the room was the iron rod that Arseny had had with him when he had stormed into my room. I only now realised that it was the bolt which kept the apartment door locked from the inside.

In the end we used our combined force to push Arseny out of the room and into the corridor. I stood in front of the door while Vanya fetched his mattress from the next room. We placed it on the floor in the hallway, to block the door to Lena's room. Distraught, Arseny watched as we demonstratively lay down on the mattress. When he realised that the path to Lena was obstructed, he retreated to the kitchen. We heard him mutter under his breath; it sounded like a prayer.

We lay on the mattress for a long time and waited to see what would happen, but Arseny remained in the kitchen. Eventually Vanya dozed off. I was sure that I would not sleep a wink all night, but Vanya's breathing was so reassuring that eventually I also nodded off.

Early in the morning I was awakened by an unfamiliar voice. A woman who I had never seen before was shaking Vanya's shoulder. As he woke up, his drowsy eyes wandered back and forth for a few seconds between me and the woman. Then he said: 'Mum.' And he added in German: 'Mum, this is Jens.'

His mother had returned from Belarus during the night. In her apartment she had found: a broken door, a misplaced mattress, her sleeping son; and a stranger. Vanya needed a while to explain the events of the night to her. I listened, reassured, because Arseny was apparently no longer in the apartment and because Vanya's mother would now put everything in order, as mothers do.

Vanya's mother, however, did something very unexpected. She *laughed*. For several minutes she could not speak because she was laughing so hard. At last she turned to me, put a hand on my shoulder and said, 'Welcome to Russia.'

Again, I spent the day in the office. When I came home in the evening, the apartment door still hung askew on its hinges. In the kitchen I heard voices. I opened the door and almost backed out of the room again. At the table sat Vanya, his mother – and Arseny. He was just about to fill three glasses with vodka. When he saw me he jumped up and ran over to me, grinning. Instinctively I wanted to avoid him, but he laid his mole claws on my shoulders and spoke to me. Hesitantly I looked at Vanya.

'He says: Come to the table and drink with us.'

Thunderstruck, I shook my head.

'He says: That's how it is in Russia – we fight, we reconcile.'

I did not want to share a table with this man for anything in the world. Helplessly I sought Vanya's eyes. He did not look happy.

'I'm tired,' I finally said. 'Sorry. It was a long night.'

In my room I switched on the ceiling lights and sat down indecisively on my bed. For a long time I stared at a spot on the wall that I had never noticed before. I suddenly felt alien, unspeakably alien, like an unwanted guest who understands nothing and does everything wrong. From the kitchen I heard Arseny's laughter and the clink of glasses, while a new puzzle piece fell into place in my head. We fight, we reconcile. I could not. I felt painfully un-Russian.

I never saw Arseny again. Lena also disappeared without a trace. When I asked Vanya or his mother about the two of them, they only shrugged their shoulders.

Eight years later Vanya was still the slender, thoughtful boy I remembered. But there was an unfamiliar intensity in his eyes, an expression of early maturity that I noticed more often in Russians in their mid-twenties than in Western Europeans of the same age. I had always explained this premature ageing by the fact that Russians finish school earlier, study earlier, work, marry and have children earlier, that they are forced to cope with everyday hardships that my own youth had been spared. But unlike most of his Russian contemporaries, Vanya took time with life. He had dropped out of his literature studies and was now struggling along as a camera assistant. At night he wrote screenplays that he hoped to make into films one day.

He was no longer living in the apartment we had shared eight years ago. Shortly after the incident with Arseny, his mother had bought a small flat, which she relinquished to her son when she moved in with a new lover a little later. In the two small rooms I recognised many things: the books, now supplemented by several rows of shelves containing philosophy, the CD collection, where more experimental styles had supplanted the guitar rock. Two cats, Pusya and Pasha, who had often slept in my bed in the old apartment, had moved with Vanya, and their preferred space in the new quarters once again was the sofa where I slept for the next two months.

The icons were unfamiliar. On each windowsill and each shelf in the apartment were small images of saints printed on wooden panels, whose unblinking eyes I sensed almost physically in the early days. Only in complete darkness did I feel unobserved. I could suddenly understand why in more pious times Russian women had turned the icons in their bedrooms to the wall before they surrendered themselves to sin.

Vanya's friends often joked about the icons. He ignored the jokes with the same patience with which the saints indulged the sins that were committed under their eyes. In his circle of friends Vanya was the only one who had his own apartment, all the others lived with their parents or shared cramped rooms in student dormitories. Vanya was generous with his privileges. Almost every evening friends sat in the kitchen. Many remained overnight, and some even had their own keys to the flat; they came and went, whether Vanya was at home or not. On the weekends you could hardly think about sleeping. In successive waves friends, and friends of friends, crowded into the apartment. Often the parties did not end for two days in a row, they just shifted in unpredictable intervals from room to room. That I slept at all on such nights was thanks to the innate Russian respect for foreign guests. As soon as I so much as yawned, someone would jump up and rouse the students who were sleeping on my sofa. They willingly vacated the space and curled up on the carpet, as undemanding as cats.

Many of the faces that passed me by in those weeks blur together in my memory, but a few are imprinted on my mind: Samer, the half-Lebanese with the girlish eyes, Sandra from Lithuania, Lyokha from Belarus, Airat, the Tartarian radio DJ with the honey voice, tiny Kseniya, bearded Kolyan, the dark princesses Nika and Yana. And Sasha – that Sasha who would dictate to me one night that there is no such thing as a Russian soul. After that, he did virtually everything to refute his proposition. I seldom saw him sober. He never slept for more than four hours and he never stayed awake for more than four hours either. He refused to talk about banalities – the more simple the questions, the more complex his answers, even if it was only about morning coffee. 'Coffee? Why do you want me to drink coffee? You don't want that? Then why are you offering it to me? Does God want me to drink coffee? If He wants it, then why is there no coffee growing in Russia? If He doesn't want it, then why does He allow you to offer me coffee?'

I choked on my coffee when I saw Sasha coming out of the shower half naked one morning. Coughing helplessly, I stared at him.

'My German friend,' he said, 'you look disturbed.'

'I'm alright,' I gasped. 'Why do you have a swastika on your back?'

He grinned. The tattoo was right between his shoulder blades. 'That, my German friend, is not your typical swastika. It's an Indian one. Look closely. It turns clockwise, not counter-clockwise.'

He had seen the symbol in a museum as a child. When, years later, friends took him to a tattoo parlour, the wheel was set in motion; it rolled out of his memory and onto his back. 'My grandfather stared at me then just like you. At first he was speechless. Then he said: "Nice". Nothing more. He never spoke much. Grandmother always said: "Leave him in peace, the war has left him speechless." I always thought that one day he would eventually begin to talk about the fascists, but then suddenly he was dead. My God, I hope it wasn't because of the swastika!'

I slept little during the two months that I spent in Moscow, and I drank too much. Nevertheless, I could often hardly wait to return to the apartment in the evening. After a while I realised why that was. Vanya and his friends associated only vague childhood memories with the Soviet Union. They belonged to the first generation of Russians who knew only from stories what their country had gone through. It was precisely this absence of memory which relieved me when I came home in the evening, disturbed by encounters with people who could not leave the past behind.

A Short History of the World

In mid-March winter turned angry. He knew his imminent end was at hand and denied it vehemently, like a child who does not want to go to bed. Spitting flurries of snow blew horizontally through the streets; the pedestrians walked backwards against them. For days the temperature dropped and dropped, until one morning I woke up and could no longer see the sky. All the windowpanes were frozen. Ice flowers entwined the icons on the windowsill.

People could not stay out on the street very long. Those who had money went to cafes to warm up; those who had none went to bookstores. I was soon tired of the cafes and their affected Western atmosphere; instead I followed the pensioners who shuffled through the bookshops in their faded down jackets. I watched them passing aimlessly back and forth between the aisles of shelves, touching the spines with frostbitten fingers, muttering individual titles. When I looked at the books closer I could not escape the impression that some of the patrons here were not seeking warmth, but consolation.

Who Finances Russia's Demise?
Genocide of the Russian People: They Call it Capitalism
Secret Fronts: How the West is besieging Russia

A gloomy whispering came from the books; shelf by shelf they murmured their rumours into the room. Many of the titles sought to bring relief for the trauma of the Soviet collapse, others dug deeper into the past.

The Viking Lie: Russia's True Origins
Occult Sources of the October Revolution
Secret Documents of the Russian Freemasons

In the middle of this jumble of conspiracy theories I suddenly discovered one familiar name: Anatoly Fomenko. I had almost forgotten about him – he was the history-obsessed mathematician I had encountered years before in Yuri's documentary. Perplexed, I looked closer at his books. Back in Berlin, I had thought the man was an obscure academic whose hypotheses had trailed away in university corridors without finding much of a hearing. That was obviously a mistake. Fomenko's books filled an entire shelf.

400 Years of Fraud: The New Chronology for Beginners
Why the Trojan War Began in the Middle Ages
Russia and the Mongols: Who Conquered Whom?

The next day I went on a search for Anatoly Fomenko. I wanted to understand what drove him to chop the world's history into pieces. It wasn't easy to find him. He taught mathematics at the Lomonosov Moscow State University and he was a member of the Russian Academy of the Sciences, but at both institutions people were reluctant to talk about him. Whomever I asked, the reactions were unequivocal. 'Don't mention that name in my presence,' one archaeologist hissed. She had spent her entire professional life deciphering Old Church Slavonic inscriptions on birch bark, which Fomenko dismissed as modern forgeries. 'Every single word that this man has ever written is outrageous nonsense,' thundered a scholar of Byzantine studies. He examined the influence of Greek culture on Russian culture, which, according to Fomenko, had never existed.

I carefully asked the Byzantine studies scholar how he explained Fomenko's popularity. I mentioned the books I had now seen in more than one Moscow bookstore.

'Very simple,' the man sighed. 'In this country nobody believes in anything anymore, and certainly not in the past. Our history has been rewritten too often. People do not trust the historians, because in the Soviet era they were only responsible for reshaping the past to the purposes of those in power. There is no longer any historical consensus in this country; everyone thinks that everything is possible. The people read Fomenko because he expresses what everyone believes: that our entire history is a lie.'

When I asked the scholar of Byzantine studies if he had Fomenko's telephone number, he stared at me dumbfounded. 'Are you crazy? Of course not!' A bit more gently he added: 'But he is easy to find. He lives in the Lomonosov University.'

'You mean he lives on campus?'

'No. He lives in the main building.'

Now I stared at him dumbfounded. I knew the university. Everyone in Moscow knows it; its cathedral-like silhouette towers over the city like the movie set of a socialist vampire film. It is the largest of seven Moscow skyscrapers for which Stalin had levelled entire neighbourhoods after the war. I knew that in its nested wings student rooms were rented out by the semester, but I could not imagine someone living permanently in this haunted Soviet castle. In my mind's eye I saw Fomenko dancing across the rooftops in the moonlight, surrounded by bats, screaming out dates and figures – a Russian Count von Count closely related to the number-crazed vampire on Sesame Street.

A few days later I was standing in front of the university building during daylight. Eventually, the obvious idea of calling Yuri in Berlin had occurred to me – he gave me Fomenko's number. The mathematician seemed surprisingly accessible on the phone. After a short conversation he had invited me to his apartment.

For half an hour I orbited the gigantic university building in the freezing cold looking for Block G, which did not want to materialise. When I finally found the right entrance, I could hardly feel my fingers. In the overheated foyer a big receptionist was sitting between tropical potted plants. She stared blankly at her television. When I asked for Fomenko, she did not look up, instead she just raised a fleshy finger and pointed to the elevator. 'Sixth floor.'

The man who opened the door for me on the sixth floor had the bushiest eyebrows I had ever seen. In tangled gray tufts they entwined the metal rim of his scientist's glasses. In front of me stood Anatoly Timofeyevich Fomenko, Professor of Higher Geometry and Topology, full member of the Russian Academy of the Sciences, defeater of history.

He conducted me into the living room. On the walls hung oil paintings and pencil drawings that I recognised immediately: They were the homemade surrealist landscapes that I had seen years earlier in Yuri's video recording. Melting watches, dancing columns of numbers, mountains made of skulls. They involuntarily made me think of heavy metal album covers.

Fomenko noticed my glances. Smiling, he pointed to the pictures. 'Old. Everything is old.'

'Don't you paint anymore?'

His answer sounded unintentionally cryptic: 'There isn't enough time.'

We sat at the living room table. The windows commanded a view of Moscow – a black and white painting of snow and concrete. There were two bouquets of lilies on the table, one white, the other pink, remnants of Fomenko's 65th birthday, which he had celebrated a few days before. Fomenko pushed the flowers brusquely to the side; they had blocked his view. In a similarly unsentimental way he had once swept aside the history of the world; it too had stood in his way.

The history he now laid out in front of me began in the early Seventies. Fomenko, at that time still a very young academic, was exploring mathematical aspects of celestial mechanics. By coincidence, he came across a paradox which had recently been posed by an American astrophysicist, a man named Robert Newton. His American colleague had encountered puzzling historical fluctuations while studying lunar motion. His findings suggested that the moon had started moving with constant speed only in the last 400 years. Before that, it seemed to have changed pace erratically at irregular intervals. Because that could not possibly be true, even though Newton did not find errors in his calculation, he presented 'Newton's Paradox' for debate.

Fomenko did not find any errors either. From a mathematical point of view, Newton's formula was flawless; the problem had to lie elsewhere. Was it possible that the historical data used by his American colleague was faulty? Newton had relied on the datings of solar and lunar eclipses as they appear in historical chronicles. As Fomenko read up on the subject, he discovered the forgotten book by a Russian scholar who at the beginning of the 20th century had dealt critically with such datings; the man had calculated alternative time spans. Tentatively, Fomenko applied this data to Newton's lunar equation. Immediately, the unexplained fluctuations disappeared. The moon moved steadily through the millennia.

The real problems, however, only started with this solution. The alternative datings deviated from the traditional ones not by a couple of days, but by centuries. For example, the Russian scholar had attributed the three solar eclipses described by the Greek historian Thucydides in his *History of the Peloponnesian War* not to the 5th century BC, but to the 11th century AD. Understandably, his contemporaries had taken him for a madman. Not so Fomenko, who found the theories plausible. Still, this raised questions that no mathematician could answer. How could Thucydides have described celestial phenomena of the Middle Ages? And if his solar eclipses had not taken place until the 11th century, was this also true for the Peloponnesian War?

Fomenko had never studied the past. But the History Faculty at his university was only a few corridors away. One day the mathematician knocked on the door of one of the historians. He submitted his problem to a white-haired scholar, who listened to Fomenko's astrophysical theories with polite disinterest. 'Young man,' he said, when Fomenko had finished, 'this is all very interesting, but what do I have to do with it?' Fomenko gathered all his courage: my thesis, he said, challenges the very foundations of your field of research. The historian frowned. 'My dear Anatoly Timofeyevich,' he said, 'according to everything I hear, you are a promising young mathematician. You should stick with your numbers. And by all means, keep your fingers off *my* numbers.'

Disappointed, Fomenko returned to the Mathematics Department. And decided to take on history himself.

When had Thucydides lived? The history books said it was: in the 5th century AD. But how did they know that? As Fomenko began to read Thucydides with the impartial eyes of a mathematician, he read about events that had occurred 'long after the Trojan War' or 'before the time of Hellen, son of Deucalion' or 'in the 48th year of the priestess-ship of Chrysis at Argos.' All datings presupposed other unspecified datings; nowhere was there a neutral zero point to be discovered. Fomenko read on, Homer and Herodotus, Xenophon and Cicero, he rummaged through the whole of the ancient world and found the same thing everywhere: dates that referenced other dates, that again referenced other dates and so on. All time spans went round in circles without any external reference point; it was a mathematical nightmare. As Fomenko read more and more, he increasingly felt that he was standing in front of a huge, unmanageable pile of puzzle pieces. The chronology of the world's history consisted of tiny parts; their positions within the total picture were impossible to guess. Someone must have arranged this gigantic chaos, having put together the time spans of all the chronicles piece by piece. But who had done it? With what methods? And above all, when?

Fomenko looked me in the eyes and made a small dramatic pause. Then he named the culprit: 'Scaliger.'

The common belief about the 16th century French scholar Joseph Scaliger is that he expanded the European view of the ancient world when he linked the history of the Greeks and Romans with the history of the Persians, Babylonians, Egyptians and Jews. Fomenko expressed it more radically: 'Scaliger drafted the first coherent chronology of world history. Unfortunately, he got it all wrong.'

Scaliger was admired by his contemporaries for his comprehensive memory, which aided him in putting together the puzzle pieces of world history. But for Fomenko, Scaliger was primarily a man. A man is not a computer, no matter how comprehensive his memory may be. Fomenko did not consider himself smarter than Scaliger; he was only mathematically superior to him. His computer told him that Scaliger had put the puzzle together incorrectly – he had crammed in too many pieces. Erroneously the Frenchman had considered chronicles relating the same events from different angles to be descriptions of different epochs. Consequently, his world history had ended up being too long, much too long. It was about 1000 years longer than the chronology that Fomenko calculated himself.

In the mid-Seventies he began to feed his computer historical dates. He gathered a small research team around him, who helped dissect thousands of chronicles into basic narrative elements: sequences of political rulers and ecclesial dignitaries, wars, popular uprisings, natural disasters, epidemics, crop failures, celestial phenomena, religious festivals, technical innovations, economic reforms. He developed a statistical analysis method that sought narrative parallels between individual chronicles. Whenever the computer discovered striking similarities in the structure of two histories Fomenko assumed that the chronicles described the same events – regardless of what era and what culture the texts were commonly attributed to.

It took years for the chaos to begin to lift. Fomenko pasted the walls of his study with sheets of paper, on which he recorded his findings. Soon, a long timeline stretched from one end of the room to the other, completely covered with hypothetical dates. Fomenko developed theories, rejected them, developed new ones, corrected them, tore sheets from the wall, crumpled them and stuck up new ones. Step by step he completed the puzzle.

In the mid-Eighties Fomenko tried to publish his research for the first time; he wrote a book. Shortly before going to press, it was banned; his theories were considered 'anti-Soviet.' This was essentially a very mild reproach, because the book did not attack Soviet historiography, but every established historiography there was. Christ's birth, Fomenko claimed, had been barely a millennium ago. Thucydides was a chronicler of the Middle Ages; the Peloponnesian War was just another term for the Christian Crusades. The Old Testament had been written after the New Testament. The Renaissance was no revival of the ancient world – it *was* the ancient world.

The book would probably have continued to be banned from publication if the tide had not turned due to an irony of history. While Fomenko was trying to shake up time, it suddenly turned itself completely upside down. Abruptly and unexpectedly the Soviet era ended. Books bearing the stamp 'anti-Soviet' suddenly came into fashion; Fomenko benefited from a wave of publications that washed to the surface what had previously been kept in the toxic cellars. His first book appeared in 1990.

Many more followed. They found readers. Fomenko's theories may have sounded chaotic, but then the times were chaotic as well.

I observed the pencil in Fomenko's right hand that had accompanied the ups and downs of his sentences like a baton. Now it stood still; Fomenko was silent. At technically complicated spots he had used the pencil to draw explanatory guidelines in the air. Now an invisible timeline floated between us, and its pencil outline was 1000 years too short. Blinking, I tried to make friends with this chronological monster. It was not easy. One single 16th century scholar had distorted the entire history of the world?

'No.' Fomenko shook his head firmly. 'Scaliger's errors are only one part of the problem. The other part is the deliberate historical falsifications that took place before his time.'

Now we were definitely venturing onto unstable ground. Behind us was what Fomenko identified as the 'scientifically validated' part of his findings, ahead of us what he called 'interpretation.' The computer, he explained, had only been able to trawl through history for statistical similarities. How these parallels had come into existence, Fomenko himself had had to piece together. He considered them the result of deliberate manipulation. Chronicles had been rewritten in retrospect – years, sometimes centuries after their creation. Names had been replaced and dates changed; the original descriptions had been so disfigured that even a genius like Joseph Scaliger was taken in by the fabrications. Only a computer had the ability to recognise the identical basic structures underneath the orchestrated surfaces of such texts.

But why should a trail of lies be drawn through history? Fomenko suspected that an ancient human disease was behind the fabrications: an addiction to the past. It afflicted peoples and their rulers whenever it came to laying claim on a territory, a throne, a belief, a culture. Whoever had demonstrably inhabited a country or ruled an empire or worshipped a god or spoken a language before all others could not be forced to share this property with new arrivals. Whoever desires a future needs a past. And the past can be feigned.

Exactly that, Fomenko believed, was what had happened to the chronicles. Parvenus had compensated for what they lacked in history by way of forgeries. They had rewritten entire chronicles in order to date their own origins far back into the past and to make their adversaries look like illegitimate impostors. Not only individual rulers, but whole peoples and nations had been attributed with a past that existed only on paper. Fomenko thought it possible, even probable, that not one of today's nation-states had been created earlier than the 16th century. Before that – at least this was what his evidence suggested – they had merely been provinces of a single, global empire. The traces of this empire had been deliberately blurred after its collapse, as new rulers bequeathed a fabricated, national past to their fledgling states.

I started to listen attentively. Fomenko's argument had suddenly taken a completely new direction. Back then, in Berlin, when Yuri had told me about Fomenko for the first time, his fragmentation of world history had seemed random to me, like the work of a maniacal mathematician who is driven by his arithmetic instincts alone. Now that Fomenko was rearranging history right before my eyes, I suddenly saw patterns that had previously escaped me. His madness had a method. As he spoke, Russia became a different country, a better one. It cast off the lies of centuries and shone brightly. Russia had not, as everyone erroneously believed, entered the stage of world history late; it had entered it early and had therefore no need to be ashamed in front of the old European cultures. It had not been established by a Viking tribe either – that was a legend the house of Romanov had started in the 17th century, to defame the extinct dynasty of the Rurikid tsars as a foreign occupying power. Russia had not converted to Christianity a millennium after Christ, but shortly after the crucifixion – so not later than the other peoples of Europe, but before them, even earlier than the Romans. And the humiliating centuries of subjection by the Mongols had never happened; on the contrary, the Mongols had been mercenaries in the service of the Kremlin. With their hordes of horsemen, Russia had dominated the world – because the power centre of that mysterious empire, whose traces had been so carefully obliterated on the threshold between the 16th and 17th centuries, had been Moscow. In all statistical probability, anyway.

While Russia grew greater and greater before my eyes, so did my doubt. Fomenko's whole theory, its derivation from an astrophysical problem, its unerring statistical methods, all of this suddenly seemed like a means to an end. Had he thought up the whole mathematical prehistory in order to let Russia shine? I quickly rejected the thesis.

Fomenko's vision of history might have motives that he did not admit even to himself, but he did not seem like a con man – he was too convinced of his mission. He was a solitary Copernicus, struggling against the errors of the centuries. He did not care that the academic world was laughing at him – one day their smiles would be wiped off their faces; then he would be the only one laughing.

He was immune to objections. When I asked him about the traditional dating methods, which so obviously contradicted his theses, he brushed them aside like annoying flies. Carbon dating, the chemical analysis of archaeological finds? 'Unreliable.' Dendrochronology, the analysis of annual growth rings in wood grain? 'Crude.' Numismatics, the chronological classification of coins? 'Error-prone.' I pulled the final card out of my sleeve – what about good old archaeology? Fomenko sighed. 'Archaeology is the most deceptive dating method of all. The entire area of research is poisoned by Scaliger's chronology. Each excavated find only confirms what the archaeologists already believe they know. They cannot think independently.'

He lifted the pencil and drew the outline of a triangle in the air.

'Take the Egyptian pyramids. That a people without any technical aids could have moved huge stones through the desert is unthinkable. Everyone knows that it is unthinkable. The archaeologists also know it, which is why they have been inventing ever newer, ever more fantastic explanations for centuries. Although the solution is really quite simple.' Again he made one of his dramatic pauses before he solved the riddle. 'Concrete.'

I looked at him inquiringly.

'Artificial stones, manufactured on site. The pyramids were assembled out of prefabricated parts. Not in the ancient world, but in modern times.'

I did not know what to say. Up to this point I had managed to defer my inner doubts and follow his argument. But the pyramids were hard to swallow.

'And,' I asked hesitantly, 'have you seen the pyramids?'

'No.' He shook his head. 'I have never been to Egypt. I can't tolerate the heat.'

I nodded stupidly.

Fomenko continued; he returned to the fabrications in the chronicles.

'Even today the manipulations continue,' he said. 'Look at what is happening in the former Soviet republics, in the Baltics, in Georgia, in the Ukraine. Soviet history is being rewritten, new countries are inventing their own history. If in a few centuries from now someone compares today's history books with the Soviet ones, they will not understand that they are speaking about the same era or the same country.'

Suddenly there was an echo in the room. Two empires had collapsed, the first in the distant past, the second, the Soviet Union, not even 20 years ago. Twice Moscow had been disempowered, twice Russia dismembered, twice history rewritten. Was Fomenko, when he evoked one empire, only seeking consolation for the loss of the other? Again I had my doubts about what had been at the beginning of his theory: eclipses of the past – or of the present.

I asked Fomenko what had become of the old notes which he had pasted on the walls of his study. I wanted to see the original timeline, the theory in its pure form.

'They don't exist anymore. I don't need them anymore. You can do all this on the computer today.'

'You didn't keep anything?'

Fomenko considered for a moment. Then he stood up abruptly and opened the door of a closet. From the inside he pulled out something that looked like a thick roll of wallpaper.

'Back then, before I discarded the notes, I photographed the whole timeline and had it printed on this canvas.' He smiled, the way a person smiles over the sentimentality of a good friend. Then he put the plastic roll on the floor beside the door. He put his left foot on its loose end; with the right he gave the rolled part a kick. With a crackling sound five metres of world history unfurled, until the roll hit the wall on the opposite side of the room. Not even half of it had unrolled – the room was too short for Fomenko's vision. But what lay on the floor was enough to take my breath away. Competing narratives ran in parallel paths from one end of the room to the other. Cyrillic letters flagged key events in history; their order contradicted everything that I had ever learned. The time was out of joint.

For several minutes we stared silently at the canvas and no longer knew what to say.

I was slightly dizzy when I finally stood alone in the stairwell. I waited for the elevator, but when it came I decided to take the stairs instead. At each window I craned my neck to get a close look at the ornamentation of the university facade, whose bizarre mixture of styles had borrowed elements from several millennia.

Some day, I imagined, an archaeological research team would dig up the ground where Moscow had once stood. A few metres below the earth's surface they would stumble across the remains of Lomonosov University, and it would not be easy for them to place this strange, timeless building in a historical context. But then they would stumble across something in the rubble that would give them still far more headaches: Fomenko's rolled-up timeline.

A Kettle of Water Minus the Kettle

In the years 1652 and 1666 two solar eclipses darkened the sky over Russia. 'For about three hours we remained at the bank and wept,' recalls a witness to the first of the two. 'The sun was darkened and the moon came up from the west; God showed His wrath to men. At that time Nikon, the apostate, mutilated the faith and the ordinance of the Church, and on account of him God poured forth the vials of the wrath of His fury onto the Russian land.'

Nikon was the patriarch whose liturgical reform incited the 17th century bloodbath of the Orthodox schism. One of his bitterest opponents, the Old Believer's Archpriest Avvakum, bestowed cosmic dimensions on the dispute about how many fingers to use while making the sign of the cross when he chronicled his memoirs in 1673. 'About 14 years later, another time there was a darkening of the sun,' Avvakum continued. 'The sun waned, and the moon came up from the west, making known the wrath of God; and at that time in the minster-church of the district the Bishop did shear the Archpriest Avvakum for a monk with others, and in the morning they cursed him and threw him into prison.'

A few years after writing these lines Avvakum died a martyr at the stake. The last his followers saw of him was his burning hand, which is said to have formed the two-fingered cross until he died. Everywhere in Russia the Old Believers watched with silent horror as their priests were murdered, one after the other. When finally the only bishop who had taken their side was also killed, there was no one left who could ordain new priests. The desperate Old Believers toyed with the idea of anointing a successor with the bishop's dead hand, but theological scruples stopped them in the end. Thus, the resistance movement was doomed to die, in the literal, as well as the spiritual, sense – without bishops no priests, without priests no sacraments, without sacraments no salvation of souls.

While the Old Believers helplessly discussed their fate, their community split into two streams. The one thought the end of time had come. Their church had fallen into the hands of the Antichrist, and if they wanted to save their souls, they would henceforth have to live without a church. The 'Priestless', as this group of the Old Believers was soon called, left the world behind them and fled into the Siberian wilderness, where they split into other, ever more radical streams, who either administered the sacraments to each other or abstained from them completely. Out of this, the more uncompromising tradition, sprang Agafya Lykova, the hermit to whom my journey was supposed to lead.

For the more moderate group of Old Believers a life without the Church was inconceivable. They ensured their survival in the early days after the schism by luring away priests from the Patriarchal Church. This method required connections and often money. Both factors forced them to live closer to civilisation than their Siberian brothers and sisters. Over the centuries, the deadly enmity between them and the Patriarchal Church gave way to a relationship of strained toleration, even if the mutual excommunications were never rescinded. A few communities of Old Believers even moved back to the cities.

One very cold March day I took a trolley bus in search of one such community which had survived in Moscow until the present day.

I did not know what to expect. The Rogozhskoye cemetery, the goal of my journey, was in a dead corner of the capital, a little east of the great Moscow ring road, hemmed in by railway bridges and industrial plants. Here, just beyond the historic city limits, Catherine the Great had granted the Old Believers a piece of land in 1771 – a gesture entirely in the tolerant spirit of Western European Enlightenment, which the Tsarina loved as much as the Old Believers hated it. I knew that the religious community had been repeatedly banned in the ensuing centuries and then unbanned again, following the zigzag course of Russian history. But I had no idea in what state it had survived the Soviet era.

A bell tower showed me the way from the bus stop to the cemetery. It was wrapped in tattered construction nets which made its free-standing silhouette look like a bandaged finger. Its long shadow pointed to the cemetery entrance. A few flat community buildings surrounded the tower, dominated by a church which emitted a weak light. Although footprints crossed the snow in all directions, the area looked deserted. It was only in the cemetery that I encountered a few people, women in headscarves and long skirts, men with monumental beards. They avoided my glances.

Without much hope I entered the church. History had taught the Old Believers to mistrust everything foreign, and my foreign brain told me they would make no exception for me.

At the entrance I was intercepted by an old woman. 'Are you a true Christian?'

I shook my beardless chin in the negative. Denial was futile.

With her forefinger the woman drew an invisible line in front of my feet. 'Do not enter the chapel. Do not speak. Do not take photographs. Do not touch anything. Do not make phone calls.'

She turned her back to me and disappeared into the darkness of the nave. There were no electric lights. Candles were burning in front of individual icons, but they only illuminated a few patches of the room. Whispered prayers filled the air. At the other end of the room I detected the silhouette of a kneeling man who was bowing again and again in front of an icon. Every time he threw his upper body forward his elongated shadow jerked through the nave like a clock pendulum.

As I left the church I noticed a man who was standing by himself in front of one of the parish buildings. He was wearing a heavy wool suit and a shirt which was buttoned up to the top, even though the tie was missing. In his hand he held a plastic bag. He stood motionless in the snow, as if waiting for something. I did not know why he struck me as more accessible than the other Old Believers – perhaps because his beard was comparatively short, or perhaps because he was standing there so idly. As I approached him he turned his eyes to me. They were like the winter sky – pale blue and infinitely far away from earth. At first I thought that he was blind. But then he nodded to me. And began to speak. And would not stop.

'... I must wait, they said, but whether I wait one hour or three or the entire day does not matter. What kind of priests are they, I wonder? They are not concerned about people; they only think about money and nothing else. Have you seen their cars? Where does the money come from, I wonder? For years the bell tower has been surrounded by scaffolding, but nothing happens. Where has the money gone, I wonder? Do not interfere, they say, do not confront the priests. For three hours I have been standing here ...'

While he spoke I could not shake the feeling that I had met him before somewhere. After a while I understood why: The scrubby beard, the eerie eyes, the monologue of suffering – he was the incarnate hero from a Dostoyevsky novel. Without knowing me, without even knowing my name, he poured out his bleeding heart to me. Each of his gestures and grimaces spoke of inner torment that seeped out unfiltered.

'... they have sent someone to spy on me, and when I talk badly about the priests, he rats on me immediately. They are Communists, at heart they are all Communists, they have thrown away their Party books and become priests ...'

While speaking, he kept reaching into his plastic bag to show me mysterious documents that he shifted back and forth in his hands for a long time before he put them back. First his passport: Vladimir Vladimirovich Semyonov, born 1961 in Donetsk. This was followed by a dog breeding diploma and then the faded programme from a dressage competition Vladimir had attended with his German shepherd. A medical certificate, a train ticket to Rostov-on-Don, a few letters of uncertain origin. Last, a tattered brochure: 'Constitution of the Russian Federation.' Vladimir opened it and read Article 2 to me: 'Man, his rights and freedoms are the supreme value.' Disgusted, he stuffed the booklet back into the bag. 'Only on paper!' It took me a while to understand that the plastic bag contained everything Vladimir possessed. He was homeless.

I could not figure him out. Was he crazy? Or just lonely, socially neglected? What he said sounded confusing, but not stupid. His flitting eyes seemed to perceive more than I gave him credit for. From the few sentences I spoke he guessed my provenance and immediately began to sprinkle German words into his sentences: *Freundschaft ... Deutschmark ... Gott ...*

His knowledge of the Old Believers was astonishing, despite his garbled delivery. He knew everything about their history, probably without ever having read a book. I learned from him how the Old Believers of Moscow had managed to build their own church hierarchy, with their own metropolitan bishop at the top: in the middle of the 19th century they had succeeded to convince a Greek Orthodox bishop of the merits of the two-finger cross.

'… they say: The Metropolitan is closer to God than you; he is above you, so how can you criticise him? But what kind of a Metropolitan is it that does not help the poor? I have been standing here for hours; I need money – not much, for him it is nothing, but for me it is everything. There … There he comes … You have to speak to him …'

His eyes fixed on a point behind my back. I turned around. A procession of clerics was leaving the parish hall. Vladimir grabbed my shoulder and pushed me up to a man whose snow-white beard reached to his belt. Surprised, the man looked at us. It was only when I noticed the crosier in his hand that I realised who stood before me: His Excellency Kornily, Metropolitan of Moscow and all Russia, spiritual leader of the Old Believers. Sheepishly I stammered my name and stretched out my right hand. A murmur went through the ranks of the clergy, half affronted, half amused. I noticed my error and tried to withdraw my hand when His Excellency grasped it with an indulgent smile. Vladimir spoke to us from the right; from the left two old women suddenly appeared, who threw themselves down in the snow in front of the Metropolitan and began to pray with whimpering voices. The clerics visibly struggled for composure; the Metropolitan withdrew his hand from mine to bless the old women; Vladimir breathlessly continued to talk while I asked myself whether I had ever been in such an absurd situation before.

When the chaos had subsided, the Metropolitan asked me a few polite questions before he referred me to one of his subordinates. The procession continued on its way, followed by Vladimir.

A young man named Gleb remained with me. He led me into one of the community houses. In his office he pulled a second chair up to the desk, then he put the kettle on and looked me in the eyes.

'What do you want to know?'

The unsuccessful start overshadowed our conversation; it proceeded haltingly. Polite, but with noticeable distrust, Gleb answered my questions, he seemed to feel uncomfortable. His broad hands were constantly moving; he put cookies on the table, put tea bags into two glasses, poured in water. My eyes were drawn to the tea bags.

'Earl Grey,' I read half aloud.

'Would you prefer green tea?'

'No, black is good. I only thought ...' I did not finish the sentence. Somewhere I had read that Old Believers did not drink anything that did not grow on Russian soil, but the objection seemed pedantic.

Gleb read my mind. 'Our ancestors did not drink tea. We do. The times are changing.'

For an Old Believer that was a remarkable sentence. But it applied, as I quickly realised, only to things like tea or Gleb's discernibly trimmed goatee, but not to the crux of the faith. The old liturgical formulas – *two* hallelujahs, *seven* altar loaves – stood unshakeable in the current of time, they still separated the Old Believers from the 'Nikonians', as Gleb called all members of the Patriarchal Church. He spoke with the indulgent patience of a teacher while I slipped more and more into the role of the slow-witted student.

Gleb pointed to his desk.

'Do you see the kettle?'

I nodded.

'You could say: water is water, whether it is in a container or not. But if you remove the kettle, the water will be lost. Without form, the content melts away. A faith without form is like a kettle of water minus the kettle.'

I pondered for a moment. 'But does it matter what the kettle looks like as long as it holds water? Isn't a cross a cross, no matter how you hold your fingers?'

Quite unexpectedly Gleb lifted his right hand and extended his middle finger in my face.

'Is that a cross?'

Perplexed, I shook my head.

'You see?'

I nodded. The argument was as drastic as it was persuasive.

An exculpatory tone crept into Gleb's voice as he explained to me why the Old Believers today accepted printed books in addition to handwritten ones and how they had managed to reconcile the use of computers with their dogmas. It sounded like theological sleight of hand, but it was

clear to me that such questions made the difference between redemption and damnation here – the computers now no longer stood between
the Old Believers and eternity. Gleb's arguments circumnavigated the
cliffs of the modern world. He justified each manoeuvre with passages
from the Bible which sounded like a method of nautical positioning:
Mark 7:19, Romans 14:17, Genesis 9:3.

I suppressed a yawn. Gleb was not an unpleasant man, but the longer
I listened to his orderly deliberations, the more nostalgic I became for
Vladimir. Maybe he was crazy, but maybe in his madness he had preserved something of the chaotic origins of the Old Believers, an anar-
chical absolutism which no longer occurred in the theologically stable
present. Vladimir was a holy fool, Gleb the Saviour's cleaning squad. My
judgment was probably unfair in both directions, but I could not help
myself – a blasphemous affection drew me to Vladimir.

He heard my prayers. Suddenly, he was standing in the middle of the
room. His confused monologue continued immediately. He seemed to
have been looking for me.

'... the church, I must show him the church. They say: he may not
enter the church, he is a foreigner, he is not one of us, but what right do
they have ...'

Gleb was silent. He seemed just as tense as the Metropolitan had
seemed earlier. Vladimir seemed to be the black sheep of the community.

'... I have spoken with Father Viktor, he has agreed, he wants to guide
him through the church, we can go there immediately ...'

I looked questioningly at Gleb. He nodded helplessly. 'If Father Viktor
agrees ...'

Vladimir pushed me out of the room. In a feverish haste he hurried
about the parish square, clasping my upper arm with both hands. He
hammered on the door of a flat brick building beside the church.

'Father Viktor! Father Viktor!'

Silence. Then an irritated bass voice. 'What is it? I'm eating!'

'... the church, Father Viktor, I want to show him the church ...'

A bearded giant flung the door open. Before I was able to say anything, he began to roar. 'Then show him the church! What has it got to
do with me?' The door slammed shut with a bang.

Vladimir did not hesitate. He clutched me by the arm and pushed me
in the direction of the church.

'… he is shaved, they say, he is not allowed into the church, he is an infidel …'

Inside two old women blocked our way. Vladimir ignored their scolding and tugged me into the dark nave, past the disapproving eyes of painted saints and horror-stricken Old Believers. I felt like an intruder, but Vladimir was unstoppable. He dragged me in front of a giant icon. In the darkness I recognised an enthroned Christ, under whose judging hands the world was coming asunder: heaven on the left, hell on the right.

'… no one shall escape Him, least of all those who think they are righteous …'

Vladimir trembled. And suddenly I understood. The Last Judgment had begun. Vladimir did not live in the past, but in the future, at the end of time. Everything could be over at any moment – that was why he was so feverish, so hectic, that was why he could not tolerate the shortcomings of his church.

'… they think they are already saved, but they understand nothing …'

Later, as we were saying goodbye outside, I told him about my trip, about Siberia, about the hermit.

'They live differently there, the Old Believers,' he said. 'They are wiser than us. They have no priests.'

A rouble note fell in the snow. I had wanted to put it into Vladimir's plastic bag, but he pushed my hand away.

On the way to the bus stop I turned around and looked back. Scanning the surface of the snow, I discovered Vladimir's silhouette at the foot of the bell tower. He was standing there motionless, as if waiting for something.

It began to snow as the trolley bus reached the ring road. Heavy flakes danced around the streetlights like squadrons of arctic moths. Spontaneously I went to Red Square – there is no image more Russian than Red Square in billowing snow.

Seamless white covered the cobblestones. A lost dog chased snowflakes. The watch guards in front of the Lenin mausoleum stared into the night; little white hills had accumulated on their hats. Snow clouds floated over the Kremlin, chopped into glaring wedges by the spotlights. The church domes, whose polished surfaces reflect all of Moscow as an onion-shaped panorama on clear days, now hung blind and dull in the sky. What was left of the aspirations of this church ensemble which had originally been built as a 'third Rome', after the original Rome and its successor Byzantium had failed? 'A fourth there will not be,' a monk whispered to Ivan the Terrible in the 16th century. The first Rome had fallen into the hands of the Pope, the second had fallen to the Turks; Russia alone adhered to the true, the Orthodox faith. But only a century later the Kremlin also fell away from Christianity – or so the Old Believers saw it, who now held their scattered communities to be the fourth and last Rome. Then, a few centuries later again, the next Messiah entered the scene, the one whose corpse is now laid out in the mausoleum next to the Kremlin wall. Again Moscow became the bishop's see of a world religion of salvation, the fifth and final Rome – a sixth there could not be, whispered Marx.

Now all of that was over. Only symbols remained of Russia's eternal search for the true faith – the red star above Spasskaya Tower, the Orthodox crosses on the domes of the Kremlin churches. Opposite, in a display window of the GUM department store, hung a light installation which displayed Russia's new old coat of arms, the double-headed Byzantine eagle. There was something desperate about it – a schizophrenic bird craning its necks in search of God knows what.

When I woke up the next morning, I began to write down the experiences of the previous day. I stayed in the apartment the entire day. In the evening Vanya came home.

'Damn traffic jams,' he cursed. 'I sat in the taxi for three hours.'

'Why didn't you take the subway?'

Surprised, he looked at me. 'You don't know?'

'What don't I know?'

'A terrorist attack. Two bombs, this morning, in the underground; 36 people have died.'

Without knowing exactly why, I set out for the city centre. In the meantime, the subway had started running again, but the cars were as good as empty. The few passengers exchanged nervous glances. Shortly before the train reached the Ring Line, a dark-skinned woman boarded, apparently from the Caucasus. Two Russians, a man and a woman, left the car immediately.

At the station Park Kultury, where one of the two bombs had exploded, a silent crowd had gathered. All traces of the attack had been eliminated; there was nothing to see. The people were staring at a shrine of flowers and other offerings which had accrued spontaneously in the middle of the platform. No one spoke. Only a bearded man with an opened liturgical book in his hands whispered a requiem. Like all the others I stared silently at the shrine, where new offerings continued to be added. A pot of crocuses. A ten rouble note. Two icons of the Virgin Mother, one made of cardboard, the other of wood. Eighteen white tea lights, nine yellow icon candles, three red grave lanterns. A lighter, a box of matches, six chocolate eggs, two Snickers bars. A handwritten note: *Vy zhivy* – 'You are alive'. Roses, carnations, asters, tulips, gerbera, pussy willows, fir sprigs.

Just as I was getting ready to go, a man walked up to the shrine. He was the type of man I characterise in my personal Moscow typology as a perestroika rocker: not young anymore, long hair, black leather jacket, very oppositional facial expression. He took two bottles of vodka and a stack of plastic cups out of his army backpack, placed them down with the other offerings to the dead, turned around and left. Mechanically, I counted the cups: 36, one for each.

The Trail of the Icons

I was rarely alone when I woke up in the mornings in Vanya's apartment. Sometimes the cats had rolled themselves up on my bed during the night, sometimes sleeping students were lying on the carpet. Sometimes when I opened my eyes and scanned the room for guests, there were only the icons. With sleepless eyes they stared at me.

I had never been particularly interested in Russian icons, and in hindsight I can no longer say why they suddenly did not let go of me. Maybe it began in Moscow, with Vanya's icons, which guarded over my sleep night after night. Maybe it was because of the images I had seen in Kiev: the Baptism in the Dnieper, the Saviour of Chernobyl – two icons that recounted Russia's beginnings and the end of the Soviet Union. In between were 1000 years that had to be reflected in other icons.

On my walks through the snowy city I sometimes went into churches to warm up. In one of them I one day discovered a large icon of the

Virgin Mother that was difficult to date. It was painted in the old Byzantine style that had dominated Russian icons until the painting of the European Renaissance pushed it aside. But the image before my eyes could not possibly be that old. And it did not look like a modern copy either, for the surface was too damaged – two vertical furrows ran through the wooden board, as if it had been broken into three parts and then been reassembled.

A young monk who noticed my gaze took a place beside me.

'The Virgin of the Don,' he whispered. 'Isn't she beautiful?'

'Yes,' I whispered back. The image was truly remarkable. The Virgin and her child had mask-like, Byzantine facial features, lacking any sentimentality. Nevertheless, or perhaps because of it, the sorrow that overshadowed their embrace was almost physically palpable.

'The painter was a great man,' the monk whispered. 'A count!' He pronounced the aristocratic title with awe. 'And a martyr. They shot him.' He hastily crossed himself.

'Shot him? Why?'

'Because he believed in God. Stalin tolerated no God beside himself.'

I nodded silently.

'It is a miracle that this icon survived,' the monk continued. 'For decades it was missing; a farmer was using it as a tabletop. But then it turned up – a miracle!' He crossed himself again.

'The painter,' I asked. 'Did he live in Moscow?'

'Yes. And he also died in Moscow. In Butovo.'

Butovo is in the southern Moscow suburbs. On a commuter train I travelled through districts of concrete buildings until the city unravelled and petered out into snowy wastelands. On the way I read the little I had been able to find about the fate of the icon painter – a few journal articles, nothing else. Vladimir Alekseyevich Komarovsky was born in 1883, the youngest son of Saint Petersburg nobility. His mother died early, followed by his father when Komarovsky was 16 years old. Just old enough to stand on his own feet, he enrolled to study art. For a while he drifted through Western Europe and became attracted to the French painting styles of the turn of the century, which he started copying upon his return to Russia.

He discovered his true passion when he was 27. It happened during a visit to the Russian Museum in Saint Petersburg, which had opened a new department for 'Old Russian Art' in 1910. Hardly anyone, including Komarovsky himself, understood what old Russian art should be. Before the 17th century there had not been any painting in Russia – except for icons. But no one in Komarovsky's time thought of these old icons and their awkward Byzantine style as art. They were regarded as primitive precursors of a tradition of painting that had only matured into an art form in the 17th century, under the belated influence of Europe. Even the names of the old icon masters – Andrey Rublyov, Dionisy, Feofan Grek – were largely forgotten. Hardly anyone actually knew what the old style of painting looked like, because in later centuries it had become so unfashionable that the icons were unceremoniously painted over in the European style.

So it happened that at the beginning of the 20th century a few conservators of the Russian Museum, who scraped the paint off the old icons layer by layer, discovered a forgotten world. They restored the images to their original condition and presented them to a public who responded at first with disconcertment, but then with enthusiasm. Russia discovered itself. Artists and churchgoers realised that for centuries they had been worshipping faces covered in European make-up. But under this make-up they now recognised features of a native Russian art tradition that had existed long before the adoption of European styles.

Komarovsky decided to become an icon painter. The years between 1910 and 1917 must have been the happiest of his life. He had found a mission, and did not yet know that it was doomed to fail. For while Komarovsky was creating a link to Russia's past, the Bolsheviks were already sketching out a future in which icons no longer had a place.

When the class struggle began, the nobleman Komarovsky fell into the category of the *byvshiye lyudi*, the 'former people'. He shared the fate of all the aristocrats, clergymen, civil servants and tsarist officers, who not only were no longer considered people, but were also deprived of their apartments, their jobs, their right to vote. Komarovsky moved in with distant relatives, whose house was soon filled top to bottom with homeless aristocrats. For a while he worked illegally as an art teacher in a village school, which led to his first arrest in 1925. He was accused of inciting peasant children as 'a member of a monarchist movement of former aristocrats'. The villagers saw it differently – they petitioned the

authorities to return their art teacher to them. Even a few Soviet dignitaries campaigned for Komarovsky, including heavyweights like Alexey
Shchussev, the architect of the Lenin mausoleum. In vain. Komarovsky
was banished to a Siberian prison camp for three years.

When he returned home, he lived, without a permanent place of resi-
dence, on small commissions for paintings. Again and again, until the
mid-Thirties, he painted icons and frescoes for the few churches that
were still open, which earned him three more arrests. After the last, in
August 1937, nothing could save him. The years of the 'Great Terror' had
dawned, Stalin suspected treason everywhere, the secret police convicted
counterrevolutionaries according to established quotas. Komarovsky's
indictment reads like the monologue of a paranoiac:

> ... *initiated a white emigrant terrorist group, with the goal to estab-
> lish a national Russia with a fascist dictatorship ... gathered coun-
> terrevolutionary elements from the circle of reactionary clergymen
> around him ... committed destructive acts of sabotage to promote
> his monarchist views ...*

The last sentence, the verdict, is concise: 'Shoot'. On 5 November 1937,
shortly after his 54th birthday, Komarovsky was executed and buried in
a mass grave.

While reading the articles I made a note of all the references to
Komarovsky's icons, in the hope that I might be able to see them. The
list was short and sad.

> *1913: Iconostasis for church in the Volga region. Church devastated
> after the Revolution, iconostasis destroyed, priest died in prison.*
> *1914: Iconostasis for church in Kulikovo. Chopped into firewood by
> looters during the civil war.*
> *1917–1925: Individual icons for various churches. All missing.*
> *1929: Frescoes for church in Moscow. Church converted into clubhouse
> for atheistic discussion club 'League of the Godless.' Frescoes not
> completed, fragments not preserved.*
> *1936: Frescoes for church in Kazan. Not completed, not preserved.*

The 'Virgin of the Don' that I had seen was Komarovsky's only preserved icon. He had painted it in 1918, one year after the Revolution, when he may have already suspected that the era of icons was coming to an end. When they arrested him for the last time two decades later, he turned, before he was led away, with a final sentence to his family: 'Pray to the Virgin.'

Butovo is the last station before Moscow's city limits. On the long ride the clientele in the carriage changed recognisably: people in urban dress got out, pensioners in rubber boots got on. The suburban railways, called *elektrichka*, are slow, bumpy trains without toilets, which to the Muscovite eye appear like rolling outposts of the provinces. During the trip peddlers roamed the carriages and pitched their chaotic assortment: road atlases, ink erasers, history books, colanders, raincoats, massage pillows, women's perfume.

In Butovo hardly anyone got off but me. Around the snowy platform Moscow drifted into dirty grey fragments: railway embankment barriers made of concrete segments, wreaths of barbed wire, warehouses, a dirty newsstand, arterial streets on concrete stilts, the construction shell of an apartment block. I walked past these urban fragments until I crossed Warsaw Avenue and left Moscow behind me.

For half an hour I walked through a stretch of forest without encountering a single person. Then, on the left side of the road, a green wooden fence appeared. The planks, nailed together without gaps, were so high that I could not see the other side. I discovered a plaque: 'Butovo Polygon. Site of mass shootings and burials of victims of political repression.' The fence continued through the forest, branching off repeatedly, following a winding layout – presumably the reason for the name 'Polygon'. An entrance was nowhere to be seen.

On the other side of the street stood a large church which seemed to have been built not too long ago. Its white tented roofs made the snow all around look even greyer. Warm, red light flooded from the front door. I entered and was immediately drawn towards the iconostasis. It was the strangest icon wall I had ever seen. On the right side of the altar door hung the usual image of Christ; on the left, the Virgin. Clustered around them there were twelve smaller images, whose bizarre brutality was so startling to the eye that the rest of the iconostasis faded into the background. An unequal battle was being fought in the pictures.

Dark figures wrapped in army coats, easily identifiable as Bolsheviks by their pointed hats, massacred defenceless Christians who had haloes hovering behind their suffering faces. Each scene of this Soviet martyrdom displayed drastic, almost cartoon-like violence. People were shot, drowned, stabbed, beaten with rifle butts, thrown into mineshafts, buried alive.

After a while I felt the gaze of three old women who were guarding a book stand in the entrance area. I went over and asked them whether it was possible to enter the Polygon.

'Of course!'

'You *must* see it!'

'Seeing as you have come here from so far away.'

'It is a special place.'

'A holy place! Have you heard about the miracles?'

'Sometimes people hear voices.'

'It's the dead. They speak. Sometimes they sing, too.'

'Like angels.'

'You must speak to Father Kirill, he will explain everything to you.'

'Just wait for an hour and then the Father will be here.'

'Perhaps you are hungry?'

'Of course he is hungry! Seeing as he has come here from so far away.'

In the end they guided me to an outbuilding and fed me cabbage soup until I could eat no more. As we were returning to the church, a priest crossed our path.

'Father! You have a guest! From Germany!'

The man who shook my hand looked like a Hollywood priest. Father Kirill – full title: Archpriest Kirill Glebovich Kaleda, head of the New Martyrs' Church of Butovo – combined the authority of a cleric with the charisma of a movie star. Under his black cassock was the body of an athlete. A gray mottled beard, which would have made other men look old, underlined the virile edges of his face. Out of metallic blue eyes he looked at me. 'Strange,' he said. 'Strange that you should ask about Komarovsky. He was shot along with my grandfather.'

Together we entered the basement of the church. In a small reception room we sat down on a sofa. Father Kirill stared momentarily into the emptiness, searching for the beginning of his story.

'I grew up with the knowledge that someone in our family was missing.'

His narrative began in the year 1892, the year his grandfather was born. Vladimir Ambartsumov was born in Saratov, near the Volga, the child of an Armenian father to whom he owed his unusual surname. As a student in Moscow he established a university bible group, the Christian Student Circle. Offshoots of this organisation were soon formed at universities throughout Russia, although the Bolsheviks were already in power. Ambartsumov was repeatedly arrested and interrogated, as the initiator of a supposedly counterrevolutionary movement. When his student circle was finally prohibited, he continued his work illegally from a decrepit building in Moscow. After his studies he was ordained a priest, and until 1931 he headed a small parish in Moscow which he abandoned with a heavy heart when increased harassment made his work impossible. Even after his resignation he kept being arrested, because the authorities suspected him of holding secret church services in his apartment. Whether this was actually true is not clear from the interrogation records that Father Kirill showed me. But then these interrogations, which moved in vicious circles, were not concerned with facts.

'In what counterrevolutionary organisations were you a member, where and when?'

'I was never a member of any counterrevolutionary organisation.'

'Then how do you explain the arrest of members of the Christian Student Circle who de facto pursued counterrevolutionary activities?'

'I am convinced that the Soviet government does not understand religious people. Therefore the Student Circle is suspected of pursuing counterrevolutionary activities. I reject this incrimination.'

'You have stated that the Soviet government does not understand religious people, whereby you have expressed your undisguised hostility towards the Soviet government. Explain this attitude.'

'I am not hostile to the Soviet government; my answer should not be regarded in that way.'

'Describe your relationship with Soviet power.'

'I think it is a temporary phenomenon, like every power.'

'Describe the content of your counterrevolutionary talks with the defendant Mikhail Shik.'

'In our meetings we discussed the difficult position of the Church

in the Soviet Union. I talked about the fact that there are cases of innocent clergymen condemned and banished to concentration camps and prisons.'

The last sentence became a self-fulfilling prophecy. In November 1937 Ambartsumov was sentenced to 'ten years of camp imprisonment without the right of correspondence.' At least that is what his relatives were told. Ten years passed. Ambartsumov did not come home. He did not come home after 11 years and not after 12 years, and only after 16 years, when Stalin died, did his relatives dare to inquire with the authorities. Ambartsumov, they were told, had died in prison, of kidney failure, in December 1943, burial place unknown.

A few years later Ambartsumov's daughter Lidiya gave birth to a child. The boy, named Kirill, grew up with the knowledge that someone in their family was missing. A grandfather had been lost; they did not know how or why. Every Sunday the family held a conspiratorial church service in their apartment – Kirill's father had secretly been ordained a priest. Sunday after Sunday Kirill repeated the family prayer: 'Lord! Grant that we learn how Grandfather Volodya died!'

The boy became a geologist. Kirill Kaleda, specialist in petrology, was in his early thirties when the empire in which his grandfather had perished collapsed. Before it collapsed completely, the empire mellowed with age; it admitted mistakes and promised to make amends. In November 1989 Kirill Kaleda entered the KGB's main building at Moscow's Lyubyanka Square. He had been summoned after inquiring about the fate of his grandfather. A middle-aged civil servant told him that on 3 November 1937 Vladimir Ambartsumov had received a death sentence and had been shot two days later, execution site Moscow, burial place unknown.

The officer handed Kaleda two final photographs of his grandfather, taken shortly before his execution. The pictures showed him from the front and in profile, a metal clamp holding his head in position. The man in the pictures was still alive, but his eyes were already staring into another world.

The officer also showed Kaleda the photograph of a man who had been sentenced and shot along with his grandfather. The man's name was Vladimir Komarovsky. Kaleda did not know the icon painter, but he memorised the name. In the photo Komarovsky had the same unearthly appearance as Kaleda's grandfather. Kaleda never found out why the two men had been shot together. He wasn't even sure whether they had known each other.

When the empire finally collapsed, the Orthodox Church gathered together what was left of itself. Lists were created, lists of victims of the Christian persecution. One day Kaleda discovered his grandfather's name on one of these lists. He was one of nearly 1,000 clergymen, bishops, priests, monks, laity and icon painters who had been shot at the Butovo Polygon.

Shortly afterwards the church set up a memorial cross on the execution grounds. A bishop gave a sermon that Kaleda never forgot. Everyone here, the priest said, had his own cross to bear – those who had been shot and those who had fired the guns. Kaleda felt his hands clench into fists in his pockets.

That summer he often drove to Butovo with his parents. His father sang mourning liturgies; together they prayed. Often they were joined by other people who had lost relatives. Disoriented, the people wandered through the unmarked ground; no grave stone pointed the way for them. The Polygon was a cemetery, but it lacked everything that constitutes a graveyard – everything except the dead. Even of the dead there was no visible evidence, and there were still people denying that executions had taken place here. Immediately beside the Polygon was a dacha settlement. The summer houses belonged to the KGB. The intelligence agency had built them in the Fifties as a resort for deserving employees. When Kaleda and his family visited the Polygon, they sometimes ran into intelligence officials who were suspicious of the muttered prayers behind their summer gardens. Stop this nonsense, they grumbled – your church is telling you fairy tales. Who do they say is buried here? It's just a few criminals, no one else.

Kaleda, the geologist, began to dig. In the beginning he dug illegally. Technically the Polygon still belonged to the KGB and investigating the deaths would have been the responsibility of the public prosecutor's office. The prosecution, however, was not keen to hassle the KGB, and since the authorities had enough on their plates in those years of upheaval, they happily left the upheaval of the past to Kaleda. After some bureaucratic back-and-forth the entire plot of land was transferred to the Church, on whose authority Kaleda now officially excavated the dead.

He found long trenches full of bones. There were so many that it was impossible to match them up. Even today no one knows exactly how many people died in Butovo. The investigations which were carried out in parallel to Kaleda's excavations yielded only basic data. The site had been enclosed by a fence in the early Thirties. For about 20 years residents and passers-by heard shots behind the fence which only ceased after Stalin's death. There were years in which hardly a shot would be heard and there were days on which the firing did not stop. A murderous crescendo echoed through Butovo between August 1937 and October 1938. Only during this period, the time of the Great Terror, did the intelligence agency document all of the executions on the premises. In just 14 months more than 20,000 people had been shot and buried, an average of about 50 per day. The youngest of these counterrevolutionaries was 14 years old. The oldest, an octogenarian archbishop, was so ill that they had to shoot him lying down, on his stretcher.

While Kaleda kept digging, the bones developed a life of their own. The Church started to declare some of the murdered clergymen martyrs. Over the years 300 people were canonised. Kaleda's grandfather was one of them. Somewhere in the mountains of bones, indistinguishable from all the other skeletal parts, there were now the bones of martyrs, Ortho-dox relics. Kaleda dug more carefully.

Other bones revealed their nature only as the KGB files gradually allowed more detailed conclusions about the shootings. Towards the end of the Great Terror, the paranoid logic of the interrogations had increasingly turned against Stalin's own henchmen – in rampant fits of panic, everybody started to denounce everybody else. Officials who had just ordered the execution of other people were now shot themselves, followed by their collaborators, their accomplices, the prison guards, the drivers who transported the convicted, finally the executioners and even the gravediggers. All the bodies were thrown indiscriminately into the Polygon's trenches. In the skeletal mountains, Kaleda realised, the bones of murderers lay beside the bones of martyrs, inseparably mixed together. It made him think of the bishop's sermon: everyone here had his own cross to bear, those who were shot and those who had fired the guns. Back then the words had seemed unacceptable to him. Now he was no longer sure.

When Kaleda had turned over every cubic inch of the Polygon, he wrote an investigation report and covered the bones with earth again. He heaped up long mounds to mark the location of the mass graves. Then he had himself ordained a priest. He built a church, a small wooden one to begin with, on the Polygon. A few years later it was complemented by the large stone church in whose basement we now sat.

There was a short pause when Father Kirill had finished his story.

'What became of the dacha settlement?' I asked. The question had been on my mind for half an hour.

Father Kirill looked at me uncomprehendingly. 'What should have become of it? Nothing.'

'You mean it still exists?'

He nodded.

'And KGB officials still live there?'

He nodded again. 'Or their families. Many of the old KGB people have died since then.'

There was no anger in his voice. I looked at him in disbelief.

'I understand your consternation,' he said. 'I felt that way for a long time myself. But you cannot build a church with anger. When our work here began, we decided to cast no stones.'

He stared into the emptiness for a few seconds, as if he was trying to remember something.

'I'll tell you a story,' he said then. 'I had a school friend, a boy named Sergey. His father was a KGB general, he had a dacha here. I had known Sergey's father since I was small. He was a shattered man. In the war he had experienced such terrible things that nobody was allowed to broach the subject in his presence. He did not even celebrate Victory Day, which everyone else does in Russia. After the war he was forced to work for the intelligence agency. He did not want it but he did not have the strength to refuse; the consequences would have been devastating. I do not know how many people there are who would have refused in his situation. It can't be many.'

He crossed himself before he continued. 'As Sergey's father lay dying, he called for a priest. I myself was not yet ordained at that time, but I knew the priest who was sent to him; he told me about it later. Ever since I myself have been a priest, I have heard many deathbed confessions, and I know that hardly anyone thinks about their sins before dying. Most people ask God to remove the pain or to provide for their families – I do not judge this, I only notice it. With Sergey's father it was different. Of course, the priest who heard his confession did not tell me any details. He only said that he had never witnessed such a radical confession.'

Father Kirill grew silent. Soft choral singing had accompanied his last sentences; upstairs preparations for the worship service had begun. I realised that the conversation had reached its end.

Father Kirill stood up. 'You have seen the icons?'

I nodded. 'They are … peculiar.'

Astonished, he looked at me. Then he realised that we had misunderstood each other. 'You mean the pictures upstairs,' he said smiling. He did not seem to think much of them. 'I'm talking about different icons. Come with me.'

He led me into the dark nave of the crypt. When he turned on the light, the dead rose from their graves. 300 pairs of eyes looked at us. The icons lined all four walls; on each picture there were five or six saints side by side, hands raised in the gesture of blessing. The martyrs of Butovo had the slim-limbed silhouettes and the mask-like faces of the old Russian icons. I could not help but think of Komarovsky, the murdered painter. I knew that he was not among the canonised, but his signature could be discerned in the style of the icons.

Silently we contemplated the images. One of the martyrs had to be Kaleda's grandfather. How do you tactfully ask about a canonised family member? When I finally formulated the question, Kaleda led me to one of the icons. Six martyrs looked at us. Father Kirill crossed himself, then he bowed his head and kissed the picture's wooden frame.

'The second on the left.'

Vladimir Ambartsumov, dead for 73 years, must have been as charismatic a man in life as his grandson. The icon abstracted his facial features, but a visible expression of willpower remained that separated him from the surrounding saints.

I suddenly had the feeling that I was staring at a family secret that was essentially none of my concern. As I was about to turn away, I heard Father Kirill laugh. I looked at him. All of the seriousness of the previous conversation had suddenly fallen away from him. Grinning, he bared two gold teeth that I only now noticed. He pointed to the icon.

'I had to have it repainted five times before it finally looked like grandfather.'

Waist-high snow covered the Polygon. From the entrance to the old wooden church a sharp-edged tunnel had been shovelled; the rest of the premises were white and unrecognisable. Only a few bare fruit and birch trees protruded from the snow. In the course of the following weeks I returned to Butovo several times, and it was only after the snow had melted that I saw the mounds of earth, overgrown with grass, which Father Kirill had raised to mark the layout of the mass graves. Now, in March, the mounds stood out only as slight elevations in the snow. They crisscrossed the premises without a recognisable system like long, chaotic scars. One of them ran straight to the dacha settlement, whose snowy roofs loomed directly behind the fence.

In search of the entrance to the settlement, I got lost twice in the forest. When I finally found it, the name plate next to the entrance struck me like a cynical kick in the gut: The settlement was called *Urozhay* – 'Harvest'.

In an Old Testament disposition, I walked around between the wooden cottages. I wanted to throw stones. But there was no one to throw them at. The dacha season had not yet started; snow covered the vegetable plots, the settlement was deserted. I was ready to leave when suddenly a sliding gate opened beside me. An old man stepped out from behind the metal fence. He limped slightly and his grey face was full of age spots.

I greeted him. Somewhat surprised, he nodded in my direction.

'You have a beautiful house,' I said.

The man looked at me, looked at his dacha, then back at me. 'What's beautiful about it?'

Only now did I look more closely at the house. It was actually not a beauty – a grey concrete annex covered the wooden façade. 'I'm from Germany,' I improvised. 'We don't have houses like this there.'

'From Germany … And what are you doing here?'

'I was looking at the Polygon.'

He stared at me blankly. 'You came from Germany to look at a cemetery?'

'It's an unusual cemetery. People were shot there …'

'Young man,' he interrupted me. 'Don't believe everything you are told. I can tell you this as someone who has had certain professional insights, unlike many of those who spread their lies today.'

'Lies?'

'Lies. Propaganda. A few priests died on the Polygon, which the Church now exploit to spread their ideology.'

'Wasn't it actually quite a lot of priests?'

'And were there no criminals among the priests? At that time there was a war, young man, a war between the Soviet Union and its enemies. There is no war without casualties; as a German you should know that. I had to deal with your grandfathers, I know what I'm talking about.'

There was a pause. Our acquaintance hadn't even lasted for five minutes, and already we had reached a dead end.

'You mentioned your profession,' I continued. 'What did you do?'

He smiled. 'I built the state.'

'You mean you worked for the state?'

He laughed drily. 'At that time *everybody* worked for the state, young man. Together we built it, our state.' He let the sliding door slam shut and turned to go. 'Lies,' he murmured. When he had gone a few metres, he turned to me once more. 'Tell that to the people in Germany! My generation no longer turns on the television, because they only tell us lies!'

Dusk fell as I reached the station. While I waited for the *elektrichka* back to the city centre, I read the announcements on the platform. My eyes were caught by a lit glass box with a notice inside: 'Categories of citizens entitled to free and discounted transport on suburban trains.' I read the list, read it again, read it a third time. What was hanging there under a flickering neon light was a compressed history of the Soviet Union.

- *Heroes of the Soviet Union (free)*
- *Heroes of Socialist Labour (free)*
- *Participants of the Great Patriotic War (free)*
- *Family members of deceased participants of the Great Patriotic War (free)*
- *Former underage inmates of concentration camps, ghettos and*

*other places of forced detention, with or without disability status
(free)*

- *Persons awarded decorations and medals of the USSR for self-sacrificing work behind the frontlines between 22 June 1941 and 9
May 1945 (50% discount)*
- *Persons awarded the distinction 'Residents of besieged Leningrad'
(free)*
- *Persons exposed to radiation as a consequence of the disaster at the
Chernobyl Nuclear Power Plant (free)*
- *Rehabilitated victims of political repression (100% discount)*

For a long time I thought about the riddle that seemed to link the first
category with the last: Soviet heroes rode the *elektrichka* free of charge,
Soviet victims with a 100 per cent discount. I could not make sense of
this nonsensical difference.

The next day I took the *elektrichka* out of the city again, this time in a
northerly direction. Once more I was looking for an icon painter, this
time a living one. Father Kirill had given me the address of the man who
had painted the martyr icons of Butovo.

Igor Drozhdin lived in a small village called Bryokhovo, whose
wooden houses cling to the edges of a Moscow arterial road just outside
the city limits. As I entered the courtyard of his house, two dogs the size
of calves rushed up to me. Shortly before they devoured me, their chain
snapped them back from their run. Behind them the front door was
opened by a man whose blonde beard reached his chest. He wrapped the
chain around his fist and tugged the gasping dogs back metre by metre.
'Now!' he cried. I rushed to the front door.

He was not an approachable man. I remember our conversation like a
disjointed dream in which one wanders lost through corridors that lead
nowhere. Unfinished sentences were followed by minutes of silence,
in which Igor's water-blue eyes lost contact with me, glazed over and
turned inward. He had to be in his mid-forties, but I wasn't even sure
about that – with monosyllabic stubbornness he eluded all questions
that concerned his own person. 'That is not important,' he repeated.
'That plays no role.'

The only matters of importance were the icons that filled his house and the adjoining workshop from the basement to the roof. Only about them did Igor speak in detail, though hardly less enigmatically than about himself. Everywhere I saw the components of his craft, the linden wood panels, the sheets of gold leaf, the mortars with the ground colour pigments, but how all of this added up into icons I could only guess. 'Not important' – Igor warded off all technical questions. 'Icons are not painted with colours.' Smiling, he jabbed his index finger into my chest. 'They are painted with blood. With blood and with tears. A painter must pray, then God will show him the way.'

Igor had been assigned the major commission for the Church in Butovo because he had experience with unusual icons. 'Most painters just copy old motifs,' he said. 'For the martyrs of Butovo there were no templates, which deterred many.' Not so Igor, who was drawn especially to the boundaries of the Orthodox canon, for reasons that I could not figure out at first. One of his favourite motifs was Alexander Suvorov, Russia's army commander in the wars of the 18th century. I knew the general's face from historic portraits, but I had never seen it on icons.

'Suvorov was canonised?' I asked.

'No.' Igor shook his head regretfully. 'Not yet. The Church is not ready.'

It took me a while to realise that military motifs were a central element in Igor's icons. Boris and Gleb, the fraternal martyrs, held swords in their hands; Alexander Nevsky, the medieval military leader, clenched his fist around his lance. Russian armies marched into battle carrying holy icons of the Virgin Mother, in front of whom the arrows of Tatar bowmen dropped powerless to the ground. 'They are mighty weapons, our icons,' Igor whispered. He handed me a dog-eared children's book. Consternated, I flipped through it – naive illustrations recounted the stories of icons which Russia had used to bring its historical enemies to their knees. Mongolian horsemen, Turkish galleys, Napoleon's cannons, Hitler's tanks – all had capitulated before the Virgin Mother.

I did not grasp it. Why did Igor deem icons weapons, what did he need them for? When I asked him, he looked at me, perplexed. 'Don't you know? The war may begin at any moment. We must be prepared.'

I never found out which war he meant. Was it Armageddon, the battle of the last days? He whispered of dark threats; sometimes specific enemies emerged, the Chinese, Islam, America. Then again, he talked about the persecution of Christians during the Soviet period, of the terror against the icon painters. From the little he told me I figured out that he had learned his craft during perestroika, at a time when icon painting was formally still punishable. 'We lived like bandits,' he said. For two decades now he had worked undisturbed, but he did not trust the peace; he lived in constant expectation of a relapse into the godless era. I wondered whether that was the unacknowledged reason why he was drawn to uncanonical motifs, to saints not recognised by the Church. A continued spirit of resistance seemed to drive him, against whomever. He seemed like a lost partisan to me, who has forgotten who his enemy is.

Nevertheless, I grasped his hand with almost childlike gratitude as we said goodbye. I had to think of Komarovsky, Igor's slain predecessor. The trail of the icons had not broken off. However strange and confused its current ramifications might seem to me, the trail led right up into the present.

On the way to the front door my eyes were drawn to an icon that I had not noticed before. The blue-white stripes of an army vest caught my eye. I took a closer look. The saint, apparently a young man, was wearing the uniform of a Russian recruit.

'Who is that?'

'The holy warrior Yevgeny.'

'Why is he wearing a uniform?'

'Because he was wearing a uniform when the Chechens cut off his head.'

Yevgeny of Chechnya

Spring came suddenly and unexpectedly. One day in early April began with giant snowflakes that grew smaller by midday and miniscule in the evening, before they changed to rain. For two days and nights water gushed from roofs and kerbs in biblical quantities, accompanied by the roar of exploding icicles. When the sun rose on the third morning, there was nothing left of the snow heaps on the roadsides. Overnight the fur coats disappeared from the subway cars, and a few days later, in the *elektrichka*, I saw the first girl's foot in sandals, red toenails glaring amid uniform rows of wellington boots.

Kurilovo, the goal of my trip, was more of a big village than a small town. In the Sixties a few prefabricated buildings had jostled themselves between the wooden houses. Since then not much seemed to have happened in the settlement. The cemetery lay a bit outside. For a long time I stumbled through the overgrown site, searching for Yevgeny Rodionov's grave. When I found it I recognised the dead recruit immediately – apparently the icon in Igor's house had been painted from the same photograph as the portrait on the grave.

Yevgeny Rodionov: 23 May 1977 – 23 May 1996.

A young man with a fiery red beard crouched between the grave stones. He was painting a fence. As I came closer he looked at me suspiciously.

'Are you the priest?' I asked.

'No,' he said slowly. 'I am not the priest. The priest was shot.'

Sasha drove me back to the settlement in his car. On the way he told me the story of the priest.

'It was a week ago. Father Alexander was on his way home from church. He saw a couple of drunk men in front of an apartment building. Of course, he had to go over and speak to them, he was that kind of man; he could not just pass people by, he always wanted to change everyone. One of the guys pulled a pistol out of his jacket and shot him in the heart. Just like that. He was dead instantly. A few hours later the police caught the men; they were completely wasted. Now the church is deserted. I take care of the cemetery, but I can't sing the Mass. No idea whether we'll get a new priest – who would want to move to a town where such things happen?'

I asked him about Yevgeny, the slain soldier. Sasha nodded. 'You mean Zhenya. I knew him by sight, from school; he was in my year. Weird guy. Wanted to go to Chechnya. They were about to send me there too, but I had no desire to come back in a coffin. My mother bribed the officers. A few thousand roubles and I could do my service in Moscow. Everybody did that. Zhenya could have done it too.' Sasha shook his head uncomprehendingly. 'But he didn't.'

He dropped me off in front of a neighbourhood of dachas and scribbled directions into my notepad. 'Look for a high metal fence. Zhenya's mother lives behind it.'

The metal fence was a head higher than me. I saw nothing, but I heard the quiet singing of a woman's voice. When I knocked on the gate, the singing abruptly broke off.

'Who is there?'

I explained myself. The gate opened a crack. A small woman with short-cropped hair scrutinised me. 'How old are you?'

'Thirty-four.'

Lyubov Rodionova smiled. 'That's how old Zhenya would be now.'

The gate clicked shut behind us and blocked out the world. Only the blue April sky hung above the fence.

In the dark living room of the dacha Zhenya's mother brewed herbal tea. She apologised for the disorder. I did not see any disorder. She apologised once more. 'When you are all alone, you no longer know who to keep order for.'

She must have told the story often. When she began, the tone of her voice changed audibly, it became softer, more melodic, as if she was singing a song that was familiar to her note by note.

'Everything began with a telegram from Chechnya ...'

The telegram reached Lyubov Rodionova in February 1996. Her son, wrote an officer of the Border Guards, had deserted; they were looking for him. Should the recruit Yevgeny Rodionow show up at home, he was to be immediately surrendered to the local military administration.

The next day Lyubov Rodionova packed cold potatoes and hard-boiled eggs and caught a train. Two days later the snow-capped peaks of the Caucasus appeared outside the train windows. She knew that her son could not have deserted; that wasn't like him. Something had to have happened to him.

When she reached the Chechen border post, a contrite officer explained the situation to her. Her son, he said, had disappeared without a trace during a night shift, together with three other recruits. At first they were believed to have deserted, but in the meantime it had turned out that the soldiers had been abducted. Unfortunately, there was no trace of them.

For an entire spring and an entire summer and an entire autumn and half a winter Lyubov searched for her son. The first Chechen war approached its end while a small, lonely woman travelled back and forth through the war-ravaged region. She spent the nights in Russian army dormitories, in the refugee tents of international aid organisations, in the half-destroyed houses of Chechen families. During the day she asked everyone she encountered whether they had seen her son.

Intermediaries put her in touch with Chechen resistance fighters. Blindfolded, Lyubov let herself be led into remote mountain hideouts, in the hope of discovering a trace. Once, she fell into Chechen captivity herself, but after three days the rebels set her free because they understood that no one would pay a ransom for her.

For a long time Lyubov searched for a living son. But gradually it became clear to her that prisoners were only useful to the rebels as a commodity, to be exchanged for ransoms or for their own prisoners. Zhenya had been missing for months and his name had never come up on the hostage market. The news of her son's death hardly affected Lyubov when she finally found the man who had murdered him. What did affect her was the way he had died.

'Your son did not love you,' the rebel said. 'Your son could have lived, but he chose death. We told him: "take off the cross you are wearing around your neck, renounce your faith, fight for our side." He would not take off the cross. We had to cut off his head. If he had loved you, he would have taken off his cross. You brought a bad son into the world, Lyubov Rodionova.'

In the end the rebels sold her Zhenya's corpse. Lyubov pawned her apartment in Kurilovo so she could bury her son. The rebels made her pay twice, first for the body, then for the head. Lyubov brought her dismembered son home in a zinc coffin. When she arrived, winter had begun in Kurilovo. When they buried Zhenya, snow was falling.

A week later Lyubov buried her divorced husband, Zhenya's father. He had not been able to bear the death of his son. Not long after that, Lyubov buried her second son, Zhenya's brother. He died in a car accident.

After the funerals, Lyubov sat alone in her dacha and thought about Zhenya, this quiet, serious boy who had vanished so suddenly from her life. She thought about the cross he had brought home one day when he was 11 years old, after his grandmother had taken him to church on holiday. 'Zhenya, what is this?' Lyubov had said, 'Take off the cross, the other children will laugh at you.' At that time hardly anybody wore a cross around their neck, and certainly not in a small town like Kurilovo.

But Zhenya had never again removed the cross. Not at home, not at school, not while playing, not while swimming, not while dying.

It took a while for the story of Yevgeny Rodionov to spread. A few years after the funeral the first journalists turned up in Kurilovo; they wrote articles; the word 'martyr' was used. After the journalists, the army came. On the anniversaries of Zhenya's death officers surrounded his tomb and gave patriotic speeches. Common soldiers sent Lyubov letters, confessing moments of fear in which they thought of Yevgeny Rodionov, the recruit who had gone to his death without blinking an eye. Then the first icons appeared. It took Lyubov some time to get accustomed to the sight of her son with a halo.

One day a call came from Moscow. It was a cleric, who introduced himself as secretary of a Church commission in charge of issues regarding canonisation. The commission, he said, had received various requests for the canonisation of her son. Could Lyubov perhaps visit them in Moscow?

She took the *elektrichka* to the capital. A committee of bearded men received her. For two hours Lyubov told her story. They asked her questions. 'Was your son a believer? How did he express it? Did he pray? Did he go to church? Regularly? How often do you yourself go to church? Did you raise your son as a Christian? What can you tell us about his martyrdom? What witnesses are there?'

'They are all dead,' Lyubov said. 'His murderers, his fellow prisoners, they are all dead.'

The Church rejected the canonisation. Yevgeny's martyrdom had not been sufficiently testified, they argued. The army protested. They protested so violently that the Church was forced to disclose their true reasons: never before, explained a member of the canonisation commission, had the Orthodox Church canonised war dead, and they saw no reason to deviate from this principle, for it was not the task of the Church to strengthen the fighting spirit of the army.

'What am I to do with a saint?' Lyubov asked. 'I need a son, not a saint.'

Listening to her was painful. It was painful precisely because she tried so hard not to care about the Church's rejection. 'I do not need any icons. I need a son.' The sentences sounded more desperate with each repetition. Her voice faltered; sometimes it nearly broke. The clerics had not believed her, she sensed it, and she could not get over it. Twice her heart had been broken, once in Chechnya, once in Moscow. She denied it, but she needed this saint, whose icons filled her living room: Zhenya, the holy warrior, a martyr with a machine gun, Yevgeny of Chechnya.

'I am not like Zhenya,' said Lyubov. 'My faith is not very strong. When I stand before the icons, I question God: Why have you taken my son away from me? A true believer does not ask such questions.'

A crucified Jesus hung between the martyr icons. Lyubov levelled an accusing finger at him. 'Christ suffered for three days. Three days! Do you know how long Zhenya was tortured?' She looked me in the eye and let the heretical question hover in the air. 'Three and a half months. Every day they tortured him. Why didn't God redeem him sooner?'

When she thought about Chechnya, she felt no hatred. Even the hatred I had observed in my Moscow friends after the terror bombing in the metro was alien to her. She knew them, the Chechen fighters who tortured their hostages to death, but she had also met Chechen mothers who had helped her, a Russian mother, because they knew exactly what it was like to search for a murdered son. 'We send our boys to their deaths, they send their boys to their deaths. Who benefits from it? A few men in grey suits. Our children die together, for things that do not concern them, that they do not even understand.'

Lyubov knew that they had sent her son to his death. But she did not realise that they now wanted to send him to war for a second time. First, the Chechens had kidnapped him; now he was Russia's hostage. As a soldier he was no longer of use; as a martyr, he was priceless. The army wanted to promote him to the rank of saint, so he could serve his country even in death. The Church had resisted the temptation to canonise Zhenya. Lyubov no longer had the strength to resist.

The name 'Lyubov' means 'love'.

Wearily, she flipped through a stack of mail. 'All of these letters,' she sighed. 'Why do people send me these letters?' She reached into one of the envelopes and pulled out a CD. 'Here. From a soldier. He sends me songs he has written about Zhenya.' She switched on a small kitchen radio and put in the CD. Plucked guitar chords. A male voice, hoarse, full of pathos.

In every Russian church
Masses should resound,
For a new saint has appeared
In the heavens of Rus.
Private Rodionov,
When you get to heaven,
Please ask God for forgiveness
For us sinners.
On the icons now appears
A saint in camouflage,
And in the heavenly host
Serves a border guard.
Who among us small souls
Dares to counter the enemy:
You will not take my cross
Unless my head falls with it.

The Return of the Wooden Gods

'Is there actually life beyond the ring road?'

We sat in Vanya's kitchen, seven Muscovites and one German. I talked about my trips to the provinces and was met by ironic incomprehension. Some of those gathered had never set foot in the regions surrounding Moscow. They knew London, Rio, Goa, but not the villages beyond the ring road.

'They don't even have Internet there, do they?'

'Internet? They don't even have electricity.'

'But somebody must live there. When you fly over, you can see houses from the plane.'

'That's only for television. So the news can make it seem as if the area is populated. In reality no one has lived there for centuries.'

'Completely different laws of nature prevail there. Watches run backwards and the rain falls sideways.'

'There must be people there who haven't heard that Lenin is dead.'

'There are entire villages where they still believe in the old Slav Gods. Real pagans.'

'Now you're exaggerating.'

'No! I saw it on television. An entire village, in the middle of nowhere, where people spit at your feet if you make the sign of the cross.'

'Where's that supposed to be?'

'Somewhere west of Moscow. I think the village is called Popovka.'

Three hours west of Moscow the *elektrichka* stopped at a small provincial station. Opposite the entrance a man stood beside an old Zhiguli; the remnants of a taxi light were stuck to the roof of the car. The driver pushed his cap back and scratched his head. 'Popovka? Where the Old Believers live?'

'The pagans.'

He nodded indifferently. 'Whatever. Two hundred roubles, but you have to walk the last stretch. You can't go there by car.'

Half an hour later the car stopped abruptly. We got out. The road traversed hilly grasslands which seemed completely deserted.

'Do you see the edge of the woods back there?'

I followed the driver's outstretched finger and nodded.

'Do you see the houses at the edge of the woods?'

I shook my head.

'That's Popovka.' He lowered his finger. I saw nothing but trees. Very distant trees. The driver grinned.

For two hours I walked through dull, wintry steppe grass, yellow at the tips, black at the roots, like the hair of a brunette that was once dyed blonde. Patches of crusted snow had survived in the shadows of isolated groups of birch trees; the meadows were covered by enormous puddles of meltwater. Toads crouched at the edges of the ponds. Their glassy eyes followed my steps.

Halfway, I cut across a small village that looked as if a plague had swept away all the inhabitants. Dilapidated wooden houses lined the road, the gardens were full of rusty scrap iron. A dog barked, but he seemed to be chained up somewhere behind the houses, I could not see him. When his bark fell silent, I heard only the smacking of my boots in the mud. At the end of the village I walked past a row of reasonably intact houses, and I briefly imagined I had perceived a movement behind a curtain. When I knocked on the front door, nothing moved. I walked on. Moscow suddenly seemed very far away.

After two hours, shortly before I reached the edge of the wood, a settlement appeared behind a hill, 20, maybe 30 houses. They couldn't be old. The walls were made of fresh timber that had not yet darkened. At the edge of the settlement a man was mowing a lawn. The slish-slash of his scythe cut through the silence from which I came. As I approached, the man rammed the blade into the ground, crossed his arms over the wooden handle and looked at me expectantly.

'Is this Popovka?'

The reaper nodded silently.

'Where the pagans live?'

'The Slavs,' he corrected. He scrutinised me from head to toe. 'You're no Slav.'

It sounded like a death sentence. Abruptly he pulled the scythe out of the ground. Instinctively, I searched for an escape route, but instead of slashing me, the man heaved his scythe onto his broad Slavic shoulders and motioned for me to follow him into the village.

'See how real Slavs live,' he said. 'See how our race is regenerating.'

I burst in on the weekly sacrificial rite. Two dozen people had gathered on the village square, most of them were wearing linen shirts and embroidered cloth belts. Towering above the crowd and the houses, the wooden body of a four-headed god arose. His chest was studded with golden sun wheels which, to my German eye, looked like many-armed swastikas. Involuntarily I compared them with the tattooed swastika on Sasha's back. They turned in the other, the German, direction, however.

Singing, five bearded men made their way across the square, wrapped in wolf skins. They had to be pagan priests, I thought, because they were carrying offerings: a pitcher of milk, a loaf of bread, cornucopias filled with mysterious liquids. They sang in a Slavic fantasy language, of which I understood only isolated scraps: '... all is God, God is in all ... Glory to the Slavs ... we have been, we are, we will be ...'

In a slow procession the men approached the tall wooden god. Several times they stopped in front of smaller idols and fed them their offerings: milk dripped from the wooden snouts of grinning wolves. The singing grew louder as the priests drew closer to the centre of the square. Repeatedly I now heard a name I recognised: 'Perun! ... Perun! ...' So it was him, the ceremony revolved around his statue: Perun, the supreme god of the Slavic pantheon. The last offerings were placed into a fire smouldering at the foot of his wooden body.

When everything was over, the scent of burnt grain filled the air. Smoke wafted across the square while the spectators scattered about the village. The reaper appeared next to me. He pushed me into the centre of the square and introduced me to the priests. From up close they looked surprisingly young, none were over 50. I had presumed them to be much older – the beards had deceived me. One after the other they shook my hand.

'Stanislav.'

'Bratislav.'

'Svyatoslav.'

'Broneslav.'

'Vladislav.'

Of course, those were not their real names. As I learned over lunch in one of the wooden houses, they were actually just called Ivan or Pyotr or Vladimir – but what pagan would want to be named after an evangelist or an apostle, let alone after the prince who had converted Russia to Christianity. They had adopted Slavic aliases, back in the time of perestroika, when Russia choked on its history and coughed up its pieces. Many forgotten gods had resurfaced at that time. One of them, the Christian God, had proceeded to conquer half the country, as He had already done once before, 1000 years earlier; but with him returned other gods who had been at home here for much longer.

'What good is a foreign god to us?' asked the man who called himself Svyatoslav, as he was piling pancakes on my plate. Now that Perun had been fed, his disciples ate. 'We have our own gods.'

They had been a bunch of bearded students back then, mostly natural scientists. They rejected the Christian God, who seemed foreign and invented to them, like an abstract ideology, hardly more true to life than the communist dogmas that Russia was just discarding. Closer to them was the idea of an animated nature, a world of gods who live in the elements, in the Russian earth, in the birch trees, the rivers, in the wind that sweeps through the fields … everything is God, God is in everything.

In the mid-Eighties, when it became possible to buy plots of private land, they decided to establish a settlement. They wanted to live the way their ancestors had lived, in harmony with the gods of nature. For a long time they searched the Moscow region for an appropriate spot, until they finally discovered the half-abandoned village of Popovka, which in Russia's ancient times had already served as a place of worship for the Slavs ...

'Wait,' I interrupted. 'How do you know that?'

They smiled. 'One can just sense it.'

Apparently I looked sceptical. 'We have unearthed ancient ritual objects here,' said the one who called himself Broneslav. 'Look at them, they are right behind you, in the corner.'

I turned around, but behind me there was only a pile of discarded tools. 'Where?' I asked.

Broneslav pointed to the pile. 'Directly in front of you.'

I looked closer. A broken millstone was leaning against the wall. Beside it was a bent pitchfork.

'That is no pitchfork,' Broneslav said. 'It is a Slavic trident. And the millstone is an altar.'

I stared at him in disbelief. Neither the millstone nor the pitchfork was anywhere near old enough to bridge the 1,000-year gap between Christianisation and the present.

'How do you know that they are not just tools?'

They smiled. 'One can just sense it.'

As the afternoon passed, I asked the how-do-you-know question a few more times, but since the answer was always the same, I learned to bite my tongue. It made me think of my friends in Moscow. They were right: different laws of nature prevailed beyond the ring road.

Most of the time I just sat there and listened whilst the village outside the windows sank into leaden darkness. It was much too late to return to Moscow and I was grateful when the priests invited me to spend the night in Popovka.

'Do you drink Russian vodka?' they asked.

I sighed. 'Well, okay. But not too much. I'll have to catch the first train tomorrow ...'

Shaking their heads, they interrupted me. 'There is no such thing as Russian vodka. Vodka didn't come to Russia until the 15th century, from the West. Our ancestors did not drink vodka. And we don't drink it either.'

Perplexed, I looked around. It was the first time I heard a Russian say that vodka was an unpatriotic drink.

'And how,' I asked hesitatingly, 'do you spend your evenings?'

With torches we went on our way. At the other end of the village we reached a small wooden hut. Thick smoke came from the chimney. We entered an anteroom.

'Take off your clothes.'

When we were all stark naked, Stanislav opened the door to the *banya*. An invisible tongue of fire licked through the anteroom and scorched my lungs. I groaned, but nobody cared, they just pushed me through the door. The room was intolerably hot, and it grew even hotter when Broneslav poured the first ladle of birch water on the furnace. With an angry hiss the water evaporated off the metal plates, and immediately the pungent steam shot up my nose. It hurt badly. And it felt good.

After the first few rounds, interrupted by ice water baths in the anteroom, I realised why the Slavs did not need vodka. The *banya* had the same effect. I felt like I was drunk, although I wasn't. When I uttered this thought out loud, I triggered an avalanche of chauvinistic enthusiasm – the Slavs hooted. They praised the *banya* as the most Russian of all intoxicants and cursed vodka, that foreign poison, with which hostile nations had flooded their country. Then their fury found other targets. They declared war on all foreign imports that had conquered and disfigured their country in the course of the centuries. The balalaika? An Uzbek lute. The matryoshka doll? A toy from Japan. Christ? The son of a Jew, a god of the Greeks and Romans, but not the Slavs. So it went – piece by piece Russia threw off its borrowed clothes, until it lay in front of me naked and unadulterated, pure, but shrunk to the size of a single, tiny village.

I do not remember exactly at what moment I started to feel uncomfortable. Maybe it began when I looked more closely at the tattoos of my fellow bathers, which I had been avoiding at first because we were naked. Bluish sun wheels rolled in all directions, flanked by runes that did not look Cyrillic, but eerily Germanic. Perhaps my discomfort began when words like 'blood' and 'soil' appeared more often in their tirades, when they talked no longer about nations, but about races, about hereditary enemies, about rulers and slaves. Feebly I formulated objections, but it was too hot and there were too many of them, and I was their guest.

Eventually, they were also overpowered by the heat. The flow of their speech grew slow and aimless, before it lost itself in song. Relieved, I lay on my bench, glad not to have to understand anything else. Yet again they sang in their Slavic fantasy language, as they had done during the sacrifice. Fascinated, I listened to the invented words and wondered whether nations had ever been anything more than communities of talented self-deceivers.

But they assured me, when I inquired, that their language was authentic, just like their rituals.

'We have studied all of that. There are people who have observed these Slavic traditions for centuries. They still exist, they are just hiding. We have found entire villages that never converted to Christianity.'

The idea was alluring: lonely pagan villages, deep in the forests, forgotten by the world, similar to Agafya Lykova's hermitage in the Taiga. But it was unthinkable. Seventy years of Soviet rule had been sufficient to almost destroy the Orthodox Church; and three centuries of Orthodox persecution had made the Old Believers an isolated minority, whose remotest hiding places had eventually been discovered. The spread of Christianity, however, had not been 70 years ago and not 300, but a full millennium. It could not be true.

'Where are these villages?' I asked.

Conspiratorial glances. 'We are not allowed to tell anyone. We have promised not to betray them.'

I nodded silently.

Although I knew that it was nonsense I could not stop imagining these forgotten pagan villages. I thought about them while we were whipping each other with birch branches, I thought about them as we stumbled back to the dark village and I still thought about them while I slowly drifted off to sleep, surrounded by snoring pagans.

The next morning I woke up early, in order to catch the train to Moscow. But the Slavs would not let me go.

'You haven't walked through the rings yet.'

They led me to an open square at the edge of the settlement. About 30 wooden posts jutted from the earth, arranged in four concentric rings. In the centre stood another, slightly lower post on which a glass globe rested, about as large as a football.

'Have you heard of Arkaim?' they asked.

I nodded. A few years before I had read the name in a newspaper: Arkaim, the mysterious ruin city in the southern Russian Steppes. When and by whom it had been built was controversial, no one knew exactly. But my pagan friends had their theories.

'It is an old Slavic place of worship, founded by our ancestors. We have recreated it.'

They pushed me into the outermost circle of their reconstructed Slavic temple. 'Follow the rings until you reach the centre.'

Expectant glances followed my steps.

'Is everything okay?' Broneslav asked as I moved from the first ring into the second. 'Do you feel normal?'

'Yes. Why?'

'There are powerful forces at work in there. Sometimes sensitive people cannot endure it.'

I continued to walk, through the second ring, the third, the fourth, until I was standing in front of the glass globe.

'Place your forehead onto the globe.'

I did it.

'Watch out! Not too long!'

I straightened up again.

'Do you feel it?'

I focused my attention inward.

'Come on, tell us what you feel!'

I shrugged my shoulders. 'Pleasant emptiness.'

Disappointed, they stared at me. I felt like a student who has failed a test.

The *elektrichka* catapulted me from the pre-Christian era back into present-day Moscow. During the ride I sat opposite an old man and his grandson. The boy stuck his nose against the glass of the train window. Outside, the graffiti-covered walls of factory buildings passed by. 'Left front!' the boy read out loud. 'Ksyusha, I love you!' – 'Spartak Moscow!' – 'Black asses, get out!'

Proudly the grandfather leaned toward me. 'He has known all the letters of the alphabet since he was four. Now he is seven and he reads Pushkin!'

That evening in Vanya's apartment I pulled a volume of Pushkin from the shelf and lost myself in his writing. The entire night and half the next day I lay on the sofa and whispered Russian verses into the cats' ears.

When I left the apartment in the evening, Moscow seemed changed. I searched for Pushkin's Russia and did not find it. Where was his sophistication, his elegance, where were Pushkin's proud Europeans? I rode to the Leningrad train station and bought a ticket to Saint Petersburg.

WIND (Saint Petersburg)

Now, city of Peter, stand thou fast,
Foursquare, like Russia; vaunt thy splendour!
The very element shall surrender
And make her peace with thee at last.

Alexander Pushkin, 1833

Peter the Great is the deity who has called us into being and
who has breathed the breath of life into the body of ancient Russia,
colossal, but prostrate in deadly slumber.

Vissarion Belinsky, 1845

It's the storm! The storm is breaking!

Maxim Gorky, 1901

Peter the Seasick

'Help a *blokadnik*!'

The man has stopped in front of me with an outstretched hand. He is old, ancient. A tightly spaced lettering of wrinkles covers his face, spelling the pride of survival.

'My pension is a joke, but do you think that matters to me? Not after all I went through in the war!'

He laughs a crow-like laugh. It is meant to drown out the horrors of the past, but to my German ears it sounds like an accusation. The blockade he is talking about is the Siege of Leningrad by the Wehrmacht, bombs and hunger, 900 days long.

'People ate the soles of shoes, tree bark, lampshades. We children didn't dare go out into the streets, for fear of being eaten. Help a *blokadnik*!'

I put a bill into his outstretched hand.

'God bless you! And from where have you come to our beautiful city?'

'From Germany.'

His wrinkles tense. For a moment I think he will yell at me. Instead he suddenly looks at me, just as embarrassed as I am – we are a hall of guilty mirrors.

'That was all long ago,' he murmurs. 'Do not think about it, young man. Explore our city instead, visit our museums – you won't find better ones in the entire world.'

And that's exactly what I did.

The boat is tiny and huge at the same time. It seems too large for the toy it is, and too small for the warship that it wants to be. The mast would look lost on the open sea, but here, in the St Petersburg Central Naval Museum, it towers over all the other exhibition pieces. Four miniature cannons line the railing; you can fire real bullets from them, though not very far. Even a much smaller man than the boat's owner would seem like a Gulliver on board this Lilliput yacht.

In 1688 a 15-year-old boy named Peter discovered the boat in the tool shed of an estate near Moscow. Even though it was half rotted, Peter saw that it could be no ordinary ship. Its sharply angled, seagoing keel clearly distinguished it from the clumsy ferryboats the boy knew.

'What kind of boat is this?' Peter asked his Dutch tutor Franz Timmermann.

'It is an English boat.'

'What is it used for? Is it better than our Russian boats?'

'If you mounted a new mast and sails, it would travel not only with the wind, but also against the wind.'

'Against the wind? Can it be possible?'

The boy couldn't get the boat off his mind. He had it dragged out of the shed and repaired. On the Yauza, a tributary of the Moskva River, it was launched, and soon people saw Peter cruising through the Moscow suburbs. It must have been a disturbing sight for the capital's inhabitants, this strange miniature boat with its gigantic helmsman, who towered over his peers even as an adolescent, and who later, as an adult, would measure more than two metres. From the very beginning, Russia was too cramped for Peter.

He was 17 when he ascended to the tsar's throne. The country over which Peter I now reigned had barely put the trauma of the Orthodox schism behind it when the struggle for Russia's future really began. The country was still largely cut off from its Western neighbours, whose religion and manners were viewed in Russia with as much suspicion as their technical innovations. Peter, in turn, knew how backward Russia looked in the eyes of foreigners. While his older half-sister Sophia was reigning on his behalf, the underage Tsar grew up on an estate outside the city walls, in the vicinity of the German Quarter, a ghetto for merchants, craftsmen and scientists from the West. The foreigners that lived here had been called to Russia because their technical knowledge was needed; at the same time they were kept away from the city like a contagious disease. Ironically, Russia's future ruler, of all people, was infected in this guarded quarantine zone with the virus of the West. Peter loved the foreign quarters, behind whose walls he let German engineers and French military experts initiate him into the secrets of their craft.

The most formative experience was the sailing trip on the Yauza. Dutch shipbuilders taught Peter how to steer an English boat against the wind. After his accession to the throne he translated the two child-hood passions that had accompanied him from this very moment into a political program: Russia had to learn to love the West – and Russia had to learn to love the wind.

In order to set the new direction, Peter himself travelled west. He did what no Russian ruler had done before him: he crossed the frontier of his kingdom, not at the forefront of an army, but during peace time, out of free will – and incognito. Under the alias Pyotr Mikhailov he signed on as a simple carpenter in the port of Amsterdam. When his true identity was discovered, he insisted on being treated as a worker, and soon half of Europe willingly played along with his charade. 'Pyotr Mikhailov' travelled from Courland over Prussia and Holland to England; he worked in shipyards, sawmills, foundries, forges, visited museums, botanical gardens, libraries and laboratories; he learned from architects, engineers, sculptors, book printers, surgeons and orthodon-tists. Peter recruited many of these European specialists as consultants on the spot. He sent them ahead to Russia with truckloads full of techni-cal instruments, while he himself went further and tirelessly asked the same questions: 'What is that? How does it work? How do you build it?'

When the Tsar returned home one and a half years later, he steered Russia against the wind. He began where it hurt his fellow countrymen most: with their beards. On the evening of his return Peter hosted a welcome banquet. Wielding a razor blade he went from chair to chair and personally shaved off the beards of his empire's highest dignitar-ies. Blood dripped from dumbfounded faces. The beard was holy – it completed man in the image of God, and according to Orthodox under-standing, whoever cut it off was laying hands on God's creation. The Tsar, however, was God's deputy on earth, which is why Peter's outrage was accepted with silent horror.

The beards, however, were only the beginning. Peter, who was deter-mined to transform his empire from the ground up, had drummers and town criers march through Moscow to beat a new time for his subjects: Ta-ta-tam! 'Shear your beards!' Ta-ta-tam! 'Take off the Russian kaftans, dress practically, like the Germans!' Ta-ta-tam! 'Rewrite the calendars – the year 7207 ends today, tomorrow will be the beginning of the year 1700!'

The nobles, in particular, feared the daily drumbeat. The Tsar imposed a new order of rank on them, in which they were able to maintain their position in society only through service to the state. Anyone who wanted to be someone in the new Russia had to work his way up like a schoolboy, had to serve in Peter's newly established institutions, had to wear foreign fantasy uniforms and bear imported titles: *Tseremonymeyster, Kvartirfervalter, Kapitenleytenant.*

The service in Peter's favourite new institution, the navy, was particularly odious. Why a Russian should love the wind was difficult to convey in a country where the wind did not taste of salt. Russia, at that time already the largest state in the world, was a beached giant – there was practically no navigable coast in the entire country. The Black Sea was still in Turkish hands, the Baltic Sea belonged to Sweden. The Pacific coast on the eastern edge of Siberia, which had been conquered by Peter's father, was hardly closer to the western Russian trade routes than the moon. In the north, just below the Arctic Circle, there was the navigable port of Arkhangelsk, but even in the few ice-free months the sea route from here to Europe led all the way around the North Cape. As a trading destination, Arkhangelsk was only serviced by European sailing ships. There were no Russian ones. No Russian knew how to build them. The entire country suffered from seasickness.

But that did not stop Peter. He had brought shipbuilders with him from Europe who were now building a fleet for him, from scratch, on the mainland. When it was finished, Peter sailed down the Don in their lead, toward the Black Sea coast. The sight of this ghostly procession of sailing ships suddenly appearing from the country's landlocked interior surprised the Turkish troops at the river mouth to such a great extent that they abandoned their fortress without much of a fight. When they did fight back a while later, Peter had already lost interest in the Black Sea. Instead he now wrested a strip of the Baltic Sea from the Swedes. Taking into account a 20-year war, he opened up a direct sea route to Europe.

On the Baltic Coast, in the windy estuary of the River Neva, Peter conjured up a city out of the marshy soil. Saint Petersburg rose up into the pale northern sky like a daydream made of stone. European architects designed Peter's paradise; Russian workers built it. The former came voluntarily and were richly rewarded; the latter came in chains, and today their bones support the foundations of Saint Petersburg.

The Tsar declared his city Russia's new capital. In order to populate it he moved the state government from Moscow to the coast and forced Russia's most influential families to build homes in Saint Petersburg. Reluctantly the country's elite settled in a city that looked as un-Russian as its name sounded. At night, when the wind blew from the sea and scudded around the houses, some Petersburg residents must have sleeplessly cursed it, this salty west wind that had turned the Tsar's head.

When Peter died in 1725 Russia was a major European power, a maritime nation, a dreaded wartime opponent and a respected peacetime ally, an empire rapidly catching up technically and economically, and by far the largest state in the world. But above all, it was a schizophrenic country. It was Western and Eastern at the same time, a mental and geographical hermaphrodite. Peter, the giant, had overstretched Russia. He had enabled his subjects to sail with the wind and against the wind – but barely had the helm slipped from his hands when the passengers began to argue about the course. Some wanted to continue straight ahead, to the West, into the future that Peter, the European by choice, had envisioned. The others wanted to turn back, into a Russian past that threatened to disappear eastward behind the horizon. The two schools of thought into which Russia's intelligentsia split after Peter's death called themselves 'Westerners' and 'Slavophiles'. They fought out their factional dispute with words in the salons of Saint Petersburg, while at heart the entire country participated. The adversaries could be distinguished by their appearance: the smoother the chin, the more European the mind; the longer the beard, the more Russian the soul. Even Dostoevsky and Solzhenitsyn remained faithful to this rule.

For the most bearded community of all, the Old Believers, Peter's rule meant a final break with the world. Once the Tsar had been the guarantor of divine order on earth; but this ruler, who turned everything upside down and reversed its meaning, had to be the Antichrist. Under Peter's reign the Old Believers' great exodus into the uninhabited expanses of Siberia began – Agafya Lykova's ancestors were among those who turned their backs on the world at that time. That is why I had travelled to the city which to this day embodies Peter's dream of the West. I wanted to see what the Old Believers had been afraid of.

Now, in late April, the wind was mild. It had lost its wintry sharpness, the pedestrians no longer feared it – with relaxed shoulders they strolled through the city, unfurling cramped winter bodies. The sun did not yet hold any warmth, but already its Nordic light shone far into the night. A few more weeks and there would no longer be nights in Saint Petersburg.

Coming from Moscow I moved through the city with the unsettling feeling of having crossed a national border without noticing. Russia blurred like a distant memory; I was now in Europe, or at least in a city that did everything it could to imitate Europe. Moscow's chaotic sprawl gave way to a precisely arranged composition of palaces, avenues and canals. The Baroque facades were reflected in the waters of the Neva – it looked as if the entire city stood on the mirror image of a sunken Europe. I felt alienated. Saint Petersburg's beauty was breathtaking, but after two months in Moscow I felt strangely uprooted. An irrational compassion overcame me; I thought about the poor Muscovites who Peter had once forced to populate his contrived dream town. They must have felt like awkward actors in a production whose only spectator was the Tsar.

Three hundred years later the past seemed forgotten. Saint Petersburg had found its role; the people inhabited their stage-set city with natural ease. Everyone I talked to asked me the same rhetorical question: Which is better – here or Moscow? Nobody waited for my reply; Petersburg's lead position was not up for negotiation. With a mixture of dread and contempt, people here looked down on Moscow, that vulgar city of money and power. But Saint Petersburg! *Severnaya Venetsiya!* 'The Venice of the North!', *Kulturnaya stolitsa!* 'The cultural capital!' It took me a while to understand the meaning of these synonyms – Venice and Saint Petersburg have little more in common than water, and culturally, the city is hardly a match for the huge and wealthy Moscow. But that is not what is meant. *Venetsiya* stands for Europe, *kulturnaya* for cultivated. Both attributes express the pride of belonging to a different, more civilised, culture. Peter would have been proud of such Petersburgers.

From the Naval Museum I walked along the Neva until I was standing in front of Petersburg's second famous ship, the battleship Aurora. In 1917 its cannons fired a volley of blank rounds into the October sky, which was the signal to storm the Winter Palace. Nearly a century had passed since then, and still the steel colossus was anchored in the Neva, an icon of the Revolution. On the waterfront, young women posed to be photographed against the backdrop of the warship – curves and edges, beauty and the beast.

The volley from the Aurora was Saint Petersburg's death knell. In a city which had been built in the name of progress, the Bolsheviks saw only fossilised Tsarism. They made Moscow the centre of their world revolution. Ironically, this shut the 'window on Europe' which Peter had pushed open. For two centuries, Russia had stared at the West from the north, for two centuries Peter's successors had imported European ideologies – until one day, Marx sneaked through the Baltic window. Saint Petersburg owed its life to a west wind; and a west wind took it away again. A west wind had united Russia and Europe; and a west wind blew the continent apart.

The Last Heir to the Throne

In the Naval Museum, Peter's boat stands in the middle of the central exhibition hall. Its mast points to the ceiling like a signpost. Almost exactly above it, on the second floor of the museum, is the office of the military historian Oleg Filatov. It is not the most pleasant workplace. In the winter, when the wind from the Neva hits the museum façade, the office is transformed into an icy, draughty hell. Although Filatov is constantly cold, he would never want to work anywhere else. He has family-related reasons.

When I shook his hand, the similarity struck me off-guard, although I had seen photos of him. With his watery blue, slightly fishy eyes and the pale blond goatee, Filatov looked like an Albino twin of the last Russian Tsar, Nicholas II, the great-great-great-great-great-grandson of Peter the Great. It is a comparison that Filatov hears often, and it pleases him. That also has family-related reasons.

We drank tea in a Georgian restaurant on Nevsky Prospekt. While Filatov told me his story, I was lying in wait for discrepancies and contradictions; I anticipated the unmasking of an impostor. In vain. However hair-raising the story might be, it did not seem to be Filatov's invention. He clearly believed it.

July 1918, Yekaterinburg, 1,800 kilometres east of Saint Petersburg: Nicholas II and his family have been held in a villa in the town centre for two and a half months. In Moscow, Trotsky dreams of bringing the abdicated Tsar before a revolutionary court and trying him personally, but things turn out differently. Civil war is raging all over Russia. The

Red Army still holds Yekaterinburg, but White Guard troops, who are advancing from Siberia to the Urals, have surrounded the city. The Tsar threatens to fall into the enemy's hands.

On the night of 16 July, Nicholas II is woken up. Under the pretext of protecting him from gunfire, they lead him and his family to a room in the cellar. Nicholas' wife, Tsarina Alexandra, asks for a chair for her haemophiliac son Alexei, the 14-year-old heir to the throne. For him and his mother chairs are carried into the cellar, while all other family members and servants, a total of 11 people, are made to line up in two rows behind them, as if for a photo. Then things happen quickly. 11 armed men enter the room, a 12th laconically reads out the death sentence. 'What? What?' Nicholas asks, before the first bullet pierces through his forehead. For several minutes gunfire echoes through the room. Smoke obscures the gunmen's view, ricocheting bullets whistle through the air – mysteriously they seem to bounce off the bodies of the Tsar's four daughters; the girls scream, but they do not die. In a panic, the murderers go after them with bayonets. The carnage lasts almost 20 minutes, before silence falls on the cellar.

That same night the bodies are removed. They are thrown into a disused mine shaft on the outskirts of the city. Despite several attempts to explode it, the shaft refuses to collapse. The overtaxed Bolsheviks wait until sunrise, then they drag the dead bodies back out of the tunnel. When they strip them, it turns out that diamonds are sewn into the princesses' bodices – that is what made the bullets bounce off during the execution. The Bolsheviks soak the naked bodies with sulphuric acid to make them unrecognisable. The mutilated remains are buried in a pit, then a truck flattens the earth. Finally tree trunks are laid across the grave in order to disguise it as a reinforced stretch of road. The Russian monarchy is buried.

So it is written in the history books.

Oleg Filatov's father hated the history books. Luckily, he was a geography teacher. In school Vasili Ksenofontovich Filatov did not have to talk about history, and at home he generally did not speak much. Only in 1988, on his deathbed, did the taciturn father disclose to his son Oleg what had really happened in 1918.

The first bullet hits the Tsar's forehead. Nicholas II falls to the ground. In falling, he buries Alexei, his son, under him. The body of the Tsar

protects the heir from fatal blows, only Alexei's arms and legs are penetrated by individual bullets. The boy hears the whistling of the ricocheting bullets and his sisters' screams when they are bayoneted. Desperately
he closes his eyes and pretends to be dead. When everything is over,
they toss him onto the bed of a truck along with the bodies of his relatives. On the way to the city limits Alexei manages to escape, and jumps
off the car. The guards throw a grenade after him which slashes his right
heel, but he gets away. He hides underneath a railway bridge, where his
pursuers do not find him.

The next morning a pointswoman discovers the badly injured boy.
She informs two Red Army soldiers, who recognise the prince but do
not betray him. They take him to a small village in the northern Ural
Mountains, inhabited by the Khanty tribe, whose medicine men are
famous for their healing powers. The Khanty nurse the half-dead boy
back to health; they rub crushed herbs into his wounds, feed him rein-
deer blood, force him to eat cooked animal eyes. The Tsar's son sur-
vives. Even the haemophilia which he has suffered from since birth, a
hereditary blood disorder considered incurable at that time, disappears
without a trace. The Khanty hand the recovered foundling into the care
of a shoemaker whose son has recently died. Alexei grows up under
a false name. He spends the majority of his life in the Russian provinces; only after his retirement does he move to Saint Petersburg with
his family. He grows old, very old.

'He is still alive,' Oleg's father said on his deathbed when he had finished the story. Then Vasili Filatov, alias Alexei Romanov, took his last
breath and died.

The son, Oleg, understood only in retrospect much of what had
remained a mystery to him while his father was still alive. He understood why he hardly knew anything about this taciturn man, about
his origins, his family. He had always wondered where his father had
received his extensive education, even though he was only a provincial
teacher and the son of a shoemaker. His father had spoken German and
English, French and Italian, Spanish, Ancient Greek and Latin. He had
played several instruments, and he had known everything, truly everything, about Russian history. And the scars! Oleg had seen them for the
first time during a fishing trip, when he was nine years old. The father
had taken off his shirt in the summer heat. Dad, the son asked, what are

those scars? Wounds from the war, his father answered, from the civil war – my family was killed, but I survived. After that, the father had never spoken about the scars again. Until his death.

When Oleg Filatov began to pass on his father's story, no one believed him. Fantasist, the people said, liar, dreamer, impostor. In the seven decades that had passed since the Romanovs' assassination, there had been dozens of self-proclaimed children of the Tsar, who alleged they had miraculously escaped the bloodbath. Filatov was not the first, and he would certainly not be the last of those who considered themselves heirs to the Russian throne. The tsarist goatee that he adopted shortly after the death of his father did not necessarily make him more credible, but I did not dare to say that to Filatov's face. I felt sorry for him. For more than two decades he had tried to prove his father's story; for more than two decades people had laughed at him. He was the hostage of a family legend.

For whatever reason, he brought his lawyer to our meeting, a patronising woman who supplied Filatov with cues whenever he got stuck. I never grasped what she hoped to gain from Filatov. I only understood that she was not the only person who nurtured his hopes. Many obscure sponsors and advocates had supported him over the years. Filatov piled expressions of loyalty from monarchist associations and Orthodox clerics on the table. He showed me medical certificates and criminological studies. Two graphologists had come to the 'categorical conclusion' that Filatov's father and the young heir to the throne had the same handwriting. A forensic pathologist had analysed photographs of both men, which, 'with high probability', showed the same person at different stages of his life. A genetics laboratory had certified that Filatov's DNA exhibited 'numerous distinguishing features' of the Romanov dynasty.

Thanks to all these dubious supporters Filatov's faith in his ancestry had stiffened over the years, until eventually he had become impenetrable to counter-arguments. They included the remains of the Tsar's family, which in the early Nineties had been excavated on the outskirts of Yekaterinburg. Initially, everything about the find seemed to speak for Filatov: forensic pathologists sorted the battered bones and aligned them through DNA tests to the individual members of the Tsar's family. In the end they found that two children were missing: neither Alexei nor his sister Maria was among the dead. On TV, Filatov watched the remains being transferred from Yekaterinburg to Saint Petersburg, where they were solemnly laid to rest in the Peter and Paul Cathedral. The day before our meeting I had visited the church, and I had seen the little side chapel with the burial niches of the Tsar's family – including the two empty niches on which all of Filatov's hope hung.

But in the summer of 2007 more body parts were discovered in Yekaterinburg. With DNA testing they were assigned to the Tsar's two remaining children. For Filatov a world should now have collapsed. But in its constant struggle with reality, his world had become unbreakable.

'Where are they, these bones?' he asked scornfully. 'Why aren't they buried? For three years they have been telling us that Alexei and Maria have been identified, but their burial niches are still empty.'

When the waitress brought tea for the third time, she could not find any place to put down the cups – a mountain of documents covered the table. Filatov pushed some of the papers aside. A photo of his father fell to the floor. I picked it up. The man in the picture looked neither particularly similar to his son nor to his supposed father. He wore his dark hair cut short, his face was narrow, the eyes melancholic, slightly dog-like. I tried hard to see the similarities between him and the young prince, but Alexei had only been photographed in childhood, and the man whose picture I held in my hand was at least 50.

When I put the photo back on the table, I looked at Filatov. Again I was stunned by the striking similarity that connected him with Nicholas II, his alleged grandfather. In my mind I stripped away all the attributes with which Filatov emphasised the likeness: the hair, combed back majestically from the forehead; the condescending expression on his face; the eccentric beard; the tailor-made suit with the silly handkerchief; his stilted phrases; the way he extended his little finger while drinking tea. The similarity remained. I wondered what Filatov felt when he looked in the mirror.

'People always think that I want to take something away from them,' he said as we were about to say goodbye. 'They do not understand that I don't want the Tsar's gold or palaces or Fabergé eggs. I do not want to be called Majesty and I do not want to rule over Russia.' He looked me in the eyes, earnestly, almost pleading. 'I only want one thing. I want to know who my father was.'

After we had parted I followed him with my eyes for as long as I could. A man with a strained aristocratic posture walking along the Nevsky Prospekt, at his side a murmuring attorney, in his head a desolate dream.

A Would-Be Saint

Sometimes Russia seemed to me like the most bearded country in the world. Not because there were conspicuously many beards – most Russian men are clean-shaven. Occasionally, however, I encountered beards that overshadowed everything I had ever seen in terms of facial hair.

Father Yevstafy beat them all. His beard knew no limits. A white-blond thicket without beginning or end proliferated from his every pore, interrupted only by a massive nose and a pair of ice-grey eyes. When Father Yevstafy was angry, and he was inclined to anger, red flushes of rage would flicker through the visible part of his face – in such moments he looked like a burning haystack.

Brusquely he shoved me through the hallway of his apartment and tore open the door to his study.

'There!' he growled. His overgrown chin pointed to an icon that was hanging on the opposite wall. 'There you have what you were looking for!'

Speechlessly I approached the holy image. Father Yevstafy stood beside me. Although I could not see his mouth, I felt that he was grinning. He was enjoying my bewilderment.

'And?' he asked scornfully. 'Do you like it?'

He knew the answer. I did not like it; I could not possibly have liked it. An eerily familiar face dominated the picture, callous and moustachioed: Stalin.

The icon had cost Father Yevstafy his church. Until two years ago he had been the head of a small parish on the edge of town. It was a perfectly normal church, with perfectly normal churchgoers, who crossed themselves in front of perfectly ordinary icons. Until one day an old woman came running out of the church screaming, because she had suddenly noticed that she had crossed herself in front of a moustachioed Pharisee. The clamour made it all the way to the Bishop, and Father Yevstafy, who had hung up the icon, was asked to submit his resignation.

Since then the image had hung in his apartment, in the city centre of Saint Petersburg.

'But why …?' I began. The whole idea was absurd. Granted, Stalin had attended a seminary as a young man, before Marx entered his life. But after that he had done his best to destroy the Church – I had seen the traces of the massacre myself, in Butovo. How could any Russian Christian want to worship his own executioner?

All of that, however, was a misunderstanding, Father Yevstafy explained to me. 'Do not believe everything you read in the newspapers!' He pushed me into a chair and slammed coffee cups onto the table. The anger blazed behind his beard. 'It is all a lie!'

Never, he explained to me, had Stalin intended to wipe out the Church. On the contrary, he had saved it. After Lenin's death he systematically assassinated the entire leadership of the Bolsheviks, until only he remained – with the sole aim to stop the Communist persecution of the Church. Granted, to disguise his true intentions, he had to sacrifice a few priests. 'But they are all in heaven now,' Father Yevstafy assured me. 'No country has as many martyrs as Russia, none has as many advocates with God. We must thank Stalin!'

Dumbfounded, I struggled for words. 'But who … Why should he … What makes him a saint?'

Father Yevstafy smiled a sly smile. He pointed to the icon. 'Look closely. He is not a saint.'

Only now did I take a more detailed look at the picture, in which previously I had seen only Stalin. Standing upright, wrapped in a floor-length military coat, his body occupied the right half of the icon. On his left side, in the centre of the picture, sat an old woman. Her eyes were closed, her right hand raised in blessing. A golden halo surrounded her face. My eyes wandered back to Stalin. No halo.

'Who is the woman?' I asked.

'The Holy Matrona of Moscow.'

Now I recognised her. I was not seeing her closed eyes for the first time – all over Moscow I had encountered icons of the blind faith healer. She had been canonised only a few years ago. Matrona Nikonova had lived in the early Soviet period, in a dilapidated apartment building in Moscow, where she secretly received followers seeking cures or advice – a blind oracle.

'Stalin visited her,' Father Yevstafy said. 'In the war, when the Germans were drawing close to Moscow. He wanted her blessing, her advice. She told him to hold out, she said: if you stay in Moscow, the Germans will not take the city.' He threw me a triumphant glance. 'And that is exactly what happened! I need not tell you, my German friend, you know better than I!'

Incredulously, I stared at him. I could not imagine that he believed the absurd legend.

'An old woman told me the story,' he said. 'She was there, in Matrona's apartment. She saw Stalin with her own eyes.'

So that was the trick. Even Father Yevstafy had not dared to have Stalin painted as a saint. Instead, he had commissioned a Matrona icon in which Stalin appeared only as a guest, a secondary character in the biography of a saint. And yet Father Yevstafy did not conceal that he longed for the day when Stalin would no longer be at the edge, but in the centre of an icon, a canonised saint with a fully-fledged halo. But he knew that the day had not yet come. 'It is too early. The people are not ready.'

I could not figure him out. There were moments when his sentences sounded like silly provocations, like the defiance of a teenager. Then he could become deadly serious, agitated, almost desperate. I looked at him uncertainly. The beard did not make it any easier to decipher the stirrings of his soul.

I carefully directed the conversation to his life story, in the hope of understanding what motivated him. He claimed to be related to Lenin by blood, but the relationship was so distant that I lost the thread as he unravelled his pedigree. As a young man he had made the most obvious career choice that a relative of Lenin could make: he became a lecturer of Marxism-Leninism. He proclaimed the word of the Saviour. At a technical college he taught budding engineers that God did not, and could not, exist.

'I was a careerist,' he said bitterly.

When God ignored all lines of argument and surprisingly stepped into his life, Father Yevstafy lost his job. He was fired and expelled from the Party after word got around that icons hung in his apartment, that he prayed. Vividly he described the Party interrogations to me, the ritualised attempts at re-education. 'You sit at a table, they talk to you, and you know that you are surrounded by enemies, enemies, enemies!'

It was incomprehensible. He had suffered under the very persecutions that he trivialised; he denied others the compassion that he demanded for himself. Had the contradictions in his life blinded him to all other contradictions? The longer I listened, the more I had the impression that the Stalin icon was the work of a desperate man. It was an attempt to reassemble the two halves of a broken biography, to reconcile the Party official with the priest. Only if Stalin was God did Father Yevstafy's life have meaning.

Obsessively, he defended the cruelty of this God, which for Father Yevstafy was only in the nature of his kingdom. 'Russia is not Holland,' he thundered. 'Russia is gigantic! It takes force, force and more force to govern such a country!'

I formulated objections, but we could not find a common language. When we said goodbye after two hours of conversation, I had the feeling that I had never glimpsed into a more contradictory world of thoughts.

On the way to the apartment door a second icon caught my eye. I recognised Alexei, the murdered son of the last Tsar. He sat slumped on a throne, in the centre of the deserted Winter Square, powerless arms folded in his lap, his face pale under a bright halo. Behind him, his right hand placed on the shoulder of the sickly heir, stood a second pseudo-saint, his head as halo-less as Stalin's. He was extremely well depicted. The wild eyes belonged unmistakably to Grigory Rasputin.

24 Centimetres

Grigory was 17 when he turned his back on his home village. No one in Pokrovskoye cried a tear for him. With a sigh of relief the village policeman struck the juvenile runaway from the registry of investigations, where a crime or two had accumulated in recent years: brawling, theft, drunkenness, rape.

On foot Grigory set off, and on foot he crossed half of Russia during the following two decades. Some say he made a pilgrimage to Greece, others claimed to have seen him in Jerusalem, but no one can testify, as so many things remain unattestable in the life of this enigmatic man. It is certain that during his wanderings Grigory became a preacher, for it is as a preacher he appears in the Tsar's diary 20 years later. 'Met a man of God,' Nicholas II noted in November 1905. 'Grigory, from the Tobolsk region.'

A puzzling affection bound the ruler of Russia to the itinerant preacher from the provinces – puzzling, because at first glance Grigory Yefimovich Rasputin was not at all a man with winning ways. Strands of oily hair hung in his face, while his beard was encrusted with bits of food. He wore tattered clerical shirts that he rarely washed; people compared his body odour with that of a goat. When speaking he made no effort to conceal his peasant origins; he was uncouth, brusque and often insulting.

Nevertheless, half the Tsar's court was soon hanging on his words. Rasputin might have been uneducated and dirty, but those who met him remembered him. More than anything it was his eyes to which he owed his charisma: stone gray, hypnotic eyes with pulsating pupils, which, it was said, Rasputin could expand and contract at will.

They attributed mystical healing powers to him. Every time the sick heir to the throne screamed in pain, because internal bleeding ruptured his body, every time the physicians had already given up on Alexei, Rasputin prayed him back to life. His divine gift gave him earthly power. The Tsarina patronised Rasputin because he alleviated her son's suffering, the Tsar protected him because he soothed the Tsarina. 'Better one Rasputin than ten hysterical seizures a day,' Nicholas used to reply when his advisors criticised the increasing influence that the preacher wielded at court. In fact, all of Saint Petersburg soon gossiped viciously about the dubious man of God, but Nicholas ignored the rumours with the same characteristic stubbornness with which he had for years been denying the revolutionary spirit brewing in Russia. Both would cost him the throne in the end. And his head.

The man who preached at the court during the day indulged himself in Saint Petersburg's filthiest brothels at night. People whispered that Rasputin's shamelessness knew no bounds, that he had relationships with married ladies-in-waiting, even that he was sharing the Tsarina's bed. If Nicholas did not drive away his rival, this could only mean that he was no longer master of his senses – a charlatan had turned his head. Even Nicholas' poor leadership in the First World War was blamed on Rasputin: he was rumoured to be a saboteur, dispatched by Kaiser Wilhelm, Nicholas' German cousin and war enemy.

Rasputin did not deny the rumours; on the contrary, he embellished them. One night he was arrested after boasting in a restaurant about nights of passion with the Tsarina. Drunk, he had climbed on a table and exposed his genitals in front of everyone, as if in proof of his abundant power. As the news of his arrest made the rounds, Nicholas' advisors breathed a sigh of relief – now finally, they hoped, the Tsar would come to his senses. But the next morning Rasputin walked free, released at Nicholas's personal insistence.

A group of young aristocrats finally decided to put an end to the nightmare. Under a pretext, they lured Rasputin into the cellar of a Saint Petersburg villa, which became the scene of what was arguably the most incompetent murder in Russian history. An assortment of poisoned food was placed in front of Rasputin. Unimpressed, the preacher washed down a few pieces of deadly cake with a few cups of deadly tea, without batting an eye. One of the conspirators finally lost patience and shot him in the back. Rasputin collapsed, but while they were still discussing how to dispose of his corpse, the supposedly dead man fled through a side door into the courtyard. When his killers caught up with him they no longer cared about matters of etiquette – they beat, kicked and choked their victim until Rasputin stopped moving. To be sure they chopped a hole in the frozen Neva and threw the dead man into it. When the bloated corpse was discovered a few days later he was hardly recognisable. The inconsolable Tsarina had Rasputin's remains buried in the garden of her summer residence.

His killers were celebrated. When one of them entered the opera house shortly after the bloody night, everyone in the hall stood up and applauded for minutes. Petersburg's aristocracy spoke of a coup that had saved the discredited Imperial family from disaster. Everyone who still thought that there was a future for the monarchy in Russia gave a sigh of relief. But it was too late.

'Tsar of Russia,' Rasputin had warned in his last letter to Nicholas. 'When you hear the bell which tells you that Grigory has been killed, no one in your family, none of your relatives' children will continue to live for more than two years. The Russian people will kill them.'

· The prophecy was fulfilled. For a few more months Nicholas rejected any restrictions of his power, even as it was rapidly slipping away from him. The bourgeois February Revolution of 1917 forced him to abdicate, but it could not appease the pent-up anger. Almost seamlessly, Russia stumbled into the October Revolution. Nicholas, the Second and the

Last, died in a hailstorm of Bolshevik bullets, less than two years after Rasputin's death.

Almost at the same time, a Bolshevik exhumation squad dug up Rasputin's remains in Saint Petersburg. His grave had become a pilgrimage site, which the authorities wanted to get rid of for good. The poisoned, shot, beaten, drowned body was meticulously burned. The ashes were strewn to the four winds. Nothing was left of Rasputin.

Nothing?

Doctor Knyazkin, who had a different opinion, led me through the basement of a Petersburg prostate clinic. At the end of the corridor, the chief physician pointed wordlessly to a glass display case. Inside there was a jar, filled with a clear liquid. I looked, looked away, blinked in disbelief, looked back again.

'Are you sure …?'

'Not 100 per cent,' Knyazkin answered. 'But there is convincing evidence.'

I swallowed. 'Did you find any medical peculiarities?'

'Well, yes,' the doctor said. He uttered the obvious. 'It is an unusually large organ. 24 centimetres. In an idle state, mind you.'

Before our eyes, preserved in formaldehyde, floated Rasputin's penis. Doctor Knyazkin cleared his throat. 'It's a long story.'

While he explained, my eyes kept wandering back and forth between him and the jar. Doctor Knyazkin was, as far as I could judge, a reasonably renowned prostate specialist, in whose presence the bizarre exhibit struck me as almost damaging to his reputation. He himself saw things differently. With appreciable pride he spread out what findings he had gleaned over the years about Rasputin's most intimate organ. Whenever patients passed us in the hallway Knyazkin proudly pointed out the historic find, and although the poor men clearly had other concerns, he infected each one with his excitement. His enthusiasm was enviable.

Knyazkin made no secret of the fact that most of his findings were based on rumours. What could be gathered from eyewitness reports of Rasputin's genitals was highly contradictory. Men who had seen the preacher naked in the *banya* described his organ as either monstrously large or pitifully small, whether out of awe or of envy. His actual and alleged lovers, in contrast, had been unequivocally overwhelmed. One of them claimed that in the arms of the preacher she had been overcome by an orgasm so powerful it had sent her unconscious. Others raved about a large, auspiciously placed wart that drove every partner into a frenzy.

Involuntarily I cast a critical glance at the jar. Knyazkin, who noticed, shook his head with a smile. 'No wart.'

Others claimed that Rasputin was impotent. It was rumoured that the only reason he was obsessed with female attention was because he had never had a woman. People whispered that he belonged to the Khlysty, a sect who celebrated their worship services with erotic orgies, in which Rasputin was attributed the role of the uninvolved eunuch priest. Others assigned him to the Skoptsy, whose followers were ritually castrated. A dubious doctor, who claimed to have performed an autopsy on Rasputin after his murder, described the dead man's sexual organ as tiny, mis-shapen and incapable of sexual intercourse.

The contradictory rumours did not stop with Rasputin's death. In post-revolutionary Saint Petersburg people soon whispered that the preacher had been ritually castrated by his murderers, as revenge for his escapades. Much like Gogol's nose, Rasputin's penis developed a life of its own. In the Twenties it was allegedly sighted in Paris, where it served as an unorthodox relic for a circle of female Russian emigrants. Rasputin's daughter Matrona, who was also exiled to France after the Revolution, is said to have been so outraged by the fertility rituals of her compatri-ots that she confiscated her father's organ. As a matter of fact, Matrona Rasputina later emigrated to California, where after the Second World War she worked as a tiger-tamer in the Los Angeles circus. According to legend she smuggled her father's genitals to America and kept them until her death in 1977. A few years later a London auctioneer claimed to have purchased a 'sensational find' from the estate of Rasputin's daugh-ter. The object turned out to be a dried sea cucumber.

Again two decades later, in 1999, Doctor Knyazkin's phone rang. A patient was on the line. It was urgent, he said, Knyazkin had to come immediately, he had never seen such a thing! Knyazkin, the prostate specialist, knew such calls well. 'Come to my office,' he replied laconi-cally, 'you can show me what you have on your mind.' Brusquely the patient interrupted him: 'Doctor Knyazkin! I am not talking about *my* penis!'

The patient, as it turned out, was the vice chairman of the Russian

Association of Antiquarians. A French colleague had offered him a wooden box, supposedly from the estate of Rasputin's former house-keeper, who had spent the last years of her life in Paris. The three of them met in the patient's home. The Frenchman unwrapped the box. Knyazkin opened it. A shrivelled and shapeless something was stuck to its bottom. Knyazkin nodded silently. The Frenchman named an astro-nomical sum. In the end they settled on 8,000 dollars.

Of course Knyazkin did not know what exactly he had acquired, and today, a good decade later, he was in fact not a bit smarter. He had long since stopped questioning the authenticity of his find. For him, what was floating before our eyes was no more and no less shrouded in mystery than Rasputin himself. In this respect, both fit together, even if they had possibly never belonged together. 'What you see here,' Knyazkin said with breathless pride, 'has possibly had a more decisive influence on the course of Russian history than the gun barrel of the battleship Aurora!'

After careful medical treatment, the shrivelled, formless something became a presentable exhibit. Despite all the studies, it could no longer be established to whom the capital trophy had once belonged. DNA testing was not an option: there was nothing left of Rasputin that would have been fit to use as comparative material. All that remained was a large, formaldehyde-soaked question mark, which nothing in the world could now turn into an exclamation mark.

Beetles and Communists

I took the express train back to Moscow. Not because I was in a hurry, but because it is the only real express train in the entire country, the sole long-distance connection where you don't book a bed, but a seat.

The journey felt like a trip into the future. Everything that usually makes up a Russian train ride had been eliminated: the motherly con-ductresses, the on-board samovar, the clothes-changing rituals, the physical proximity, the carry-on food, the feuding families, the drunken soldiers, the rumbling heartbeat of the wheels. Even the typical odour was missing, that mix of engine oil and onions and bedclothes. The air strongly smelled of nothing at all. Solitary cappuccino-drinkers and laptop-typers filled the soundproofed compartments. My seatmate dis-creetly moved her elbow away as I sat down. Without looking up from her computer she replied to my greeting, then grew silent, like the rest of the carriage. There was the same awkwardly maintained anonymity that I was familiar with from the commuter trains in Western Europe. Twenty more years, I thought, maybe 30, then all of Russia will look like this.

For most of the four-hour trip I just stared out of the window, glad to live in the present. The country that flew by outside looked as if it was in a hurry.

Halfway along the route someone tapped me on the shoulder. I turned around, but there was nobody there. When I turned back around the face of my seatmate was chalk-white. With a hysterical finger she pointed to my shoulder and shouted a word I did not understand: '*Maiskizhuk! Maiskizhuk!*' I fumbled with my shirt. A huge insect flew off and disappeared through the open compartment door. My neighbour sighed with relief.

Back in Moscow, in Vanya's apartment, I consulted the dictionary. I was leafing through it when a scratching sound distracted me. Irritated, I raised my head. Directly beside my face a fat May beetle was crawling over the window pane.

The next day I saw them everywhere. Disoriented, they crawled through hallways and underground subways, they dug their claws into the hair of panic-stricken pedestrians, adhered squashed to windshields or simply fell from the sky, exhausted.

A particularly fat specimen dived right into Alexander Gurtsev's soup. It struggled with all six legs, desperately trying to cling to a beetroot cube. Gurtsev removed the beetle from the soup and resumed our conversation, unperturbed. He was the last Muscovite who would have been afraid of insects.

We spooned our soup in the middle of the forest. Gurtsev was the only person who lived here for kilometres around. The old wooden house in which he was quartered was a fair bit behind the beltway, hidden between dense pines and birches. The Academy of Sciences had built it in the 19th century, as a forest research institute. Until the end of the Soviet period, forestry scientists had worked here, including Gurtsev. Together with his colleagues he studied the surrounding forest areas. In a small garden behind the institute building they tended to endangered plant species, some of which had been on the verge of extinction since the 19th century.

Then, in the capitalist chaos that followed the unravelling of the Soviet Union, the Academy ran out of funds to pay their employees. There was also no more money for the maintenance of the remote research institute. The house fell into disrepair. In the institute garden the famished forestry scientists planted vegetables. Unfortunately, after the first potato harvest, a few of the endangered species had to be struck from the Red List for good.

Gurtsev's heart bled. He had spent the greater part of his professional life in the old forest institute, which was now crumbling before his eyes. One day he decided to save what could be saved. He packed his suitcase, turned his Moscow apartment over to a friend and moved into the forest.

He dug new beds for the endangered plants. Then he converted the house into its current condition. All that remained of the original construction were the thick tree trunks which made up the walls; the rest Gurtsev had completely rebuilt. The roof was covered with solar panels, the cellar filled with huge batteries and in the garden stood a wind turbine that he himself had made. Hand-dug passages tunnelled under the house, part of a complex heating and ventilation system that Gurtsev had designed himself. He had enclosed the sunny side of the building with greenhouses in which he grew potatoes and vegetables all year round. What he consumed in terms of food and electricity, he produced for the most part himself, living almost independently of the outside world.

After Gurtsev had shown me his kingdom, we sat on a bench in front of the house for a long time. He was a taciturn, focused man in his mid-fifties, whose terse sentences sounded like axe blows in the silence of the forest.

'Forget Moscow. Washed-up place. Drains everybody dry.'

We had met through a mutual acquaintance, Father Kirill, the priest from Butovo. Gurtsev was not religious, but just like Father Kirill, he had lost his grandfather at the Butovo Polygon.

'Sad story. Was a brave man. Says my mother.'

His grandfather, a miner from the provinces, had become a revolutionary long before the Revolution. In the late tsarist period he had fought for better working conditions in his mine, without joining a political party. As a strike leader he was arrested and exiled to Siberia, where he met his future wife, Gurtsev's grandmother. Both moved to Moscow when the political prisoners were released from the tsarist camps in 1917. The grandfather was no longer in a revolutionary mood when he returned from exile; he stayed out of politics. Only occasionally he met with former Siberian companions in Moscow. At their gatherings they often spoke about a former fellow prisoner, whom some of them had met in exile, a Georgian named Iosif Dzhugashvili. They marvelled at the meteoric political career of this man, because everyone who knew him remembered him as dull and untalented. They marvelled a bit too loudly, for when the Great Terror began, Iosif Dzhugashvili, by now better known under the nom de guerre Stalin, thinned out their ranks. Gurtsev's grandfather was condemned as a 'left deviationist'. In 1937 they shot him; in 1991 they disclosed it to his descendants.

For Gurtsev, then in his mid-thirties, the news was just another reason to hate Moscow. Who knew, he thought, perhaps his grandfather would have survived if he had returned to the province after his exile, instead of going to the capital. Perhaps then his grandson would have also grown up elsewhere, not in this washed-up Moloch that had been growing ever more washed-up since the end of the Soviet Union. When Gurtsev went into the forest, it was only partly the concern for endangered plants that compelled him. Primarily he was happy to turn his back on Moscow.

'The city drains the whole country,' he said bleakly. 'All of Siberia exists only so the capital can exist. Raw materials, food, energy, people – everything is absorbed by Moscow. The place is on the brink of collapse. The traffic! Millions of cars idling motionless day after day, with the motors running for hours. It's as if they only import all that gasoline to toss it onto the street in Moscow and set it on fire.'

Here in the forest the city was invisible, even though it was so close. You could not even hear the highway. Complete silence surrounded us, broken only by the frantic coloraturas of a nightingale.

Nevertheless, Gurtsev remained dependent on the city that he hated. He had financed the modifications to the house with a part-time job which he told me about reluctantly. A few kilometres further south a wide arterial road cut through the forest, the famous *Rublyovka*. It is lined by the mansions of Moscow's super-rich. Alexander took care of their trees. In the millionaires' gardens he pruned orchards, protected pine trees from beetles and advised oligarchs where to find Lebanese cedars or Canadian maples for their property.

One of his customers visited him in the course of the afternoon. A maroon jeep stopped in front of the house. I expected a pimped-up oligarch bride and was absurdly surprised when a discreetly dressed, not at all disagreeable woman in her forties got out of the car. She greeted Gurtsev affectionately, like a long-lost friend. Then she pulled a roll of money out of her handbag, and without batting an eye, she handed over 200 dollars for a bucket of insect repellent.

'It is *soooo* beautiful here, Alexander,' she whispered. Her gaze swept through the treetops. 'But isn't it terribly lonely? One can barely come to visit you! The forest roads are *soooo* bad, I had to take the *suuuper*-large car.'

As her truly large car disappeared between the trees, Gurtsev looked at me, shaking his head. 'Do you know what is strange about our Russian millionaires? Their mansions are huge, but their plots are tiny. In America the rich build themselves a new house if they can see their neighbour's chimney smoke on the horizon. And here? The *Rublyovka* looks like a colony of dachas: one house next to the other, separated by enormous walls. Russia is the largest country in the world, but no one dares to use the space, not even the rich. We all live as though we're in a pioneer camp.'

Until evening we sat on the bench in front of the house, while the lengthening shadows of the trees wandered over the forest floor. When they were pointing almost due east, Gurtsev revealed his dream to me.

'A plot of land for everyone. Russia is huge, there is enough for all. Give the people land, free them from the cities. Let them work, let them live.'

He had devised a plan, a plan for the salvation of Russia. Everyone could live as he did, self-sufficiently, independent of the outside world; it was only a question of will. And of knowledge. He, Gurtsev, could teach the people what they needed to know to survive. His house in the forest was the nucleus of a revolution.

I listened to him, fascinated. Although he was talking about solar cells and wind power, the story he told was centuries old. Generations of civilisation-weary intellectuals had dreamed the same dream – the dream of a return to Russia's anarchic peasant roots. Gurtsev might be a dreamer of the 21st century, but at heart he was a student of Tolstoy. A line of tradition even connected him with the Old Believers, although he was neither religious nor hostile to technology. What united them, despite all the obvious differences, was their faith in the Russian soil.

While Gurtsev continued to talk, I mentally said goodbye to Moscow, with a strange urgency. The encounter with this urban hermit had reminded me of the purpose of my journey. I suddenly had the feeling I had stayed in Moscow much too long. I wanted to go, to Siberia. Gurtsev's dreams and the shadows of the trees showed me the direction.

As we said goodbye, Gurtsev gave me a few telephone numbers of Siberian friends. Most of them were forestry scientists, wood people, like Gurtsev himself.

'We Russians have always been a people of the forest,' he said. 'Always.' He sighed. 'We just forget it sometimes.'

The May beetles disappeared as suddenly as they had appeared. Belying their name, they exhausted themselves within three late April days. I saw the last dead beetle disappear in the rotating brushes of a road-sweeper that was cleaning up the city centre for the big parades. Another species now descended on Moscow, also predominantly active in May, and also threatened by extinction: the communists.

On the 1st May a red veil lay over the city. I stood at the roadside while the May Day parade passed me by, and wondered, amazed, where these battalions of retired proletarians hid themselves when they were not carrying Stalin posters and Lenin banners through the city. There was something unreal about their procession, something ghostly. It looked like a funeral march. Solemnly the Revolution carried its icons to the grave.

Eight days later, on Victory Day, I recognised some of the withered faces that had caught my attention at the May parade. Again the streets were full of Communists, but they were not the dominant force among the general euphoria that still electrified Russia 65 years after Hitler's defeat. It was not the first Victory parade I had witnessed in Moscow, and once again I noticed that the celebrations seemed to be getting larger, not smaller, with the passing of time since the war. Perhaps because the 9th of May is more or less the only public holiday that this huge divided country can still agree on.

The last red pennants and victory flags still lay on the sidewalks as I drove across Moscow in mid-May to make my farewell visits. Then one day it was time. While I packed my bag, a party was in full swing in Vanya's apartment. A few of the students spontaneously decided to take me to the station. The train to Krasnoyarsk was already on the tracks when we arrived.

My train car was the second-to-last; I had booked a seat in the cheap open compartments. Vanya stowed my backpack inside the car, then we emptied one last bottle of champagne on the platform. In the glaring spotlights the students blinked like stray bats. They seemed out of place. Their straggly hair-styles, the carefully planned carelessness of their clothes, their whole urban lifestyle separated them from the proletarian passengers of the *platzkart* class. More than one close-cropped head turned in irritation at our round of champagne.

When the bottle was empty we all stared at the train that would carry me away over the magic border of the beltway, deep into a hinterland that none of us really knew – neither me, the foreigner, nor them, the city dwellers. 'Send us a text message as soon as the clocks run backward,' one of them joked. We laughed, more out of duty than amusement; the joke suddenly sounded stale in this setting. Then a tremor went through the train and the conductress urged everyone to board. We hugged. No one laughed when Vanya touched my forehead, my chest, the right, then the left shoulder with three fingers.

Inside the train car the overhead lights were not yet turned on; a warm semi-darkness enveloped the passengers. Stillness reigned, the kind of stillness only a crowd can produce. Men talked in whispers or stared out the window in silence while their wives rustled blue and white bed linens. Every now and then children's laughter broke the general commitment to silence, followed by a mother's whispered admonition, '*Tikho, tikho, tikho.*' It was only when the train began to move and its mechanical sigh became a steady background noise that the tension in the car dissolved.

I shared my four-seater with a grey-bearded man and two younger women. After boarding we had greeted each other briefly, but now, as the train rolled through the Moscow night, no one spoke. Outside the windows the brightly lit city centre gave way to the darker backdrop of the outlying districts, and when there was no longer any obvious reason to follow the endless parade of prefabricated buildings, my fellow travellers went to sleep. I withdrew to my berth and observed the tangled play of shadows that flickered over the drawn curtains, the nervous afterglow of a nervous city.

A child cried quietly in the dark, tormented by the train's eerie rumbling. For a while I listened to the mother's soothing, '*Tikho, tikho, tikho,*' before I fell into a dreamless sleep.

WATER (Siberia)

This was done at the origin's birth,
When our mother created the earth.
Snow white mountain summits rose
And stood firmly and peacefully in repose.
Brooks tumbled from an icy fault,
Channelled through beds and did not halt,
Flowed into valleys from the mountainside,
United with rivers broad and wide,
Joined to the powerful flowing stream,
The face of the earth an eternal beam.

Opening lines of the Chakassian Saga 'Altyn-Chyus'

Pour a pint of boiling water over six tablespoons of dried wild ginger
leaf and leave for two weeks in a dark place. In the morning give
the patient a 100 ml dose of this brew, followed by 100 ml of vodka.
Repeat the procedure at noon. In the evening give the patient only
100 ml of vodka, which should induce vomiting. Administer vodka
again, another 200 to 300 ml. Vomiting should be repeated. Once
the patient refuses vodka, force down 100 ml wild ginger brew.

Recipe to treat alcoholism, Tatyana Lagutina, 2006

Tears wet the face of the Son of Man.
The predestined enlightenment had been fulfilled!

The Last Testament, Book 1, Chapter 6, Verse 69

Trans-Siberian Chocolate

When I woke up in the morning, Moscow was already a distant memory. In the frame of the train window hung a painting of monochrome austerity from which the nocturnal journey had extinguished every urban element. Pale yellow steppe grass occupied the lower half of the picture, stone grey sky the upper, sharply divided by the knife blade of the horizon. Every now and then birches crossed the picture, straws in the boundlessness of Eurasia.

I woke up very early. Almost everyone in the train cabin was still asleep, only my grey-bearded compartment neighbour nodded a silent good morning to me. He sat at the window reading. His book was called *The Murderess with the Tender Eyes*.

The conductress brought me tea. I blew over the edge of the cup to cool it, as I stared, not fully awake, into the infinity behind the train window.

'Marsh and grass and birches,' said the bearded man, who had guessed my thoughts. 'You'll see nothing else until shortly before Novosibirsk. If you are travelling that far.'

'Further. To Krasnoyarsk.'

'I'm from Novosibirsk. And you – you're not from here?'

'From Germany.'

He whistled through his teeth. 'You have the longer route.'

Thus began the ritual bargaining I have so often experienced on Russian trains: your life story for mine.

Volodya was a native Siberian. He made a distinction between three classes of Russians: city-dwellers, steppe-dwellers and forest-dwellers. For the first two he had little time. His own world began where the first coniferous forests make their stand against the grassy plains of the steppe. Volodya spent every free day in the wooden labyrinths of the Taiga. 'People always tell me what they experience on holiday, in Turkey, in the Crimea, in Europe. Who needs that? Give me a tent and a shotgun and I'm happy.'

He pressed an invisible rifle to his shoulder and aimed from the train window. Silent shots convulsed through his body, as he killed invisible game along the route.

The train was not Volodya's preferred means of transportation – at heart was he a motorist. Earlier, in the Soviet era, he had been a race car driver. He showed me photos of his machines: converted Ladas, souped-up Zhigulis, welded together from parts Volodya and his racing comrades stole from socialist production. In those days they had worked as mechanics in a Novosibirsk agricultural machinery combine. 'They paid us the minimum salary, we did minimal work. We didn't give a damn about the tractors, we just needed the tools, the spare parts. It was all there, we just had to help ourselves. No one checked us, no one asked questions. Those were heavenly times!'

But the time when Volodya had driven racing cars himself was long past. 'I'm too old,' he said regretfully. 'I don't understand the sport anymore. Everything has become more difficult. You can't do anything anymore without money. If I went into the combine today and said: "Kids, mill me a bumper," they would say: "Volodya, bring us material to mill."' He laughed a short, dry laugh. 'Market economy.'

Today he worked as a trainer. He showed me photos of the drivers he trained in Novosibirsk: boys with shaven heads, most of them hardly of age. With paternal tenderness Volodya commented on the photos. 'Maxim, very good boy, he'll have a bright future.' – 'Here, Sasha, he has driving in his blood.'

The training job was on an honorary basis, Volodya earned his money as a freight transporter. With his truck he transported race cars from one competition to the next. He had just come from Moscow, where he had left his transport vehicle until the next race. In a few weeks he would pick it back up. If there was no competition taking place, he transported building materials, furniture, cars, anything that came up. Next there was a house move pending; Volodya would transport a friend's belongings all across Russia. 'His wife desperately wants to live in the south. Now they are moving to the Black Sea.' Volodya shook his head uncomprehendingly. 'What good is the Black Sea to a Siberian? My friend doesn't really want to go, but his wife is constantly harping: "the climate, the climate." I don't understand what is wrong with our climate. Our summer is a real summer, our winter a real winter. At the Black Sea there is not even snow. His wife says: "I don't need snow, I never liked snow." She'll see what it means, a life without snow. That is not for Siberians.'

He asked me about the goal of my journey. When I told him about Agafya Lykova, Volodya nodded. He knew the story.

'The Taiga attracts people,' he said. 'My cousin works for the police. Last summer he was sent into the wilderness. A hunter had found a corpse in the middle of the forest. It took him a week to battle his way to the spot. In the end he found a small wooden hut. Inside was an old man, eaten away by insects, his beard reaching down to his chest. The hut was almost empty. All they found were animal traps and dried meat. No one knew the fellow. No one knew how long he had lived there alone.' Volodya let the story take hold, and then laughed his dry laugh. 'Siberia!'

As we talked, the carriage slowly started to spring to life. Blue and white sheets glided from sleep-crumpled bodies, mountains of laundry transformed into human beings. Greetings were muttered, unknown bed neighbours furtively examined; outside the toilet a procession of toothbrushes formed. Collectively our Trans-Siberian community awoke and prepared for a day of sustained idleness.

Around noon I roughly knew the destinations and life stories of all my immediate neighbours. Masha (Moscow – Irkutsk) had a man at Lake Baikal and another one in the capital. The Siberian drank, but was the better lover; the Muscovite had money but no soul. Sergey (Yaroslavl – Yekaterinburg) sold gems from the mines of the Urals and did not let his sample case out of his sight for a second. Tamara (Moscow – Chelyabinsk) was a policewoman; in her professional life she solved criminal cases, on the train, crossword puzzles. Sonya (Kiev – Chelyabinsk) was studying German and did not grasp the difference between *die gleichen* and *dieselben*, those peculiar German words that mark the difference between things that *look* identical and things that *are* identical. 'The birch trees outside the window,' I explained, 'are *die gleichen* as yesterday, but not *dieselben*.' Sonya nodded, enlightened. 'Is word for trees, yes?'

In the afternoon I took a short nap. When I came to again, I was suddenly no longer sure whether I was really seeing the birch trees outside the window for the first time. The monotony of the landscape was confusing. Had the train moved at all while I slept? Or was a tapestry of unchanging landscape transported past the windows, as had been done at the World Exhibition in Paris in 1900, when the Trans-Siberian Railway was presented to an astonished public for the first time?

The glamorous luxury cars which Parisian society strolled through at the exhibition were never used in Trans-Siberian reality. Far simpler models commuted between Moscow and Vladivostok when the line was completed in 1904. The first symbolic cut of the spade had been performed 13 years earlier on the pacific coast by a young boy named Nicholas, who did not realise that he was digging his own grave – three decades later Tsar Nicholas II rolled to Yekaterinburg in a Trans-Siberian carriage, towards his execution.

Before the line was put into operation, Siberia was linked with the Russian west only by a rough, unpaved dirt road which was barely accessible for the major part of the year – in the winter snow hampered the journey; in the spring, mud; in the summer, dust. The relationship between the two parts of the country was loose, geographically and mentally. Even in the travel notes of Chekhov, who crossed the Eurasian landmass in a horse-drawn wagon shortly before the construction of the railway line, the inhabitants of Siberia spoke of Russia as if it were another, distant country. The endless trip over the Siberian tract must have made it feel like such.

Despite all the hardships, however, the road was hopelessly congested, even during Chekhov's time. Year after year, since serfdom had been abolished in 1861, a stream of land-seeking farmers flowed into the vast expanses of Siberia. On horse-drawn carts people transported their entire belongings eastward, for 1,000s of kilometres. It happened that at their final destination they bumped into former neighbours, who had fled from serfdom years before to seek their fortunes in Siberia. For centuries the sparsely populated areas east of the Ural Mountains had attracted people who wanted to evade the state's reach. Runaway serfs hid in Siberia, wanted criminals, escaped convicts, deflowered girls, dishonoured men, illegitimate children. The Old Believers were the most famous, but not the only community of sectarians who awaited the apocalypse deep in the wilderness. They shared their exile with all those outlaws, exiles and madmen who the state itself transported east so they would not cause any more damage in the Russian heartland.

Just a little earlier, there had not even been a road to Siberia. When the first bands of Cossacks crossed the Urals in the 16th century, they dragged dismantled rowing boats over the mountains. Siberia was conquered by water. The Cossacks used the branched river system that traverses the entire land mass between Moscow and the Pacific. From the Volga they worked their way forward to the Kama, from the Irtysh to the Ob, from the Yenisey to the Angara, from the Lena to the Amur. Piece by piece they wrested the country from the Tatar tribes who had dominated it since the collapse of the Mongol empire. The Tatars called their realm *Sibir*: 'sleeping country'. The Cossacks, who adopted the Turkish word, woke Siberia with violence. When they reached the Pacific in 1639, not even 60 years after the beginning of the campaign, they had moved Russia's border more than 5,000 kilometres to the east. Each year they had annexed an area the size of Great Britain to the already huge tsarist empire.

Siberia's proportions are somewhat terrifying. Towards evening, as the train car sank into sleep, I lay on my bunk and stared forlornly into the dark, endless nothing outside the window. I had been travelling for 24 hours and we had not even reached the Urals yet. I knew that Siberia, if you were to separate it from western Russia, would still be the largest country in the world by far. Any attempt to fully comprehend it suddenly seemed presumptuous to me, and each random inspection arbitrary. Depressed, I pulled the bedcovers over my head and thought about Agafya Lykova. It was reassuring to have a goal, however difficult it might be to reach.

In the middle of the night I woke up, without knowing why. When I looked at my watch I realised that the train had to be passing the Urals, the boundary between Europe and Asia. Before my departure I had been looking for a train that would cross this magic threshold in daylight, but I would have had to change more than once and had finally abandoned this romantic idea. Was that why I had now woken up?

I pushed the curtain to the side and stared intently out of the window. In the light of a sickly crescent moon I could see the outlines of low hills, but nothing more. The Urals are not high mountains. In most places they are hardly suitable as observation points, let alone a continental barrier. A forgotten cartographer, who found no other plausible landmarks, declared them to be the junction of the Siamese twin continent Eurasia. Under my pointlessly searching gaze this demarcation revealed its complete arbitrariness. For half an hour I waited impatiently for a change that did not want to take place. One continent stayed behind, another emerged under the wheels. And in between unchanging birch trees the train rolled on uneventfully. Nothing ended, nothing began. Europe and Asia refused to act out their eternal marital quarrel before my eyes.

The next day the landscape stayed the same; there was just more of it. Fewer and fewer cities or even villages interrupted the monotony of the swampy meadows. When houses appeared, they clung to the railway embankment, huddled closely together, as if they were afraid of the emptiness behind their backs. Sometimes I could hardly believe that we were crossing the most populous part of Siberia, that the genuine emptiness only begins further north of the route, where the climate does not permit agriculture, where only conifers grow, and at some point not even those anymore.

At every stop old women surrounded the train cars. They sold dumplings, boiled potatoes, beer and dried fish. I had not carried any provisions with me and relied on their regular deliveries. When the stops became rarer, I miscalculated my meals and had to bridge half a day with one bar of Alyonka chocolate. The earnest face of a wide-eyed girl was depicted on the old-fashioned wrapper. In Moscow I had always wondered why the little Alyonka on the picture looked so scared. Until Vanya explained it to me one day: 'She's afraid of Stalin.' I have had a weakness for the brand ever since.

'You are eating Russian chocolate,' Volodya said. It was an observation, not a question.

'You don't?' I asked.

'Of course. Nothing else. I do not like your German chocolate. I still remember, back in the time of perestroika, when all of this stuff from the West suddenly appeared in Russia. All we ate were *snickersy* and *marsy* and *raidery*.' He uttered the foreign names with disgust. 'It took years for us to realise that this stuff does not taste like chocolate at all. I'm really glad that Alyonka is back in the shops now. And Red October! Have you tried Red October?'

I nodded.

'And?'

'It tastes good.'

'Which do you like better, German or Russian chocolate?'

'I like both.'

Volodya looked at me searchingly; he did not seem to believe me. 'If I offered you a piece of German chocolate and a piece of Russian chocolate now, which one would you take?'

I laughed. 'Both.'

'But which one would you eat first?'

While I was still thinking it over, an elderly man from the next table, who had been following our conversation, intervened. 'You need to ask differently,' he said to Volodya. 'You do not really know whether he would eat the piece he desires first. He may save the one he likes most for last.'

Volodya took note of the objection thoughtfully. 'Okay,' he said. 'He will only be allowed to eat one.'

Both men looked at me quizzically. And not just them. The policewoman opposite squinted over the edge of her crossword puzzle. The gem salesman looked at me with unconcealed curiosity. Suddenly the fate of two nations hung on my choice between two fictitious pieces of chocolate.

'I don't know,' I said honestly. 'Sometimes one, sometimes the other.'

My spectators nodded, disappointed.

In the afternoon, as we stopped in Omsk, a large family boarded the train. I counted 15 people who hustled down the aisle behind one another, packed with plastic bags and screaming babies. They were not Russians. Because of their dark skin I thought they were Caucasians at first, but Volodya, who eyed the new arrivals suspiciously, enlightened me. '*Tsyganye*,' he whispered gloomily. In Russian the word has the same connotations as 'gypsy', but it is used without scruple. I have never heard a Russian talk about 'Romani people'.

The *Tsyganye* made it hard to like them. They cracked sunflower seeds and spat the shells into the corridor. Wordlessly, they grabbed napkins and sugar cubes from the surrounding compartment tables. The men stretched their legs across the corridor and would only retract them under curses when asked by passers-by on the way to the toilet. Suspicious and taciturn they fought off my attempts to start a conversation.

As the sun was setting, a little black-eyed girl stood in front of my seat and stared at me. 'Give the child chocolate,' her mother called. Smiling, I broke a piece from the bar. The girl snatched it, clutched it tightly in her clenched fist and continued to stare at me. With her wide-eyed gaze she looked a bit like a dark sister of the blonde chocolate Alyonka. 'Give her more!' the mother yelled. 'Give her the whole bar!'

Volodya suddenly jumped up from his seat. 'Shameless woman!' he shouted. 'Call off your child or I'll send her packing!' I put a calming hand on his shoulder, but it was too late. Crying, the girl ran into her mother's arms, and the entire family stared at us full of hostility. Volodya shook his raised forefinger. 'Behave like human beings!'

After he sat down, he grumbled to himself for a long time. 'There weren't any people like that in the past! Back then everybody worked, instead of begging!' The Russian passengers murmured their consent; they shot conspiratorial glances at Volodya and me. Imperceptibly the front lines had shifted in the carriage. Just half an hour ago I had been the stranger, the exotic foreigner who understood nothing about Russian chocolate. Now the Russians and I were suddenly on the same side. We were Europeans. We had common enemies. Asia bonded us together.

At night, when Volodya and I were already lying on our bunks, we exchanged a few final words. We knew that our acquaintance ended here. Before dawn we would pass through Novosibirsk, where Volodya would disembark. Worlds separated us, but we had spent three nights and two days together in a confined space. I had drunk Volodya's cognac, he had questioned me about German cars. I knew his racing stories, he knew the goal of my journey. A Trans-Siberian friendship united us.

'If you come to Novosibirsk sometime …' he said, without finishing the sentence.

'Then I'll ask for Volodya, the race car driver.'

'I can show you the Taiga.'

'That would be nice, Volodya.'

'There are not many people who know the Taiga. Even in Siberia there are not that many anymore.' He sighed. 'And I don't know why. You tell me. Why do people go to Egypt, what do they want in Turkey? Everyone is looking for something, and no one sees what is outside their own front door.'

'Maybe,' I said, 'people want to travel, because they could not in the past.'

Volodya sighed again. 'In the past, it was different. You could not travel, but no one wanted to travel, because we had the Taiga. Siberians loved the Taiga. And today? God knows what they love today. I do not understand people anymore.'

'Volodya,' I said hesitantly. It was dark, we could not look into each other's eyes, but that made it easier to ask questions. 'Why is it that so many people in Russia only see what they have lost?'

He was silent for a long time. Just as I thought I must have offended him, I heard his dry laughter. 'Maybe because we always thought we had nothing to lose.'

Do Bees Have a Five-Year Plan?

When I woke up the next morning, snow was falling. I stared incredulously out of the train window. White flakes danced between bare birch trees. I had travelled backwards in time, from the Moscow spring into the Siberian winter.

My chills amused the seven Siberians with whom I grilled *shashlik* under the open sky a while later. Vladimir, a friend of Alexander Gurtsev, the forestry scientist from Moscow, had picked me up at the station in Krasnoyarsk and invited me to his dacha. His friends laughed at my optimistic summer outfit. While they wrapped me up in thick layers of spare work clothes, they told winter jokes.

'In Siberia you can tell the season from the down jackets. In the winter you wear them closed, in summer, open!' – Laughter. – 'In Siberia it is only cold for one month in the year. The rest of the year it is *very* cold!' – Laughter. – 'Of course there is a summer in Siberia. Unfortunately, I had to work that day!' – Laughter. – 'An African comes to Siberia and asks …' And so on, an endless exchange of geographical gallows humour.

In the evening we fell asleep beside the dacha's stove, warmed by jokes and vodka. When we woke up the next morning, winter was over. Defiant remnants of ice swam in the rain barrel next to the veranda, but their fate was sealed. Overnight the temperature had risen a good 15 degrees. There was a tense buzzing in the air, a pressure like that from a sneeze held in for too long, as if 1,000 buds were ready to burst. A few more hours and an ephemeral spring would sweep away the winter and initiate the shortest of all seasons, the Siberian summer.

Vladimir came up behind me on the terrace. 'Just a few days,' he said, 'then everything here will be green.' It sounded sad. Like every farewell. And Vladimir was not the man to take farewells lightly.

He was in his mid-fifties and worked for a local forest protection agency. In the Soviet era he had liked his job. Today it depressed him. 'Our job is to watch and do nothing while clever capitalists deforest the Taiga and sell it to China,' he said. A penchant for sarcasm, maintained over decades, had dug sharp creases into the corners of his mouth. 'The Chinese are smarter than us. They buy the trees from the stupid Russians for a few bottles of vodka, turn them into furniture and sell it to the West. Eventually the entire Taiga will be standing in European living rooms, without us having earned a kopeck. That is how capitalism works in Russia: everyone thinks only of himself, and in the end we all remain poor.'

In this sea of market economy Vladimir's dacha was the rescuing ark. In the garden behind the house he had gathered all the conifers of the Taiga: pines, larches, firs, spruce, all planted in biblical pairs, two specimens of each type. '*Pinus sylvestris*,' he murmured as he showed me the garden. '*Pinus sibirica. Larix sibirica. Picea obovata. Larix gmelini. Abies sibirica.*' Like a Noah of the forest he walked among his creatures.

'And that there?' I pointed to a freshly ploughed field behind the dacha. Young seedlings stood in the furrows. Vladimir's face darkened. 'Those are Artyom's experiments.'

Artyom was Vladimir's stepson. I had met him the previous evening: a restless twenty-something whose eyes flickered with suppressed rage. Vladimir led me through Artyom's field. '*Pinus sibirica*,' he said, pointing to the saplings. 'Siberian pine. The king tree of the Taiga. Artyom grows them and sells them to customers in Moscow.'

The seedlings were 30, maybe 40 centimetres high. I tried to imagine that one day they would shade the villas of rich Rublyovka residents in Moscow. Not a stupid business model, I thought. But Vladimir seemed to think little of his stepson's ideas. 'Trees are state capital, not objects of speculation,' he said. 'I have explained that to Artyom a thousand times. He doesn't want to hear it. Says I should not interfere.'

'He's trying to build up something of his own,' I said carefully. 'Few people in Russia have the courage to do that, I think.'

Vladimir snorted. 'That may be. But that is not the problem in this country. The problem is that no one wants to build something together.'

At the other end of the field Artyom was working. He was digging holes for fresh saplings. For a while we stood next to him and watched without speaking. Then Vladimir said: 'See that you finish before sunset, Artyom. Are you listening? Don't leave the plants outside overnight again.'

I saw the anger flicker in Artyom's eyes. Abruptly he threw the spade aside. 'Are you starting that again?' he shouted. 'I'm fed up with it! Don't interfere! What do you know?' He stared at his stepfather full of hatred. Vladimir ground his jawbone nervously. I searched for a conciliatory sentence, but before I could think of one a female voice cried from the dacha, 'Men! Food is ready!'

Nothing releases tension as well as a plate of borscht. It must be the colour, I thought; beetroot quenches the thirst for blood. While we were spooning our soup, I observed Vladimir and Artyom from the corner of my eyes. They looked reasonably calm. In the eternal drama of fathers and sons the intermission curtain had fallen; actors and spectators stood chewing at the buffet.

'The bees,' Vladimir cried suddenly. 'The bees are coming out!'

He ran to the garden. Artyom and I followed him. The awakened bees whirred around a wooden box painted pale blue. Silently we observed their dance. Vladimir pointed out patterns in the apparent chaos of their movements. Some of the swarm crawled around the entrance of the hive in entwined loops. 'Those are the dispatchers,' Vladimir explained. 'They signal to the others where the food is.' Then he pointed to the box. 'In there sits the central committee, giving out directives: so and so much food for such and such part of the hive. Then the worker bees fly off and meet the requirements. Exactly like in socialism.'

Artyom and I had to laugh.

'Do the bees have a five-year plan?' I asked.

'Of course,' Vladimir said. He smiled, but you could tell that he found the joke inappropriate.

'And a party?' Artjom asked. 'A politburo? A KGB?'

Vladimir avoided his stepson's mocking gaze. Without answering, he turned to the bees. The three of us silently watched the swarm, moving as if it was steered by a common will. A dream suddenly hung in the air, one that had long been declared dead. Communism seemed tangible, possible, desirable, for one short spring moment.

'The bees are smarter than us,' Vladimir said quietly. 'They know that a planned economy works. And us? We shatter everything that we have built.'

'Planned economy! Ha!'

Artyom drove me back to the city in the late afternoon. His anger had dissipated, now he seemed amused. 'Vladimir will never change. He is too old to change.'

Outside, beyond the car windows, dense conifers passed by, interspersed with occasional birch trees. The landscape was completely different from the open plains I had contemplated from the train for three days. What I was now seeing were the first outposts of the Taiga, that endless forest in which Agafya Lykova lived.

During the ride Artyom talked about his business. When I asked whether he also delivered to customers in Krasnoyarsk, he stared at me in disbelief. 'Sell pines in Siberia?' He laughed. 'Look around you!'

The unmistakable green of the *pinus sibirica* gleamed left and right of the route.

'If someone here needs a tree, he just goes into the forest and digs one up. No matter who owns the forest, no matter if it is a nature reserve, no matter whether three other trees fall with it! Everything belongs to the people!'

A wrinkle creased his forehead. The rage had returned.

'I don't know how long it will take before this way of thinking is finally out of our heads. Decades, probably. And by then there will be nothing left of the Taiga. It is being plundered. People take chainsaws into the forest, load up their trucks and sell the stuff to China. The police stand by and collect kickbacks. That is Vladimir's planned economy for you! Everyone robs everyone else, and in the end we all remain poor.'

I had to suppress a laugh. The drama of fathers and sons, I thought, is a drama of mirrors and echoes.

At the Krasnoyarsk University dormitory, the receptionist persuaded me to share a room with a young soldier. 'He is a stranger in town. Just like you. Surely you will find things to talk about.'

We did find things to talk about. Zhenya was an army accountant from Novosibirsk. He had been reassigned to Krasnoyarsk for a few weeks, to examine the finances of the local military branches. The local military branches made every effort to prevent Zhenya from examining them, which was why he had not been properly sober for days. In addition he was, as he mentioned in passing, an Old Believer.

I was speechless. With a few sentences Zhenya had disproved all the ideas of the Old Believers I had acquired through reading. He worked for the *state*? In the *army*? As an *accountant*? He *drank*? Confused, I searched for any sign of the world-detached, service-refusing, money-despising, abstinent beard lover of my fantasy – but there was only the clean-shaven reality.

Zhenya laughed. 'That is all long gone,' he said. 'Things used to be strict for us in the old days. But today …' He made a dismissive gesture with his hand. 'We live in the world after all. The way you imagine it, one can only live in the forest. Like your Agafya Lykova.'

I had come to Krasnoyarsk because I was looking for three people who had visited Agafya Lykova in the Taiga: a photographer, a doctor and a linguist.

I found the photographer first. His name was Valery. He had a long white beard that he shook vehemently when I asked him whether he was an Old Believer. 'For god's sake, no! Vodka?' We drank half the night.

Valery talked about Agafya. He had met her only once, a long time ago. 'If I could, I would go back every year. But it has become too difficult. In the past there was a geologists' settlement near her hut, but it was abandoned 20 years ago. Since then you can hardly get there. You need a helicopter. Or healthy legs. I don't have either.'

I found the doctor in a Krasnoyarsk polyclinic. Doctor Igor Nazarov confirmed the rumours I had heard about the death of Agafya's three siblings. 'Flu,' he said. 'Ordinary influenza viruses, introduced from the outside world. The Lykovs had no defences against such diseases because they do not occur in the Taiga. When the geologists appeared amongst them, they died like flies.'

Only Agafya and her father survived. Doctor Nazarov had visited both of them several times. Since the death of her father, however, he had only seen Agafya a single time, and that was already 15 years ago.

'You want to visit her?' he asked.

I nodded.

'That will be difficult. You'll need …'

'…a helicopter?'

'Exactly. Or a robust physique.'

Doctor Nazarov's physique was impressively robust for an octogenarian. But the journey to the Taiga exceeded his powers. He seemed to have resigned himself to the fact that he would not see Agafya again in this life. As we said goodbye he asked me for a favour. 'If you really manage to do it, please take a gift to her for me.' He pressed a bill into my hand. 'Buy her a kerchief. Dark, with red flowers. She likes those the best.'

I gave him my promise.

The linguist wore two scarves and three jackets, one over the other. In the Krasnoyarsk Literature Museum the heating had failed, and the spring sun had not yet managed to expel the winter cold from the dark wooden villa. Galina Alexandrovna was a small, slender woman in her forties. She spoke so hurriedly that the breath clouds in front of her mouth were more sharply outlined than her sentences.

She showed me copies of letters Agafya Lykova had written to distant relatives. Fascinated, I examined the large Slavonic letters – more paintings than alphabet – that filled the pages in irregular lines. As in the liturgical books I had seen in Moscow, the words followed one another without punctuation. I had trouble reading the handwriting, but with Galina Alexandrovna's help I deciphered the opening formula that began each letter.

LORD JESUS CHRIST SON OF GOD HAVE MERCY ON US AMEN AGAFYA KARPOVNA WROTE THIS ON THE FOURTEENTH OF DECEMBER IN THE YEAR SEVEN THOUSAND FIVE HUNDRED AND NINE A DEEP OBEISANCE

I looked questioningly at Galina Alexandrovna. '7509?'

'Since the creation of the world. The Old Believers still count this way. That was one of the facets of my doctoral thesis.'

'You wrote about the Old Believers?'

'About the traditional denominational lexicon in Agafya Lykova's written utterance.'

'Ah.'

'You know, this woman is of vital importance to linguistic research. Imagine an individual whose semantic awareness is formed in a completely hermetic micro-society! Only as an adult did she come into contact with carriers of normative idiolects! Do I have to explain to you what kind of lexical disruptions such a shock triggers?'

'Um …'

'I wish I could visit her again. There are so many unanswered questions! Her anthroponyms! The varieties of her sacred lexicon …'

'What keeps you from visiting her?'

Galina Alexandrovna sighed. 'It is too difficult. Since the geologists' settlement was closed you can only get there on foot. I did it once, but only because I was naive and underestimated the Taiga. It was dangerous. I will not do that a second time.'

My search for the four geologists who in 1978 had discovered the Lykovs in the Taiga was unsuccessful. They were the first people from the outside world to have spoken with the hermits. The little that I learned about their fate sounded like a pitch-black joke about Siberia's hardships. One had drunk himself to death. Two had vanished without a trace in the chaos following the perestroika period. The fourth, a woman, had died during a Taiga expedition. A bear had killed her.

Krasnoyarsk hurts the eyes, especially when you examine the city from above. A flat, undeveloped mountain rises above the skyline. You can climb to the summit and look for the 'best and most beautiful of all Siberian cities' that Chekhov described. But you won't find it. It is buried under an industrial carpet of factories and smoking chimneys. The old Krasnoyarsk fell victim to a war that raged 4000 kilometres further west. When the Germans advanced on Moscow, Stalin had entire factories in Western Russia dismantled and rebuilt in the Siberian hinterland. Still today their fumes darken the sky over Krasnoyarsk.

The city is lovely only where it draws the eye downward, away from the sky. On Peace Prospect there is a small monument to Pushkin, the European by choice, who never visited Krasnoyarsk in his life, which makes the statue all the more touching. A few old wooden villas still remain in the city centre, witnesses to a better time, or at least a less gray one. The Yenisey cuts a gigantic swath through the city, a river that looks like silver lava, pouring towards the Arctic Ocean with majestic lethargy.

On a park bench in the city centre I thought about further steps. I did not notice the old man who took the seat next to me until he started speaking.

'How old do you think I am?' he asked.

'50,' I lied. To my eyes he looked 60, but Russian men usually look older than they are. When guessing I always subtracted a few years. This time I was completely wrong.

'70!' he cried triumphantly. 'I am 70! And my virility is undaunted!'

'Congratulations.'

'Shall I tell you my secret?'

'Absolutely.'

He pressed a small glass vessel into my hand, filled with a brown liquid. On the label there was a familiar name: *pinus sibirica*.

'Siberian pine oil,' the man said. 'Fortifies the immune system, improves circulation, strengthens the nerves, slows the aging process and …' – winking, he put his hand on his crotch – '… increases virility! Take it. I'm giving it to you! If you need more, you know where to find me. Shall I tell you my second secret?'

'Yes, please.'

He looked around conspiratorially to the left and right. Then he leaned over to me, whispering, 'Jesus is alive.'

I had to laugh. 'That is no secret. Half the world is talking about it.'

'He is alive! He has returned! His name is Vissarion, he is the Son of God. He is risen! He lives in the Taiga, not far from here. Go there, see for yourself!'

The glass with the pine oil broke in my bag on the way home. I was just washing the brown stains out when my mobile rang. From the breathless voice I recognised Galina Alexandrovna, the linguist.

'You are still in Krasnoyarsk?' she asked. 'Very good. I have phoned around a little and there is someone who can take us to Agafya by boat, upstream along the Abakan, then continuing by foot through the Taiga. It will be difficult, but he wants to try it.'

'Great,' I said. 'But didn't you say that you would never go back …?'

She sighed. 'I have been thinking about it. I believe it is necessary. The research, you understand, the issue is too important …' She murmured a few technical terms that I barely understood on the phone. 'Unfortunately, the earliest we can travel is in two weeks,' she continued. 'The snow in the mountains is melting, the river is not yet navigable, the current is too strong. Can you wait that long?'

'Yes.'

'Good. I will call you the moment the river level drops.'

When she hung up, I went to the closest bookstore and bought a map of the Krasnoyarsk district. I was looking for the kingdom of God. It was only a few hundred kilometres away.

Messiah of the Mosquitoes

It is written in the Last Testament, Book 4, Chapter 41, Verse 26: *What is predestined takes place. And on Mount Zion, the worthy children of God gather!*

The mountain appeared unexpectedly. Behind a bend in the road it suddenly flung the dress of pines from its body and bared its peak, as effectively as an experienced stripper.

For an entire day I had been crossing the steppes south of Krasno-yarsk, by train, bus and *marshrutka*. Shortly after the provincial capital of Abakan the first groups of trees had broken through the monotony of the meadows, birch trees at first, which gave way to conifers as the mountain appeared on the horizon. At its foot, the dense Taiga barred the view in all four directions.

I had not yet seen many Siberian villages, but Petropavlovka was so out of the ordinary it was hard to overlook. The village roads were too clean, the vegetable gardens too cared for, the wooden houses too new. But most perplexing was the good mood of the villagers. They beamed. They sang. They said hello.

Petropavlovka and the villages Cheremshanka, Zharovsk and Gulyayevka belong to the kingdom of God that the pine-oil salesman in Krasnoyarsk had told me about. About 4,000 people live in the set-tlements at the foot of the mountain. God Himself lives on the summit. That was why I had been standing at Petropavlovka's bus stop with a few of God's children since early morning, for it was written in the bus schedule that the mountain could be reached twice a week, on Tuesdays and Saturdays, passengers should please register their names in advance.

The bus was an old pickup truck. There was a slight dispute as we climbed up to the open bed, because Sasha had not registered his name on the list but, nevertheless, wanted to go along. The drivers laughed at him, Sasha whined, Sasha was allowed to go along. He sat next to me, a giant with a child's face. As the truck drove away he began to talk: it was always the same with him, he had no control over himself, he always acted before he thought, and because he wanted to change, he was here, and that was why he had left his wife and child behind in Chelyabinsk, because they did not want to come along to the mountain.

And as Sasha finished, Elvira began to talk; she had been born in a train compartment in Germany during the war, and then she became a mathematics teacher in the Soviet Union and the greatest atheist of all time, and then one day someone gave her a book, and in the book was a photo, and Elvira saw the man in the picture and thought, my goodness, that is truly the Lord God, and so she went to the mountain.

And as Elvira finished, Janis began to talk, the Latvian who had owned an import-export company in Hamburg, and then one day one of his drivers had an accident, and they kept him alive in the hospital for three weeks, and when he died, the company owed half a million Euros for medication and had no insurance, and Janis sold the company and paid the debt and accepted it, it was fate, and he went to the mountain.

And Sergey began to talk; he had once been a colonel in the Soviet Rocket Forces, and his days were filled with the work of destruction, and at night he sought peace, and he read the novelists and the philosophers, the mystics and the materialists, the gurus and the ufologists, the Qur'an and the Vedas, the Old Testament and the New, and at the very end he read the Last Testament, and only then did Sergey understand, and he went to the mountain.

And Ivan from Belarus began to talk and Grigor from Bulgaria and Hermann from Bavaria and Vladimir from Kazakhstan, and they all sat together in the bed of a rusty truck, and they came from many countries, and one goal united them: the mountain. For it is written in the Last Testament, Book 3, Chapter 10, Verse 6: *And many came to the teacher who lived in this country, and those who had newly arrived.*

The biography of the man who had changed the biographies of my fellow passengers so dramatically is very well documented. At the time of my journey, in the year 50 of the Era of the Dawn, it filled 19 volumes; a new one came out every year. In Petropavlovka someone had pressed the first volume into my hand, and when my fellow passengers had exhausted their enlightenment stories, I opened the Last Testament and began to read.

Once, on the 14th of January 1961, the predestined birth took place. According to the will of the great creator, the parents did not know the nature of the child who had appeared to them and gave the small one the name Sergey. (LT 1,1,1–2)

Sergey Anatolyevich Torop was the only child of a Siberian construction worker. The Last Testament describes the father as an honest, albeit godless man, who gave his son into the care of the grandmother early on. Sergey grew up with her, far away from home, on the Black Sea. The starry southern sky united in his memory with the voice of his grandmother, who in the evenings, when they both lay together in the grass, would whisper praise for the creator of the heavens.

Sergey was a gentle, dreamy child. He painted. An early portrait of his grandmother peeling potatoes was widely praised for its attention to detail. When Sergey was seven years old his parents' marriage was on the rocks, and his mother brought him home to Siberia, to the provincial town of Shushenskoye. It is unclear whether it was the separation from his grandmother or a general tendency towards melancholy that overshadowed Sergey's school days. He suffered. The dreams of his classmates were foreign to him. They aspired to professions that Sergey found abhorrent, they sought recognition in a society he did not associate with.

He was a loner. In his room in his mother's house he created his own world, which he filled with glass flasks and test tubes at first, later with sports equipment, only to return in the end to the painting utensils of his childhood. After the tenth grade he left school. Instead of looking for work, he painted. His mother increasingly lost patience with him. When Sergey was still living with her in his mid-twenties, she gave him an ultimatum: job search or eviction. Sergey became a traffic cop, but only because he liked the work hours: late patrol, evening to midnight, dreaming under the starry skies.

But in the summer of 1989 any contact with the dirty ways of human society came to an end. Because something mysterious and powerful approached the doors of Sergey's house, and his heart felt this. (LT 1,6,1–2)

It was the time of perestroika. Change was in the air, something was coming to an end, something new was on the rise, but what exactly it was, nobody knew. In the newspapers there was talk of things that had not been talked about before; in people's conversations hope mixed with apocalyptic fear. There were discussions about nuclear annihilation, about environmental destruction and overpopulation, pandemic diseases, planetary disasters. Sergey, who had suspected for a long time that something was wrong with the world outside of his room, read a newspaper notice one day which talked of mediums endowed with extrasensory powers and of dark prophecies from a world beyond our own.

According to the words of this world, man has already lost all opportunities for salvation, because he has developed inside himself a detrimental force, and a sorrowful sacrament awaits the human race in the coming years. The Son of Man did not let this notice go unheeded. His face grew dark and he sank into deep thought ... And from his chest that burned with flaming fire a cry rang out into the far reaches of the Universe: 'No! There must be a way out for humanity!' (LT 1,6,8–13)

Something stirred in Sergey; he did not know what it was. He felt the disaster that was developing, he knew that someone had to prevent it. But was this someone ... could it be ... was it possibly ... himself?

A little later the next clue came. By that time Sergey was living exclusively from his painting, he had chucked the job as a traffic cop. One day a priest knocked on his door. He said he needed two icons, Saint Nicholas and the Virgin Mother – could Sergey do it? Sergey had never painted icons. He did not go to church, he was not even baptized; his relationship with God was unclear. But he was young and needed the money.

Soon the first paint touched the prepared surface. Sergey did not follow the formal requirements of icon painting, but created a living image and allowed Nicholas to walk on a cloud ... The creation process continued, and soon the second image was completed – Mother Mary, also walking on a cloud. (LT 1,6,34–39)

Sergey delivered the icons to the church. A deacon received them and chatted with Sergey for a while. Then he spontaneously offered to baptise him – since he was already here, it was no big thing really, and after all, an unbaptised icon painter, wasn't he hoping for follow-up orders? Sergey felt as if he was being blackmailed. Politely, he asked for time to think.

A little later the priest summoned him to the church. The man was visibly nervous; he rubbed his hands, spoke evasively, until finally he came out with it – he had bad news for Sergey. His icons had been rejected by the church authorities.

He complained that the saints walked on clouds with bare feet, that their garments fluttered in the wind, that the hands of the miracle worker Nicholas were too large, like a peasant's, not as fine and noble as they should be with a saint. (LT 1, 6, 56)

The priest proposed compromises: here a few additional brush strokes, there a minor intervention, away with the clouds, shoes on the feet – after all Sergey was a professional, wasn't he? But Sergey found the priest's manoeuvring just as offensive as the deacon's blackmail attempt. Should such people be allowed to call themselves God's servants?

Bitterness touched his heart. Only quietly did short sentences resound from his mouth in response to the waiting client: 'I will not change a hair. I cannot betray the image which I myself have seen.' (LT 1,6,57–62)

Sergey returned his fee to the priest and took the icons back home, where he threw himself on his bed in threefold despair: he was broke, doomsday was approaching and no help could be expected from such a church.

And while He remained in deep thought and grief, He sensed something great develop in Him, and it awoke and arose ... Tears wet the face of the Son of Man. The predestined enlightenment had been fulfilled! (LT 1,6,66–69)

The 18th of August 1991 was a memorable day – for the country, for the world, for the universe. In Moscow Boris Yeltsin climbed onto a tank and called for resistance against the Communists' coup. In Siberia, Sergey Torop stepped before a crowd of people and revealed himself as the Son of God. In hindsight, it is difficult to say which was the greater event: in Moscow a coup was staged against perestroika; in Siberia, against the apocalypse.

Henceforth, Sergey called himself Vissarion Christ, and he began to gather disciples. First he gathered them in his home town, but soon lost sheep were flocking to Siberia from all parts of the crisis-ridden country. When the city grew too narrow for the young community, Vissarion led his disciples out into the wilderness, into the Taiga – and up the mountain.

Thus began the hard and arduous days of construction of the future in the Siberian land. (LT 3,10,4)

Halfway up the mountainside the gasping of the motor stopped abruptly and the car discharged its load of pilgrims. The muddy road ended, we would have to walk the rest of the way. For two hours we followed a narrow path that snaked uphill between the densely packed pines. Anemones and cowslips lined the way, awakened by the warmth of spring, just like the insects. They were everywhere. Several times we had to stop to pluck ticks from each other's skin. Mosquitoes attacked us in thick swarms, as purposeful and unyielding as a biblical plague.

I hiked alongside a veteran who had witnessed the exodus of the community in the early Nineties. Stepan was not yet 50, but the hardships of the Taiga had aged him prematurely; his body was as sinewy and emaciated as an old man's. He told me how in the early years the disciples had slept in tents at 40 degrees below zero, how they had cleared the mountaintop with axes because Vissarion taught them that chainsaws disturbed the balance of nature.

While he was speaking, I tried desperately to keep the mosquitoes at bay. Stepan seemed hardly to notice them. But that was deceptive. 'You never get used to them,' he said, smiling. 'You just get used to the fact that you don't get used to them.'

Secretly I opted for the apocalypse. Better an end with terror, I thought, than this endless mosquito martyrdom. Vissarion had to be a remarkably charismatic man if he had inspired his disciples to live in these hostile surroundings. The dreamy traffic cop from the Last Testament was still fresh in my memory, and I had a hard time recognising him in Stepan's stories.

Late in the afternoon we reached the Abode of Dawn.

'The what?'

'The Abode of Dawn,' Stepan repeated. 'The heart of the community.'

We were standing at the edge of a large, deforested clearing just below the mountain summit. There were about 80 wooden houses distributed loosely around the site, many of them decorated with fantastic roof structures. I let my eyes wander. Beyond the cupolas and peaks and towers, pristine pine forests stretched to the horizon. Birds of prey circled weightlessly above the slopes. Below the clearing glimmered a cold blue mountain lake. For one short moment I forgot the mosquitoes. Whoever's son it was that lived here, the Heavenly Father was kind to him.

A meeting between Vissarion and his disciples was scheduled for the next day, like every Sunday. Overnight, I was lodged with a young couple. Ruslan came from Lenin's native city, Ulyanovsk. Lisa came from Tchaikovsky's native city, Votkinsk. They had met in the Abode of Dawn.

Over the course of a Vissarionist supper (no meat, no dairy products, no alcohol) they told me their story. Lisa's parents were Soviet atheists, Ruslan came from a family of Tatar Muslims. Both had read the Last Testament without ever having had any contact with the Old or the New one. Whether Vissarion was the returned Christ hardly seemed to matter to them – for them he was 'the Teacher', as they called him.

'He teaches us how people can live together without hurting each other.'

Ruslan had worked as a programmer until a few years ago. One day his former boss had pressed the Last Testament into his hand and, thus, lost his favourite employee. Before he went to the mountain, Ruslan turned the small company he had established alongside his job over to a friend. The company installed heating coils on dacha roofs, and the friend had by now grown rich. 'Whenever I visit Ulyanovsk, my old friends say: Ruslan, that could have been you.' He shrugged his shoulders, smiling.

'Yes, it could have been me. But what kind of a life would that have been?'

While he spoke, Lisa hung on his words. Their infatuation was physically palpable. Whenever their glances met I had the feeling of being swept out of their field of vision by a sudden wave of love. They gave the abundance of their happiness to the community. 'Four and a half days a week we live for others!' Ruslan said. He counted the gifted hours on his fingers, a rosary of self-sacrifice: 'preparation of the liturgy – half of Sunday; construction brigade – all day Monday and Tuesday; on Wednesday there is the community meeting – again half a day; Thursday …' At the end of the list he looked into my eyes euphorically. In his metal-framed scientist's glasses I could see a tiny reflection of the kitchen window, and an even tinier one of the Taiga behind it, a thousand pine trees in two lenses. 'Everyone helps everyone. No one demands anything, no one has debts, and everybody has enough to live on. Isn't that wonderful?'

They showed me their wedding photos. The ceremony had been a few years earlier, and the two people in the pictures, receiving their teacher's blessing in wide, white robes, were clearly newcomers to the Taiga. Ruslan especially had changed: the once chubby bridegroom was now an athlete, with hard muscles on his arms and chest. Lisa too had grown thinner. But both still had the same watery blue eyes which in the wedding photos made them look almost like brother and sister. Their expression was one of childlike trust, coupled with a constant fear of hurting others.

'The important thing is to avoid negative feelings,' Ruslan said. 'Always, at every point. When there is conflict, we ask the teacher how we should act. Tomorrow you will hear his replies.'

After the meal I helped the two with the garden work. The sowing season had just started. It was the most important time for the self-sufficient settlement; the yield of the short summer had to last through the long winter. Although dusk was approaching, the air was still filled with the warmth of spring, and the work was sweat-inducing. Afterwards, Ruslan sent me to the shower, a small wood cabin in the garden. The icy water felt good, but suddenly one of the damp floorboards gave way under my foot. I broke through into the muddy ground with a crash. When I confessed the mishap to Ruslan, he assumed an earnest expression and looked straight into my eyes.

'Forgive me, please, for this.'

I laughed. 'Forgive me for ruining your shower.'

'The shower should not stand between us. I will fix it immediately. And Lisa will take care of your wound.'

'That's not necessary.'

'You're bleeding.'

'The scratch should not stand between us. I would rather help you with the repair.'

It took Ruslan five minutes to remove the broken plank and put in a new one. As a symbolic contribution I handed him the hammer and nails. As we looked into each other's eyes once the job was done, I felt as if I had learned my first Vissarionist lesson. Never had a conflict been resolved more thoroughly.

I awoke in the middle of the night. Some animal cried in the darkness, I could not classify the sound. Ruslan and Lisa were fast asleep. Quietly I stepped out the door. In the light of an almost full moon the sleeping settlement lay before me. With their cupolas and peaks and towers, the moonlit houses looked like bizarre chess pieces, and the mountain summit like a brooding player hunched over them.

What game was being played here? I was no longer sure. From the distance Vissarion's mountain had seemed like the make-believe world of a charlatan, and his disciples like pitiable fools. But Ruslan and Lisa were not stupid, and their honest enthusiasm directed my thoughts in a completely different direction now. What Vissarion promised his followers was in essence not very different from what Lenin had once promised the world: the breakthrough into a new era, the creation of a fraternal community, without chains, without exploitation, without money. With their youthful spirit of sacrifice, Ruslan and Lisa seemed like the Komsomol members of communism's pioneer years, who set out into virgin Siberia to build a paradise on earth, undeterred by all climatic opposition. They were the new humans, who would realise their dream against all human experience.

I, however, had felt like a hopeless cynic in my conversation with Ruslan and Lisa, unable to believe that any tool for world happiness could hammer out the dents in the world, not socialism and not Vissarionism. All I could see was new dents. And old patterns. The church of the Last Testament would fail like the church of the Communist Manifesto had failed, and even in their failure I recognised similar historical steps: Vissarion had not converted mankind, but here, on the mountain, his dream was intact; the world revolution had failed to take place, instead the motto was now: Socialism in one country.

Of course there were differences, fundamental ones, and perhaps they were more important than the similarities. But as I saw the cupolas and peaks and towers spread out before me in that moonlit night, I could not shake the feeling that a long-lost game was repeating on this chessboard.

And from their mouths gushed many questions. And the truth flowed in response. (LT 3,10,6)

Silence set in. First the singing stopped, then the murmurs, finally the rustle of clothes. Motionless, the disciples waited, some kneeling, others sitting. Their sudden silence made the chirping of the birds sound shrill.

For several minutes the clearing lay as if frozen. Then from the left a figure dressed in white stepped from the curtain of pine trees. It approached slowly, walking steadily along a paved stone path. Step by step the Son of God became visible, recognisable: the slim body, the long girlish hair, the dark beard, the Mona Lisa smile. Vissarion took his place under a purple parasol. With a gesture of his hand he inaugurated the audience.

A young man stepped to the microphone in the middle of the clearing.

'Teacher, I would like to ask you something. My wife and I, we … intimacy between us has grown rare. She is always tired, or she has women's problems, or she fears getting pregnant …'

'What is your question?' Vissarion interrupted. His voice was a purring singsong.

The man cleared his throat. 'The question is … I see her less and less as a wife … more like a sister … it is …'

Vissarion interrupted him again. 'Love can take many forms, and one of them is the love between brother and sister.'

The man collected his thoughts; he was struggling for words. 'But it is … when I want to and she does not … that triggers a physical frustration … and I do not know by what means … how on earth can I …'

'Do not swear,' Vissarion said, smiling. Faint laughter went through the ranks of his listeners. 'Ask nothing of each other. Do not strive for something that looks good from afar but cannot be obtained. There is a long path before you. Follow it with patience, follow it together.'

The man nodded, thanked Vissarion and left the microphone. Involuntarily I wondered whether his wife was sitting in the audience. But after I had listened to the interplay of questions and answers for a while, I realised that no one here was afraid to talk about intimacies in public. Every other question concerned marital affairs: how to deal with hurtful remarks, different eating habits, unwanted advances, the unfulfilled wish for children? Almost all other questions revolved around housekeeping: Was it contrary to the laws of nature to castrate a horse? Was detergent spiritually harmless? When my neighbour's goat relieves itself in my garden, does the manure belong to my neighbour or am I allowed to fertilise my field with it?

Sometimes Vissarion responded succinctly, almost brusquely, as if he wanted to signal that the question had been answered often enough. Then again, certain questions seemed to please him, and he replied at length, expanding on the topic and branching off into related matters.

After a few questions I noticed a gaunt, long-haired man who sat a few steps away from Vissarion, in front of a recording device. I had seen him in photos – it was Vadim Redkin, once a singer in the perestroika rock band 'Integral', now Vissarion's evangelist. He was the one who transcribed each of the teacher's sentences into the ever-growing Last Testament. In the course of the previous day I had browsed this holy scripture again and again, with growing fascination, because no human topic seemed to be alien to it. My favourite question was the one about the mosquitoes. There are, one man had asked, people who are constantly bitten by mosquitoes and others who are almost never bitten. What does this difference mean? Do mosquitoes prefer saints or sinners?

Put yourself in the place of the mosquito. Would you make a dive for something if its consumption disgusted you? (LT 6,28,23)

Yesterday I had laughed about these words, today I felt their consolation – I put myself in the place of the mosquito and found it easier to endure their sting. Vissarion's truths might be simple, but I slowly began to understand the grateful smiles on his disciples' faces. It is good to have someone who takes simple questions seriously.

The tone only changed during one of the last questions, asked by a young woman in a maroon velvet dress. Her demeanour lacked the humility displayed by the previous speakers, she spoke whingeingly, almost accusingly. 'I really need to say something general about our architecture in the settlement, teacher. Because somehow we have run out of steam, you know? In the past we designed ambitious projects, and now? It's all right as long as you can somehow live in it. Architecture is an expression of the human spirit, we must by all means continue to develop in this area, especially now, when the whole world is in a creative crisis ...'

Vissarion interrupted her, smiling. 'Your observations are correct. But you overlook something. Nothing that happens to me happens by chance – everything happens inevitably. Creative work used to play a greater role in our settlement, because it had to be so at the time. Today other things take centre stage. I myself have ceased to paint and will probably never take it up again, and that, too, did not happen by chance.'

The last sentence was apparently news – a murmur went through the crowd, and the next woman to ask a question took up the theme. She had to be about 40, a slender, pretty woman in a short summer dress. Her voice was a pleading whisper, and I figured out what Ruslan and Lisa later confirmed: Vissarion was not giving this disciple the kind of love for which she longed.

'Teacher,' she breathed, 'I was perturbed to hear that you do not paint anymore. You say everything is inevitable, but what happens to us? I look around me and find disturbing signs everywhere. In the past the only people included in the community were those who were ready to accept great hardships. Now it is enough if someone does not smoke and drink. The requirements continue to drop and ... and you do not paint anymore ... I am worried ...'

I pricked up my ears. Was this only a rejected lover speaking, or was the stagnation she complained of the next stage in the foreseeable withering of all utopias?

Vissarion's answer was long.

'Tanya,' he began, addressing a questioner by name for the first time. 'Each of us should concentrate on our own duties. It is not your duty to worry about me. What you are doing is very dangerous.' The same mild murmur of his voice now only emphasised the sharpness of his allegations. Had he not stressed often enough that his programme was focused on generations, on centuries, on eternity? Didn't Tanya see for herself how petty it was to measure eternity against a moment? Did she trust him so little?

Tanya made timid attempts to defend herself, but Vissarion would not let her speak again. When he had finished, there was silence. No one stepped up to the microphone. Vissarion waited a few seconds, then he ended the audience.

'Beware of the sun,' he said in conclusion, addressed to the whole community. 'The sun shines very brightly during this season, it has a strong effect on people. Be careful with it.'

He stood up and slowly returned the way he had come. When he was just a few steps away from the edge of the forest, he stopped and turned around again. His disciples waved silently, until their god had finally disappeared between the pines.

As I left the clearing along with Ruslan and Lisa, someone tapped me on the shoulder. I turned around. It was Vadim, the evangelist. 'The teacher,' he said, 'is ready to answer your questions.'

God's son received me in the study of his house. His handshake was one of acquiescing gentleness, his smile impenetrable and embracing at the same time. Vadim and I took a seat, and in silent expectation Vissarion returned my gaze.

'Perhaps you would first like to learn something about me?' I asked.

Smiling, he shook his head. 'That is not necessary.' Mild indulgence sounded in his words. I could not tell him anything that he did not already know.

In the same tone he answered my questions – as if he had anticipated them, as if he had put them into my mouth himself, to be able to give me answers that had long been waiting for me. No, naturally it was no coincidence that the return of Jesus had occurred in Russia, as nothing happened by chance. Russia had long been prepared for the return. The Bolsheviks had destroyed the foundations of all religions, and so a society had emerged which was able to approach God in spiritual freedom, which could find its way back to Him unencumbered.

And yes, naturally it had had to happen in Siberia, in a place that was still largely unaffected by the self-destructive actions of mankind.

He spoke slowly, his head tilted back slightly, a never-failing smile on his lips. He looked in my direction, but I provided his gaze with no place to rest, his half-closed eyes flirted with the infinity behind my back. I caught myself examining his words and gestures for traces of the man he had once been, the contract painter and traffic cop Sergey Torop. It was an obvious thought, but when I became conscious of it, I felt petty – instinctively I was waiting for the unmasking of an impostor. In vain. There was no indication that this man did not believe in what he said.

Meanwhile we had penetrated deeply into the ramifications of Vissarionist doctrine. It seemed, like so many Christian revival movements before it, to wrestle with an old dilemma: if God is omnipotent and good, then why does He not prevent evil? Vissarion solved the contradiction through division of labour: there were two Gods, an old one and a new one. The God of the Old Testament had created the world, but He was indifferent to His creation, the fate of the people did not concern him. All He had been able to give the world was faith, while hope and love were alien to him. Only another, younger God, the God of the New Testament, had sent His son to mankind as a glimmer of hope – and now that son had returned, with the Last Testament and its message of love.

'In those days,' Vissarion said, bridging the 2,000 years between His first and second appearance on earth with a vague wave of the hand, 'in those days I was not yet in a position to show humanity the laws of their spiritual development. Many things I could not say; not everything could be recorded; the circumstances did not permit it.' In those days, he continued, God's word could only be delivered in parables. Only now was Christ able to provide specific instructions for every situation in life, and only those who heeded them would be able to overcome the self-destruction instilled in man.

As a third, half-pagan deity, Mother Earth was enthroned in the Vissarion pantheon: nature, the personified creation. Between her and humanity there was discord, fuelled by alien powers that wanted to drive the world to extermination. Their most effective tool was money. Distributing it among men was entrusted to the chosen people of the Old Testament, the Jews, who were powerless to break out of their destructive role, because their indifferent God did not stop them.

Besides the evil aliens there were also good aliens, but at about this point I lost the thread. Vissarion talked further, about the transmigration of souls, about energy waves. His voice was gentle and insistent, it flooded the room. I felt immersed in answers, but as I read through my notes later I could barely make sense of what we had talked about for a whole hour. My questions seemed even more pointless to me than his answers.

At the very end of our conversation, however, one sentence suddenly roused me. One day, Vissarion said, when the Last Testament was completed, his own presence would no longer be necessary. A little too hastily I blurted out the question which one is reluctant to ask a god: 'And then? What will happen when you are no longer present?'

Vissarion laughed, with amusement, not defensively. 'There will still be students,' he said, 'and a Scripture will remain, one that leaves no questions unanswered. There will be no need to write commentaries which distort my words, as has so often been done in the past.'

Vadim, the evangelist, nodded vigorously. Vissarion searched his eyes; a knowing smile crossed the room. They were a committed team. They had safeguarded themselves against the mistakes of their predecessors. Their plan was watertight, their Testament the Last.

Back at the foot of the mountain, in Petropavlovka, bad news was waiting for me. The warm weather of the last few days had accelerated the thaw in the mountains. All the rivers had broken their banks, including the Kasyl, which I had crossed on my way to the settlement. The riverside road was flooded, the bus service discontinued, the valley cut off from the outside world. At the thought of being stuck indefinitely in the kingdom of God, the hair on the back of my neck bristled. I only now became conscious of my inner tension – for days I had nodded and smiled at all attempts at conversion, and I could not do it any longer. I accepted gratefully when a pilgrim couple offered to take me along in their jeep, which they hoped would be able to get through the flooded road.

Sasha and Ira were 'from the area.' They lived, as it turned out, near Novokuznetsk, a good 400 kilometres away, a Siberian puddle jump. It was their first visit to the kingdom of God, but they wanted to return. Perhaps forever. Sasha talked about the construction company he had founded. 'I always thought I needed that – my own company, a car, a house. But then you work and you work, and in the end you ask yourself: What for?'

We reached the riverside road at midnight, in the pouring rain. As far as the headlights could reach, the asphalt was under water. I pulled my shoes off and walked in front of the car to find the shallowest route, while Sasha followed behind slowly. In a few places the water was up to my knees, but we made it through. Our cheering was shared, our motives different.

Two hours later Sasha stopped at a train station in a small, deserted town. 'I'll be right back,' he said. Ira and I sat in the car, too tired for conversation. I looked out the window. The rain had stopped, the clouds had cleared, a perfect starry sky beamed above the train station. Not far away, I thought, a bearded man now stood on a mountain and contemplated the same stars as me and Ira, and a million other children of men, and Sergey Torop knew it, and he knew that the stars were the same ones he had contemplated as a child. Only he, Sergey Torop, was no longer the same.

I wondered where Sasha was. My eyes scanned the dark station square. A drunk was leaning against a wall, retching, a finger stuck in his throat. I looked closer. It was Sasha.

'Ira,' I cried. 'Your husband, what is wrong with him?'

She turned around, but she could not see Sasha from the front seat.

'Is he vomiting?'

'Yes.'

She sighed. 'I knew that it was starting again. It's his liver. He stopped drinking a long time ago, but he is sick, very sick.'

I opened the car door. Ira held me back. 'Leave him alone. Afterwards he'll be better.'

Silently we waited. It was quiet on the station square, only Sasha's retching pervaded the darkness.

'He felt better on the mountain,' Ira said quietly.

About a year later, long after my return from Russia, Vissarion's evangelist Vadim published the 20th volume of the Last Testament. I discovered the text on the community's website. It describes the year 50 of the Era of Dawn, or in secular terms, the year 2010. Chapter 17 begins with the following verse:

On 30 May, after the Sunday sacrament, the teacher sat in the study of his house, where he answered the questions of a writer from Germany named Jens. Jens knew the Russian language well, he was writing a book about Russia ...

In disbelief I read the transcript of our lurching conversation, 75 bible verses long. It did not sound much more comprehensible than it had in the Taiga, but suddenly it took on a meaning which lay beyond the words. I had travelled to Vissarion to make him a character in a book. Only now did I realise that he had done the same thing with me.

You Shall Know Them by Their Beards

Sasha and Ira dropped me off in Abakan, the provincial capital of the Republic of Khakassiya. It was already dawn when I fell asleep in a land-scape of withered flowers, in a hotel room which had not been wallpa-pered for a long time.

The next morning I took a bus to the small town of Shushenskoye, named after the river Shush. Vissarion had spent a number of years here in his youth, but that was not the reason for my visit. I was searching for traces of a different god.

Moscow, 23 February 1897. At the Kursk train station a young man is waiting for the Trans-Siberian railroad. Ahead of him lies a two-month journey that will end in Shushenskoye. The train compartment is cramped, but not half as cramped as cell 193 of the Petersburg detention centre, from which the young man has just been released. For the crime of disseminating revolutionary literature, Vladimir Ulyanov is to serve the remaining three years of his sentence in Siberian exile.

Compared with the subsequent nightmare of the Soviet camps, the tsarist system of exile is relatively comfortable. Members of the upper classes – Ulyanov comes from a land-owning family – can organise their lives in Siberia more or less freely. The young man takes up resi-dence in a medium-sized country house. He receives mail by the bundle from revolutionary comrades, and he sends back equally large bundles. He buys a hunting rifle and an Irish Setter named Shenka. His neigh-bours regularly see the two stalking through the surrounding woods. In summer he bathes twice a day in the Shush, in winter he impresses the small town residents with the elegant momentum of his ice skating. 'When he would skate over the ice with his hands buried in his pockets,' recalls an admiring witness, 'nobody could catch up with him.'

On the side, the young man finds time to complete a book that is later adopted into the canon of the holy scriptures of the Soviet Union: *The Development of Capitalism in Russia*, published in 1899 under the pseudonym Vladimir Ilyich Lenin.

The skates hang on the wall as if Lenin had just hung them up to dry. A great man with small feet, I think involuntarily. It is a quiet day in the former home of the revolutionary. There are six of us: the tour guide, a Russian family and me. The hunting rifle hangs on the bedroom wall, above the two beds in which Lenin and his wife slept. Nadezhda Krupskaya was arrested shortly after Lenin's departure. When they banished her to the West Siberian city of Ufa, she asked to be relocated with her betrothed. The authorities gave their consent, but, as Lenin wrote to his mother, 'under a tragicomic condition: if we do not get married immediately, she has to return.'

The wedding ceremony took place in Shushenskoye, in a small church that was demolished after the Revolution. Apart from the church, every single stone in the city has been preserved, even if Lenin so much as walked past it. On his centennial birthday, in 1970, the entire historical town centre was freed of inhabitants and turned into a pilgrimage site. Millions of workers were then herded through their redeemer's place of exile.

Today, with the stream of pilgrims having subsided, the museum has a discernible public relations crisis. Self-consciously they have renamed the site an 'Open Air Museum for Siberian Village Culture at the Turn of the Century.' It is a curious place: a pilgrimage site which hides its saint so that the absence of pilgrims is not as noticeable.

Lenin's house alone still exudes the spirit of the old Soviet personality cult. We stand before His bookshelf in reverence; we contemplate ourselves in His shaving mirror. The tour guide recites details from the saint's vita, then she turns to the group. 'Any questions?'

A young boy wants to know where the toilet is.

'At the main entrance.'

No, says the young boy, he wants to know where Lenin went to the toilet – why is there no toilet in Lenin's house?

Everyone laughs. Except the guide. Her answer is tight-lipped. 'Personally, young man, I find this question irrelevant.'

The mother steps into the breach. 'Surely Lenin had a chamber pot under his bed,' she whispers to her boy. 'Remember, the woman just told us that Lenin had a maid. Surely the girl looked after the chamber pot.'

'Questions?'

I hesitate. I have heard rumours that the maid looked after more than Lenin's chamber pot. When I ask, the guide looks at me as if I had spit in her face.

'What?' her voice cracks. 'Who? Who said that?'

'An old man at the bus stop.'

'Lies!' She shakes her head vehemently. 'Lenin had a mission, young man! He wrote books here, he established a party, he had no time at all for such nonsense! Haven't you seen the beds?'

I had indeed seen the beds. They stand at right angles to each other, Lenin's head at Krupskaya's feet, separated by a chaste bedstead.

'You mean …?'

'Yes, I mean! Lenin was a very busy man!'

I cannot figure her out. She is young, not much older than me, she cannot have been working here for very long. No one forces her to believe in a Lenin who did not go to the toilet out of sheer missionary spirit.

She seems relieved when she says goodbye to the group.

Galina Alexandrovna, the linguist, confirmed to me on the phone what I had suspected: the river had continued to rise and was not navigable for the indefinite future.

To pass the time, I decided to travel to the neighbouring republic of Kemerovo. I had heard of a small Old Believer settlement called Kilinsk where distant relatives of Agafya Lykova lived.

According to my map, there were just 350 kilometres between Abakan and Kilinsk, but it was clear to me that the number meant little. Distances in Siberia have an unreal, intangible quality. At a crawl, the trains pass through kilometres and kilometres of nothing, in which the eye loses any sense of the distance travelled. The timetables in the trains, the clocks on the platforms, the departure times on the tickets, everything ticks according not to local, but to Moscow standard time. The passage of the hours blurs. The passengers wait stoically, and every conversation about distances ends with dismissive hand movements – two days, that is nothing, 1000 kilometres, that is nothing at all. At some point you start feeling the same way.

When I bought my ticket I understood that it would be a long ride. I had to make multiple changes, travel around mountains and forests, cross an internal administrative border and switch to another time zone. I almost missed the departure of the overnight train in Abakan because I forgot to convert the departure time to local time. Moscow plus four, I drummed into my head, plus four, plus four. I drummed it into my head a little too thoroughly – the next morning, in Novokuznetsk, it was only Moscow plus three, and I missed the intercity bus to Tashtagol. The next one left two hours later. Fifty kilometres outside the city limits the front axle broke. No one knew when the replacement bus would come. No one knew whether one would come at all. No one but me asked questions. Eventually I stopped asking questions too.

When I finally arrived in Tashtagol, I had been travelling for 24 hours, and I was still 30 kilometres from my destination. Buses to Kilinsk ran only on Mondays and Fridays. It was Tuesday. All the motorists I approached turned me down. 'Forget it. That's at the end of the world, no one will go there today.'

The only available accommodation in Tashtagol was an employee's apartment on the upstairs floor of the bus station. Two of the three rooms were unfurnished. The lights did not work in any of them. I locked the door behind me and went for a walk.

In another life Tashtagol could have been an idyllic mountain settlement, a well-frequented spa town, a popular ski resort. In this life it is a collection of crooked wooden houses and battered concrete buildings, scattered in the mountains like car parts after a traffic accident. The main street was deserted. Next to a waste container a pig and a dog were fighting over scraps. World War slogans in various stages of fading adorned the facades of the prefabricated buildings: '40 years of victory!' – '50 years of victory!' – '65 years of victory!' It looked as if the city was slowly celebrating itself to death.

Depressed, I walked down a side street which turned into an unpaved dirt track just beyond the city limits. I followed it until a fenced cemetery appeared on a mountainside next to the road. The entrance was nowhere to be seen. I jumped the fence and climbed uphill between the grave stones.

By now I knew the Russian cemeteries. I knew the serious looks of the portraits on the grave stones, the roughly-welded metal crosses, the primary colours of the painted fences. I knew that the grave stones were either adorned by an Orthodox cross or by a Soviet star. In Tashtagol I saw both symbols on the same stone for the first time. Timur Stepanovich Ganabin, 1903–1967, not an indecisive man according to his portrait, wavered in death between this world and the beyond. The cross was chiselled into the top left corner of the stone, the star into the top right. Puzzled, I looked at this forced marriage of opposing symbols, which now not even death could part.

The cemetery was large, it stretched out all the way up the mountainside. Having reached the top, I looked back down at the city. From the distance Tashtagol looked almost cosy. Chimney smoke hovered above the vegetable gardens. Mixed forests of birch and pine trees wound green-on-green patterns around the city. Behind the trees shone the snowy peaks of the Altai Mountains.

A narrow path ran crosswise over the mountaintop. At its end stood a small caretaker's house. As I approached, two black shadows shot out of the door and rushed up to me. My heart skipped a few beats before a man's voice called the dogs back. In the entrance to the hut leaned the cemetery keeper.

Gena was 56, but he could have also been 76, or 46 – his body was an undatable ruin. Never had I seen such a destroyed man. Everything about him was crooked and out of joint. A striped army vest hung on his shoulders like a construction net spread out to protect passers-by from splintering parts. Only the scars seemed to hold his deformed body together. In tangled lines they ran up from both arms over his shoulders to his neck. One split the bridge of his nose, another went right through his lips and down to his chin. His disfigured face was hard to read. For a long time I did not understand whether my presence was welcomed or not.

But Gena was glad to have a chance to talk. He had been raised in Kazakhstan. Twenty years ago he had been evacuated, together with all the other Russians. 'That was in fashion back then,' he said dryly. He had brought his mother with him, his son had stayed behind; he did not mention a wife. Shortly after their arrival in Siberia his mother had died. Gena was alone.

He had drunk himself half dead, for decades, until his body eventually gave up its resistance. He had been on the wagon for four years now. He took care of the cemetery, and in return he was allowed to live in the hut.

'And before that – well, you can see where I was before.' He pointed to his shoulder. Between the scars I recognised the tattooed outlines of a church. Gena counted its domes out loud. 'One, two, three, four. One for each year.'

I looked at him blankly.

'Everybody did that in jail. It was in fashion back then. Four years, four domes.'

'What for?'

'A guy bumped into me. Back then I had too much strength in my body. Could not handle it.'

'He's … dead?'

Gena shrugged his shoulders. 'Didn't know what to do with my strength.'

As we went into the hut, I understood why he had been leaning in the doorway. His legs did not obey him. His gait was an uncontrolled stumble.

The hut was tiny. A bed, a stove, nothing else. On the wall hung two sweaters and a winter jacket. Gena was wearing everything else on his body. In the summer he washed in the river, in the winter in the snow. For his work he received no wages, only the hut. Visitors to the cemetery brought him tea and cigarettes, and each Sunday a large glass of kasha. Porridge was the only thing his stomach could still tolerate. He fed half of it to the dogs.

He made tea. The stove was cracked, the pipe did not fit properly, smoke escaped from all the gaps. My eyes watered. We shared a yellow plastic cup and filterless cigarettes. The dogs had lain down on the bed, Gena petted the larger one's head. Sometimes he spoke to me, sometimes to the dogs. Sometimes I was not sure who he was speaking to.

His pale eyes radiated a late-discovered tranquillity. I sensed Dostoyevsky, the old Russian story of blood and penance, crime and punishment. A murderer, guarding the dead. But when I asked Gena about God, he laughed like a tractor.

'God? I grew up under the Communists. Back then we all made fun of those bearded ones with their icons. Now nobody laughs anymore. Now they all crowd into the churches. It's in fashion now.'

He pulled the dog towards him and gently bit his ear. 'Right, Timka? We have survived the Communists, we will also survive the priests.'

The next morning I rose early. After a long search I found an old man who agreed to drive me to Kilinsk, although he actually needed to go in the other direction. 'German?' he asked again and again. 'Really? German?' The last Germans he had seen in Tashtagol had been prisoners of war.

Just beyond the city limits the asphalt road turned into a rough dirt track. The old man cursed at each pothole. We passed a village, then another one, then nothing for a long time. 'And so it goes, on and on,' the man said. 'Two more villages, then Kilinsk, then another two villages, then nothing more. Only Taiga. The road leads all the way to Mongolia. But I don't know anyone who has ever driven that far.' Uncomprehendingly he shook his head. 'You won't find anything but Old Believers in the villages here. Strange people. They really want to live at the end of the world.'

Amazed, I looked out the window. Every trace of human life had disappeared from the landscape. Dense, pristine Taiga surrounded us, dissected only by the dusty path through which we made our way. Each time the next deserted valley appeared behind a mountain top, and the next, and the next, I thought: they have done what they could. The Old Believers could not have found a better hideout.

After one and a half hours the road emptied into a narrow, treeless valley. A few dozen wooden houses lined a small creek. On the bank, two bearded men watered their horses. They stared suspiciously at the car. The driver put a hand on my shoulder. 'Do you want me to wait? You can't get away from here.' With gratitude I refused.

The two bearded men looked at me in silence as I approached. I mentioned a name I had read in a two-decades-old issue of a Krasnoyarsk newspaper. Wordlessly, they pointed to a house on the other side of the creek. I thanked them. They stared silently.

The village looked like a blind spot in world history. I walked past houses that leaned into the mountain slopes so crookedly it seemed that in the course of the centuries they had melted into the landscape. On the wooden facades hung harnesses and antiquated tools whose purpose I could not guess. Only a few scattered cars and power lines tied Kilinsk to the present.

I edged my way across the creek on a wooden beam. Uncertainly, I stopped at the garden gate of the house the bearded men had pointed to. I called out the name I had read in the newspaper, once, then once again. It was not until the third time that the front door opened. An old woman stepped into the garden. She looked at me suspiciously. I gabbled a few prepared sentences: I was on my way to see Agafya, her relative – perhaps she wanted to give her a message, to send her a letter?

The woman said nothing. I saw that she was trying to place my accent. 'Germany,' I said. 'I'm from Germany.'

She cleared her throat. Then she asked me whether I had a chip in my palm. Or in my forehead.

I asked her to repeat the question – surely I had misheard it.

'Do you have a chip in your palm?' she repeated. 'Or in your forehead?'

Dumbfounded, I looked at her. 'I … I don't think so.'

She walked over to me through the garden, opened the gate and pushed past me. 'Wait here.'

My eyes followed after her in surprise, until she had disappeared between the houses. A quarter of an hour passed. In the meantime, two girls walked by in long dresses and headscarves, staring at me in confusion. When I greeted them, they turned their eyes away. I felt increasingly uncomfortable. I had not expected to be received with open arms. But I had also not expected to feel like an alien.

When the woman returned, a second, somewhat younger woman was walking beside her. With questioning glances the two stopped in front of me. Nervously, I began to explain my presence in more detail. I talked about my journey, about my interest in the Old Believers, my encounter with the Metropolitan in Moscow. After a while, the younger woman began to smile reluctantly, and a little later the older one too. Their faces gave away an inner conflict, as they seemed to ponder which commandment was the more urgent: hospitality or loyalty to their faith. In the end they asked me to take a seat on a bench in the garden. 'Wait,' they said, before they disappeared into the house.

Again a quarter of an hour passed. When the women returned they placed a small table in front of me and loaded it up with food. Herbal tea, red cranberry juice, black bread. Honey laced with bee wings and pieces of honeycomb. Potato soup. Everything was recognisably self-made, self-planted, self-harvested.

'Eat,' they said. Hesitantly I reached for the spoon. I assumed they would sit down with me. They laughed nervously. 'That is not possible.' I understood. They could not eat with a heretic.

The two of them were sisters. They forbade me to write down their names. Only God, they said, could command the name of a Christian, it did not belong in a newspaper or a book. And not in a register either, they added. This last sentence did not refer to me, they were now talking about the national census, which was imminent in Russia. Again, the government would send officials into their village, again they would distribute passports to the Old Believers. And again they would burn them, just like the last time.

'Do you have a passport?' the younger sister asked.

I nodded.

'That's where the chip is. Or do you Germans plant it into your hands already?'

I shook my head.

'So it is only the Americans. But surely it will soon be the same with you.'

It took me a long time to figure out what the chip was all about. No one in Kilinsk owned a television. But occasionally colourful magazines found their way into the Taiga, which the Old Believers read as if they were apocalyptic letters. In each line they discovered encrypted references to the imminent end of the world as it has been predicted in the Scriptures. Why else would the magazines constantly report on 'stars', stars in human shape, which did not shine in the heavens, but in the cinema and on red carpets? Mark 13:25: *And the stars will fall from the heavens.* Why were all the men in the magazines beardless? Isaiah 7:20: *When that time comes, the Lord will shave off your beards and the hair on your heads and your bodies.* Why did the magazines report about a false Messiah named Vissarion? Mark 13:20: *For false Christs and false prophets will arise.* What were those barcodes that were now printed on all food and products? Revelation 13:17: *And that no man might buy or sell, save he that had the mark, or the name of the beast, or the number of his name.*

The chip also came from the magazines. In foreign countries, it was written, people were not only issued with passports, but the passports now also contained a chip. The chip was Satan's seal. For now it was in the passports, but soon it would be implanted in humans, as John had prophesied in the Revelation, chapter 13, verse 16: *And he causeth all, both small and great, rich and poor, free and slave, to receive a mark in their right hand, or in their foreheads.*

From the younger sister's words I gathered that she had lived outside the village for a while, in the world. She spoke about this period only in vague terms and with bitter regret, as if about a mistake that was long past. The older sister, in contrast, had apparently never left the village.

There was no church in Kilinsk, as I had supposed. The Old Believers here were of the priestless denomination. They celebrated their services in their houses. I did not learn any details. 'We cannot talk about that,' the sisters said.

Both were distant cousins of Agafya Lykova. The hermit had visited them in Kilinsk twice. Both times the geologists had flown her in on a helicopter. During the first visit Agafya had only stayed for a few days, over Easter, at a time when her father was still alive. The Old Believers in Kilinsk, who had only learned about their relatives' fate from newspaper reports, received Agafya like a lost daughter. They knew that her father would not live much longer, they implored her to stay with them. Agafya said neither yes nor no. As she flew back, tears flowed.

Shortly after the death of her father, Agafya had returned. That second visit was more difficult, because there was more at stake. Agafya had not come as a guest, but as a potential neighbour.

In the helicopter she had brought water supplies for three months with her. She explained that during her first visit the water had not agreed with her. The people in Kilinsk did not understand. They had been drinking the water since their birth. Their fathers had drunk it, and their grandfathers, and the fathers of their grandfathers too. Agafya did not touch it.

The cars bothered her. The power lines bothered her. In the sky there were too many planes for her, and in the houses too much light. When she was served the rare food items that the people in Kilinsk bought in the shop instead of producing them themselves, Agafya pushed them aside. She argued about matters of faith, about minute details which no one in Kilinsk had given any thought to before Agafya appeared.

In the end they offered to build a hut for her, only for herself, alone, outside the village, in the forest. Before Agafya climbed into the helicopter, she promised to think about it.

She never returned.

Twenty years had passed since that last visit. The two sisters had tears in their eyes as they spoke of Agafya. It had not been easy with her, they had argued. But she was a relative. She was a sister in faith. And now she was alone.

In the end the sisters pressed a handwritten letter and a large jar of sunflower oil into my hands. 'Tell Agafya that we pressed it ourselves, that it is not from the shops,' they urged me. 'Otherwise, she will not take it.'

I promised.

'Someone must drive you back to Tashtagol,' said the younger sister.

I nodded. I had long since abandoned the vague hope of spending the night in Kilinsk.

While we were waiting for the car, the sisters showed me a young pine tree standing in one corner of the garden. It looked miserable. Its peak hung crookedly to the side, the needles were discoloured in a reddish hue.

'Agafya brought it with her,' said the younger sister. 'We don't know what is wrong with it. It won't take root here.'

Three young men drove me back to Tashtagol. They were all the same age, in their mid-twenties. All three were Old Believers, but none of them saw his future in Kilinsk. They worked out of town, as a driver, a mechanic and a security guard. They commuted between two worlds. The differing degrees to which they seemed to be attached to the world they came from could be read on their faces. One wore an untrimmed Old Believer beard. The second had a token goatee. The third was clean-shaven.

Grinning, the shaven one looked at me. 'Do you know what unites the three of us?' He did not wait for my answer. 'Our sins!' The shaven one and the one with the goatee roared with laughter, while their bearded friend managed a tortured smile. Apologetically, the shaven one put a hand on his shoulder. 'Don't get cross with me.' Then he turned to me. In explanation he pointed to the bearded one. 'He's not sinning much since he got married.'

We talked about Agafya. The three were too young to remember her visit to Kilinsk.

'I'm related to her,' the bearded one said.

'First time I've heard that,' replied the shaven one.

'You're related to her, too.'

'Nonsense.'

'You are. Her father was an uncle of your … No, wait, a great-uncle …'

For a quarter of an hour they tried to unravel the family relationship. In the end they concluded with resignation that in Kilinsk almost everyone was related to everyone else. The shaven one and the one with the goatee sighed. They were unmarried. The chances of finding an unrelated Old Believer girl in Kilinsk were practically zero.

Where to, Arkashka?

The status reports Galina Alexandrovna made by telephone about the water levels had slowly become routine. When I returned to Tashtagol, my mobile showed a missed call – in the Taiga there had been no signal. I called Galina back. The river was still not navigable.

With no specific plan I drove back to Abakan, the capital of the Republic of Khakassia. Along the way, on the overnight train, I read an old children's book that a friend in Moscow had given me for the journey: *Timur and his Squad*, by Arkady Gaidar.

'Good book,' said my compartment neighbour. 'But Gaidar was not a good man.'

The man was about 60 and discernibly not a Russian. From his vaguely Mongolian features I concluded that he had to belong to one of the Turkic-speaking minorities of Siberia, presumably the Khakassians, the natives of the region.

'Why wasn't he a good man?'

'He fought against my people. He was an enemy of the Khakassians.'

I had heard that Gaidar had been stationed in Khakassia in the civil war – my friend in Moscow had mentioned it when he gave the book to me. But I did not know anything else.

'There is a village, north of Abakan, in the steppes,' said my compartment neighbour. 'Solyono-Ozyornoye. Go there, they will tell you everything.'

When we arrived in Abakan I had finished reading *Timur and his Squad*. It is not a long book. The story is simple: a nameless war is raging in Russia. All men are at the front. A 14-year-old boy named Timur dreams of defending the fatherland, but he is too young. Instead of fighting, he spends the summer in a dacha settlement near Moscow. Together with a few friends he founds a secret society. At night they sneak through the settlement, secretly carrying out household chores that the local women are unable to finish in the absence of their men.

The book was published in 1940, shortly before the outbreak of the great war that Gaidar anticipated in *Timur and his Squad*. When the war became a reality, Timur's adventures had grown so popular that they also became a reality. Throughout the Soviet hinterland children's brigades were formed that supported the population with voluntary work assignments. The 'Timur movement' was born. As an organised part of the Soviet youth organisations it outlasted the war. Timur rose to become the model child of socialism: a selfless hero whose youthful energy is entirely committed to the common good.

In schools throughout the Eastern Bloc the book was compulsory reading. Although I only read it on the train, I had heard friends in Berlin mention the title. They had read *Timur and his Squad* as students in the GDR, at about the same time I was busy filling the Russian hole in my children's puzzle a few hundred kilometres further west.

The autonomous Republic of Khakassia is one of the smaller puzzle pieces in the structure of the Russian Federation. It is slightly larger than Belgium, but has fewer inhabitants than Luxembourg. Dense Taiga covers the southern, almost uninhabited, part of the region. The Abakan River, of whose water levels Galina Alexandrovna regularly kept me informed, has its source in the far south, in the foothills of the Sayan Mountains. The stream crosses half of Khakassia before flowing into the Yenisey in the regional capital of Abakan. Somewhere along its banks, deep in the Taiga, is the hut where Agafya Lykova lives.

The village of Solyono-Ozyornoye, which my Khakassian compartment neighbour had mentioned, is in the northern, more densely populated part of the Republic. From Abakan I took a minibus that rumbled through the open steppes for two hours. On the way, I read a biography of Gaidar that I had found in a bookstore in Abakan. The writer's life story was short and bizarre. When *Timur and his Squad* was published, he was 36 years old. One and a half years later he was dead. A Moscow newspaper had hired him as a war correspondent. A German bullet found him on the front. He left behind a confused life that had little in common with the world of his children's books. The memoirs of the journalist Boris Saks describe him:

> *His mental illness regularly drove Gaidar into psychiatric wards …*
> *I was young at that time, had never experienced such a thing, and*
> *that terrible night made an awful impression on me. Gaidar cut*
> *himself. With razor blades. They took one blade away, but as soon*
> *as you turned around he would cut himself with another. He locked*
> *himself in the broom closet and would not answer. They broke down*
> *the door, he had cut himself again. In an unconscious state they*
> *carried him away, all the floors were covered in blood. I thought he*
> *would not survive this … Later, in Moscow, I once saw him in his*
> *underwear. His entire chest and both arms were covered with huge*
> *scars, one beside the other …*

Gaidar came into the world in 1904, in a small town near the Ukrainian border. He was born Arkady Petrovich Golikov – only later, as a children's author, did he trade his real name for a pseudonym. His own childhood ended early. He was ten when he ran away from home to follow his father, who had been sent to the front in the First World War. When they found Arkady and sent him back, he struck out at his rescuers, crying: 'I want to fight!'

His school career ended in the fifth grade. They threw him out because he had threatened a classmate with a loaded gun. The bewildered parents did not stop the 13-year-old when, in 1917, he joined the Bolsheviks, a few months before the October Revolution. Gaidar was 14 when he registered with the Red Army. He was 15 when he was wounded for the first time, in a fight with Ukrainian counterrevolutionaries. He was 16 when he commanded his first unit.

At 17 they promoted him to serve in the Special Assignment Troops, an elite squad employed to put down the last counterrevolutionary resistance at the end of the civil war. As a commander of this unit Gaidar was transferred to Khakassia in 1922, with orders to eliminate the Cossack leader Ivan Solovyov, who had holed up in the Taiga with his followers. It was a duel that had a lasting effect on Gaidar's biography. Even in 1940, when he was working on his last children's book, the mission in Khakassia still seemed to preoccupy him. *Timur and his Squad* depicts the battle between two gangs of boys. Their ringleaders in the book bear the nicknames 'Commissar' and 'Ataman'. The former is the rank designation of a Soviet elite officer, the latter the title of a Cossack captain.

Timur was making to cut off Kvakin's path. Kvakin saw him and halted. His vacant features registered neither surprise nor fear.

'Hiya, Commissar!' he said quietly, cocking his head to one side. 'Where you off to in such a hurry?'

'Hiya, Ataman!' Timur replied in the same tone. 'I was off to meet you.'

When the Red Army Commissar Gaidar arrived in Khakassia in 1922 to track down the Cossack Ataman Solovyov, he set up his headquarters in a small village in the north of the region. It was the settlement which my Khakassian fellow traveller had mentioned: Solyono-Ozyornoye.

Shortly before I reached the village a peculiar argument broke out on the minibus. On the rearmost bench sat a young man with a large brown plastic bottle in his hands. He looked worn out, like someone after a night of drinking. Periodically he raised the bottle, took a large sip of beer, and sank back into his seat, moaning. Suddenly, the bus braked abruptly.

'Young man,' the driver yelled over his shoulder. 'No drinking on board!'

I had never heard this sentence before in Russia. The drinker in the back seat looked equally surprised. 'What? Come on, it's been a tough night, I have to get rid of this hangover …'

'If I see the bottle one more time, you're getting off.'

We rode further. Initially the man refrained from drinking. Then he began to throw nervous glances towards the driver, to snatch the bottle to his mouth in unobserved moments and quickly make it disappear again. A couple of times it went well, then the driver braked again.

'Last warning.'

The game was repeated. When the driver stopped for a third time, his voice was toneless. 'Young man,' he said. 'You're getting off here.'

No reaction.

'Young man!'

Nothing.

A hand shook my shoulder. I turned around. It was the driver. 'Young man!' he said. 'You wanted to go to Solyono-Ozyornoye. We are here.'

I thanked him and got out – which is why I unfortunately never learned how the dispute ended.

Solyono-Ozyornoye means 'Salt Lake'. I looked in every direction, but there was no lake in sight. A few hundred wooden houses were crowded together in the steppe, surrounded by kilometres of nothing.

The first thing I saw in Solyono-Ozyornoye was a corpse. The man lay motionless by the roadside, in the middle of a puddle. I stood next to him indecisively. An old woman came walking along the road. In passing, she kicked the dead man's bottom with all her might.

'Son of a bitch! Get up!'

The corpse moaned, stood up and staggered on his way.

I asked the old woman about Gaidar. She deliberated for a moment. 'Speak to the Kozhukhovskys,' she said. With vague gestures she described the way.

The village consisted of three long roads. The middle one was called Ulitsa Gaidara. There was a memorial plaque at house number 20: 'In 1922 the writer A. Gaidar, fighter for the Soviet forces in Khakassia, lived in this house.'

I found Polina and Georgy Kozhukhovsky in an old wooden house at the southern edge of the village. At first I mistook them for siblings, but after a few minutes I realised that the two were one of those married couples who become increasingly similar in old age.

Georgy's grandmother Agrafena had been a housekeeper in the Red Army headquarters during the civil war. She had washed Gaidar's laundry and cooked for him.

'Everyone in the village called her the Red Grunya,' Georgy explained.

'Because she was a Communist?'

'No. Because she continued to paint her lips into old age.'

'Did she talk about Gaidar?'

Georgy hesitated.

'She deified him,' Polina chipped in. 'Such a golden boy, she always said, such a good one, such a handsome one.'

Georgy was silent.

'Come on, tell him!' Polina said. 'Gaidar committed sins. The Khakassians hated him. Tell him what the Red Grunya said.'

'I can't,' Georgy said. 'It's too political.'

'Coward!'

A little later Georgy's son Alexei turned up. He led me to the village cemetery, to show me a cross that the local Cossacks had erected for Gaidar's adversary Solovyov a few years earlier. The Cossack captain had been born in Solyono-Ozyornoye. The village had kept its famous son a secret for a long time – during the Soviet era Solovyov was considered a criminal, a counterrevolutionary warmonger, a non-person. Now his funeral cross stood proudly in the steppe.

'Is the Red Grunya also buried here?' I asked Alexei.

He shook his head. 'She spent her last years in a retirement home in Abakan. That's where she was buried. I was still small when she died, I hardly remember her. Father told you the story about the sabre, I suppose?'

I made a vague hand gesture, which he accepted as a response.

'The Red Grunya talked about it constantly. Gaidar took a Khakassian boy hostage, a 12-year-old. His relatives allegedly fought for Solovyov. Gaidar gave them an ultimatum. When time ran out, he cut off the boy's head. With a sabre.'

The steppe wind blew dust across the cemetery. A plastic bag got caught on Solovyov's cross, broke free, tumbled on.

An undated entry from Arkady Gaidar's diary reads: *Dream according to scheme No. 2 … I saw people I killed in my childhood.*

Gaidar was posted in Khakassia for only two and a half months. It was enough time to make him a despised figure among the local population – and a hero of Soviet propaganda. In the Sixties, long after his death, a film was made about his fight against Solovyov. In *The End of the Taiga Emperor*, the red Commissar Gaidar single-handedly hunts down the white Ataman Solovyov, to the cheers of the Khakassian populace.

The reality was quite different. Gaidar did not succeed in eliminating the Cossack captain. Solovyov voluntarily turned himself over to the Red Army in 1924 and was executed. By that time Gaidar had long since been withdrawn from Khakassia. The authorities had received frequent complaints about him, there was talk of atrocities committed against the civilian population, of looting, of excessive violence. A specially appointed commission of inquiry ruled drily that Gaidar's actions lacked 'operational effectiveness' and recommended that the 18-year-old commander be executed. He was court-martialled and accused of illegal shootings. Gaidar admitted them, but explained that the victims had been 'bandits', at whose execution he had merely neglected 'legal formalities'. He was pronounced guilty. The sentence was lenient: dismissal from service, combined with a ban on holding responsible positions.

What followed were Party reprimands, nervous breakdowns, mental institutions and children's books.

His literary career began with a name change: Arkady Golikov became Arkady Gaidar. The pseudonym is not a Russian word, but a Khakassian one. It means: 'Where to?' According to legend, it was the only Khakassian word the red Commissar knew. When he rode through the Khakassian villages, he shouted: 'Gaidar? Gaidar Solovyov?' – 'Where to? Where did Solovyov go?'

Among the Khakassians, word quickly spread that this battle cry did not bode well. Panic broke out whenever the Commissar neared their villages. '*Where to!*' cried the Khakassians. 'Here comes *Where to!*'

Gaidar liked the nickname. All of his children's books were published under the Khakassian pseudonym that made him famous. In fact, he became so famous that in the Thirties there was talk of rehabilitating him as a Party member. Stalin, usually not squeamish when dealing with Russia's minorities, was against it: 'I can forgive him. But can the Khakassians forgive him?'

A Khakassian folksong runs:

The earth of the Fathers blossomed yellow
And the bank of the Yus lay like silk
Once it was filled with songs
Before you showered it with tears – Golikov!
Old and young lie on your path

With bullets and fire my people are wiped out
Do their curses not reach you?
You black soul – Arkashka!

A Khakassian historian in Abakan advised me not to take all the horror stories about Gaidar seriously. 'He has blood on his hands, that is certain. But some Khakassians make him personally responsible for everything the Russians have ever done to our ancestors.' The historian sighed. 'You know, our history is a difficult cross to bear. There are people among my compatriots who still dream of a separate state, an independent Khakassia.' Shaking his head, he bent over the table and wrote two large numbers in my notebook, a one, followed by a two.

'Twelve per cent. We make up twelve per cent of the population of Khakassia. What kind of independence are we talking about?'

In the library of Bolshiye Arbaty, a village south of Abakan inhabited exclusively by Khakassians, I discovered an edition of *Timur and his Squad* shelved between Russian translations of Khakassian epics and Khakassian translations of the Bible.

Tatyana Antipovna did not understand my surprise. 'It is a good, sweet book. How is a book to blame for its author?'

She was a quiet woman in her mid-forties, whose voice made up in charisma what it lacked in volume. We had met each other at the village school where Tatyana worked as a teacher. Now we drank tea together with three other Khakassian women. Valentina was also a teacher, Nadezhda and Stepanida worked in the library.

In a desk drawer, under the file-card box that contained the lending forms, the four women had stored away a nondescript sheet of paper. Thirty-seven handwritten Khakassian names were listed. 'It took us several years,' Tatyana said, 'to gather the names of all the victims.'

The massacre had been exactly 90 years ago that summer. In 1920, during the civil war, a detachment of Russian soldiers had turned up in Bolshiye Arbaty. They rounded up all the male inhabitants on the edge of the village well and shot them, one after the other. Then they threw the corpses down the well, blew up the shaft with a hand grenade and disappeared.

Twenty years ago, Tatyana and her colleagues had started to document the names of the victims. At that time all the witnesses of the massacre had long been dead. There was no longer anybody in Bolshiye Arbaty who personally remembered the events of the civil war, which for 70 years had been talked about only behind closed doors. No one in the village knew who had caused the carnage. It could not have been Gaidar – he did not arrive in Khakassia until a year later. Tatyana and her colleagues were not even sure whether the murders had been committed by red Bolshevik troops or by their white, counterrevolutionary opponents.

'We will never find out,' Tatyana said. 'When you ask the old people in the village, all they say is that they were Russians. That is what their parents told them. Red or White – back then hardly anyone here understood the difference. To the ordinary people in the villages a Russian was simply a *Khasakh* – a Cossack. There was no other word in our language. People still saw the Russians as the conquerors of the 17th century.'

Tatyana fell silent, as if the bitter overtones of her words suddenly made her uncomfortable. She did not bear the Russians any ill will, neither the Cossacks nor the Communists. 'Khakassia was no paradise before the Russians came,' she said. 'My grandparents lived in yurts, my parents could neither read nor write. Who knows whether I would be a teacher today, if everything had turned out differently. Who knows whether there would be a school here at all.'

It was not until the Revolution that the Khakassians were abruptly plunged into a world which had hardly touched their lives while they had been subjects of a distant tsar – superficially Christianised, inwardly faithful to the shamanistic spirit world of their ancestors. Tatyana's father had hardly spoken a word of Russian – it was not until the Second World War, on the front, that they had drummed the most important orders into him. Now his photo hung in the village school, on a memorial board for the veterans, with a black band in the top left corner.

'If your father hardly spoke any Russian,' I asked, 'why did he call you Tatyana?'

The question had preoccupied me for hours. The woman sitting in front of me looked like a daughter of Genghis Khan, but she was named after the hero of a Pushkin novel.

Quadruplicate laughter was the response. Tatyana laughed, Valentina laughed, Nadezhda laughed, Stepanida laughed. 'Do you think our parents chose these Russian names?' Tatyana shook her head. 'There were no others. If you wanted to give your baby a Khakassian name, the people at the hospital would say: that is not on our list – pick another one.'

In the first decades after the Revolution most Khakassians had carried two names, just as before the Revolution they had practiced two religions – outwardly the Russian one, secretly their own. They had given up both habits at some point. Of the four women in the library, only Stepanida, who was a good decade older than her colleagues, also had a Khakassian name: Ulukh Rod.

'It means: "Grow large". I was tiny at birth. I was born two months too early.' She smiled. 'The name saved me.'

It was only in their children's generation that Khakassian names were slowly coming back into fashion. Just like the Khakassian language which was now in public use again. In Soviet times the Khakassians had avoided speaking Khakassian, because they knew that Soviet people did not like it when other Soviet people expressed themselves in an un-Soviet manner.

When I asked the women to say a few Khakassian sentences, Nadezhda pulled a book from one of the library shelves. It was an old Khakassian saga called *Altyn-Chyus*. Nadezhda opened the book at a random page and began to read. The verses had a strong rhythm, and although I did not understand anything, I heard the rhymes in the Turkic word endings. After a few lines Nadezhda abruptly broke off. A peculiar silence suddenly hung in the library. 'Perhaps that is not the best part,' Tatyana said.

I did not understand what she meant until the women translated the verses into Russian for me. They told of an infant, the only child of a steppe king, who one day fell into the hands of the evil witch Ku and her accomplice Alyp-Khartaka. Later, when I found a Russian translation of the saga in a bookshop in Abakan, I reread the verses:

Alyp-Chartaka pulls out his sword
And six times turns the steel.
Alyp-Chartaka pulls out his sword
And six times lets it reel.
His sword is wide, as the moon is wide
Three pood weighs his sword, he holds it high

And with cruel laughter he grabs the babe
And casts it down on a flat stone slab.
He lifts the blade, he makes it flash,
And begins to cut the babe, to slash
And smites him with delight, and tortures him long
And plaintively the infant sings this song:
Oh, Alyp-Chartaka, why torment me?
Kill me more quickly, have mercy on me!
My red blood, let it faster run dry,
My white soul, let it faster fly.
There laugh Alyp-Chartaka and the witch Ku
The life of Alyp-Khan's son is through.

Outside the evening sun was setting. A long, narrow shadow crept across the dusty village square, ending just before the entrance to the library. Where it began, about a hundred metres away, a stone stele towered in the sky.

Silently we approached the collapsed village well. The terrain was overgrown with stinging nettles. The stele had been erected here by the women only a few years before, as a grave stone for the victims of the massacre. Tatyana explained that a shaman had come to Bolshiye Arbaty for the dedication of the stele, beseeching the spirits of the dead for forgiveness.

'There are still shamans?' I asked in surprise.

'Yes,' three voices answered simultaneously.

'No,' answered the fourth voice. It was Stepanida, the oldest of the women. 'There are no shamans anymore. They are long gone.'

'But one of them was here,' said Nadezhda.

Stepanida smiled wryly. 'He just calls himself a shaman. The real shamans are all dead.'

For a few days I drove back and forth across Khakassia in search of shamans. Along the way I saw stone steles everywhere. Like swords they jutted out of the steppe, lonely landmarks in boundless emptiness, hundreds, sometimes thousands of years old. Some of them stood right in the middle of fields. Apparently even the Soviet bulldozers had not dared to flatten the old gravestones of the steppe peoples.

It was not only the stones that had survived. The ancient animist rites had also returned. Along the roadsides I sometimes met Khakassian families who hung colourful ribbons on the steles or left offerings: a banknote, a chocolate bar, a gnawed chicken bone, a glass of vodka. 'Our ancestors did this,' they explained to me. 'The spirits like it this way.' They laughed sheepishly, as if they themselves were not quite sure whether after all these years the old magic still worked, whether the spirits had not long since disappeared from the steppe, because too much blood had soaked the grass.

It made me think about 'Altyn-Chyus', the Khakassian saga that the women in Bolshiye Arbaty had read to me. Khakassia felt a bit like the fairy-tale realm from the narrative, which no longer has a ruler because the king's only child has been slain. Enemies overwhelm the orphaned kingdom and devastate it, until there is nothing left to recall its former inhabitants – nothing but the song of a steppe bird:

He leans to the west and weeps his song
He leans to the east and wails his song
And it's always the same, unchanging sigh:
The only son of Alyp-Khan was I.
My killers are Alyp-Chartaka and Ku
On the shore of the river they saw it through.
Into the earth they let my red blood flow,
And a tree began from the earth to grow.
A cuckoo now sits on the broadest limb,
He has my voice and moans this hymn.

My search for shamans was unsuccessful. All I found were shady faith healers and folk musicians, who tried to sell me herbal potions and shaman drums.

'Give it up,' a Khakassin in Abakan advised me. 'There are no shamans anymore. The Russians have killed them all, for fear of their magic. They were powerful, our shamans. Why do you think Gaidar went crazy? The shamans made his soul sick so he would vanish from Khakassia.'

But then I did find a shaman – in the closing verses of 'Altyn-Chyus'. He appears out of nowhere, after centuries of hardship, in order to return the murdered infant to his rightful rule over the lost steppe kingdom:

He gathers the child's bones, collects them all,
Barely a handful, delicate, small
While spells swell swiftly from his throat,
He lifts the cuckoo from his coat,
And to bind the cuckoo then he tears
From the tail of his horse three slender hairs
And winds and coils the hairs, the three,
Three times around the cuckoo, and whispers he
And enshrines the cuckoo, thrice entwined,
Between the bones, savagely confined,
He burns wild herbs, blows the smoke that swells
On the cuckoo and bones, and chants his spells.
And the blood that once to the earth withdrew,
Draws back into the infant's body
And the soul, that once to the heavens flew
Flies back into the infant's body.
And the infant, trembling, slowly revives,
He stretches, he breathes – he is alive!

Blood and Vodka

The next phone call from Galina Alexandrovna was the turning point. The river level had dropped. The linguist asked me to travel to Abaza, a small town in southern Khakassia, at the edge of the Taiga. It was the hometown of the man who had promised to take us to Agafya.

On the journey the landscape changed drastically. Shortly beyond Abakan the steppe developed goose bumps. Tiny hills bulged under the grass. As I drove south, they grew higher and higher, until the over-stretched blanket of meadows finally ripped open and revealed the first cliffs. Scattered formations of birch and pine trees marched across the hilltops, scout patrols of an army that grew stronger in the foothills of the Sayan Mountains, until up behind a mountain ridge the Taiga suddenly lay before me, an army of wooden soldiers posted from here to the horizon. Through dizzying hairpin turns the bus rolled down into the valley of Abaza, Khakassia's last outpost before the wilderness.

San Sanych picked me up from the bus station. He was in his mid-forties, a man with small, quick eyes that twinkled with a constant sarcastic smile. He threw my backpack into the trunk of a jeep and showed me the city centre, which consisted of a few dozen concrete buildings. Beyond them Abaza looked like a dacha settlement: low wooden houses, surrounded by vegetable plots. We turned into an unpaved path that ended at the edge of the woods. San Sanych's house was the last in the row.

'Completely self-built,' he said proudly. As if to prove it, he showed me his left hand, on which the forefinger was missing.

San Sanych was a teacher. At Abaza's only school he taught a subject with the curious name 'Fundamentals of Safe Living'. He instructed Russian students how to protect themselves against Russian threats: alcohol poisoning, terrorist attacks, sexually transmitted diseases, nuclear accidents, savage animals. To supplement his teacher's salary, he leased the top floor of his house to tourists who came to Abaza for fishing or hunting. Occasionally he organised boat tours, mountain hikes and Taiga expeditions.

San Sanych's actual name was Alexander Alexandrovich, but like many Alexander Alexandroviches, he used a shortened form of his first name and patronymic. San Sanych's father had also been called San Sanych, just like his grandfather. Unfortunately, the family memory did not extend any further back, because the grandfather had died early – he had tried to save a church from being destroyed by the Bolsheviks, which the Bolsheviks had very much resented. The grandfather's widowed wife, who had to make ends meet with an orphaned son, decided in her plight to become an agitator for atheism. Until the end of her life she taught students and collective farm workers that the god her husband had died for did not exist.

In the two weeks I spent in San Sanych's house, I heard the story about his grandparents more than once. The first time I found it very touching. The second and third times I still found it sad. By the fourth time the effect had worn off, and by the tenth time I began to understand why San Sanych's wife Natasha usually left the room when her husband held forth. Even at the 100th repetition he told his stories with a facial expression that demanded absolute attention and applause for every punch line.

In retrospect, I don't understand why it was not clear to me from the beginning that our encounter was ill-fated. I saw the signs, but I was too fixed on the goal of my journey to take them seriously.

The first sign was another call from Galina Alexandrovna. She was in hospital, with bronchitis. I remembered the icy office in the Literature Museum, the clouds of breath in front of Galina's mouth, the jackets and scarves she had worn one over the other, unfortunately to no avail. 'I can't come with you,' she said regretfully. 'It's a shame, but it won't work.'

I wished her a speedy recovery and said goodbye with an uneasy feeling. It was clear to me that my journey would be much more difficult without the linguist. For Galina it would not have been the first visit to Agafya, and according to what she had told me, the hermit trusted her. But I was a stranger and a foreigner at that. How Agafya would react to me was difficult to foresee.

San Sanych had never met Agafya either. As it turned out, shortly after my arrival, he did not even know the part of the Taiga where she lived. When I asked him how we would find the way, he looked at me resentfully. 'Don't you trust me?' I soothingly assured him of the opposite. 'We just have to follow the river,' he said. 'It's simple.'

The river, however, was still not navigable. A fresh flood of melt water had caused the levels to rise again, and an end to it was not to be seen. Every morning I took a walk with San Sanych's dog, a Collie named Tishka, straight through a forest to the riverbank, only to find that the Abakan continued to swell. The sight of the flood was terrifying. Although the river is a good 200 metres wide in Abaza, it raced through the settlement at a speed I had never seen, or even thought possible, in any other river. Huge branches shot downstream, sometimes complete trees, uprooted, defoliated and scrubbed clean by the water. When the current hurled them ashore, they shattered on the pebbly banks with terrifying crashes.

In order to bridge the time while we waited, San Sanych introduced me to a few of his friends. I met Misha, the boat driver who would take us to Agafya. He looked like a caricature of a Siberian *muzhik*, a real man: broad and uncouth, with slow, impassive expressions and a red-veined drinker's face. Misha had two passions: he collected tsarist coins and sexist curses. The latter he used with such frequency that I rarely understood his sentences at first attempt.

'Jens! *ЁБТВОЮМАТЬ*, your shoe, *БЛЯДЬ*!'

'What?'

'*ЁБАННЫЙВРОТ*, it's undone, *БЛЯДЬ*!'

'I see. Thank you.'

'*НАХУЙ!*'

I met San Sanych's friend Sergey, the most exotic inhabitant of Abaza. He was an instrument maker. His house was stuffed with self-made didgeridoos and shaman drums, which he sold at Siberian folklore festivals. The business was going well; Sergey had almost enough money saved to realise his life's dream. He wanted to emigrate. Abaza was not remote enough for him. He was drawn to a tiny island named Sonsorol, located in the middle of the Pacific. It had 23 inhabitants; Sergey wanted to be the 24th. So far he had only seen the island on pictures, but through the Internet he was in contact with two residents who supported his relocation plans. 'They both know the Governor of the island,' Sergey said proudly. I wanted to argue that with 23 inhabitants, every second one was presumably related to the Governor, but I bit my tongue. Sergey meant business. He had already filled out the visa form for the Pacific Republic of Palau. Now he was teaching himself the local language. Fascinated, I leafed through his rudimentary Russian-Palauan dictionary:

Mere direi – Babushka
Haparu ma hatawahi – Spasibo
Hoda buou – Do svidaniya

I met Sergey's brother Grisha, a drilling worker. In the Eighties he had worked in the geologists' settlement whose crew had discovered the Old Believer family in the Taiga. Grisha had met Agafya and her father several times. Unfortunately, he was hard-pressed to come up with any stories about them. In contrast to his extroverted brother, he was a withdrawn fellow, he almost seemed depressed. When Sergey and I visited him, Grisha was in a particularly dark mood. He was in the hospital. During an assignment in the Taiga he had suffered a tick bite. 'Encephalitis,' he said wryly. 'Occupational hazard.'

I had heard bad stories about the long-term effects of tick bites. Grisha smiled gloomily when I asked about them.

'Forget the ticks,' he said. 'The mosquitoes are much worse. Around this time of year they won't give you any peace. Sometimes there are so many of them that they block out the sun. You will no longer know where your body stops and where the mosquitoes begin. Hey, what's that scared look on your face? Don't worry, you get used to the mosquitoes. The *mozhki* are much worse …'

'The what?'

'*Mozhki*. Tiny bastards that creep through every hole. Not even a bee-keeping mesh will stop them. When they bite, you yowl in pain. They are not like mosquitoes that leave you with a neat little sting. *Mozhki* rip the flesh from your body. If they really help themselves, you won't recognise yourself in the mirror. But don't worry, you get used to the *mozhki* eventually. The *mokretsy* are much worse …'

'Grisha, thank you, that's enough really …'

'… and even worse …'

'Enough!'

'… are the *slepny*.'

Back at San Sanych's house I discovered a school book with the title *Fundamentals of Safe Living for the Sixth Grade, published by J. L. Vorobyova, Distinguished Life-Safer of the Russian Federation, Hero of Russia*. On page 136 Ms Vorobyova writes: 'In the Taiga, between May and September, swarms of bloodsucking mosquitoes, *mozhki*, *mokretsy* and *slepny* attack every living creature. They crawl under any clothing and into the nose, ears and mouth. Their bites are painful and can trigger nervous breakdowns. Getting used to them is impossible, and there is virtually no way of protecting yourself.'

Depressed, I slammed the book shut. If even a 'Hero of Russia' capitulated to the insects, how would I survive the Taiga?

The wait dragged on. On the fourth day the river level slowly began to drop; on the sixth it rose again. During my morning rounds with Tishka, the dog, I had made it my habit to mark the water level by sticking a branch into the shore. If the water did not reach up to the branch the next morning, my mood was instantly lifted. If the branch was submerged, it deteriorated.

Abaza's recreational opportunities were quickly exhausted. The local museum staged an exhibition about the Great Patriotic War. The local Lenin monument was made of gilded concrete. A discotheque named 'The Geologist' was frequented by underpaid mineworkers and unemployed steelworkers. The local iron mine was still in operation, while the steel mill, once Abaza's raison d'être, had closed decades ago.

I took long walks with Tishka, the dog. I read my way through San

Sanych's library. I sorted through my notebooks. I sorted through them once more, and then sorted through them again. The most notable diversions were the evenings when San Sanych fired up the *banya*. The small bathhouse stood in the garden, substituting for a shower. Like most of the houses in Abaza, San Sanych's house had neither a bath nor a toilet. There was an outhouse in the back of the garden. The water came from a self-drilled well.

Sometimes I wondered whether San Sanych was satisfied with his life. 'Siberia has no use for educated people,' he said once, while we were sitting in the *banya*. 'Siberia just needs slaves. We are supposed to work so the Muscovites do not have to work. We are a colony of Europe.'

He was not at bottom a disagreeable person. But something nagged at him. A stifled ambition seemed to eat away at his soul, an inner surrender to external adversity. I tried not to hold it against him when he turned his irritation on the outside world, but the longer I lived with him, the more difficult our relationship grew. His monologues increased, and San Sanych grew more and more offended when he realised that I was not listening. He made me feel that my fate was in his hands – how would I find my way around the Taiga without him? Did I know how to scare up firewood, how to ward off bears, how to repair a boat? Often he spoke in preaching tones about his loyalty to principles, about his abstemious lifestyle: no meat, no cigarettes, no alcohol. When he did open a bottle of wine one evening, I realised quickly why he generally avoided drinking. The alcohol compounded his unpleasant traits, it made him pushy, arrogant, and irritable. Natasha, who entered the kitchen at one point, turned on her heels when she saw our wineglasses.

On the tenth day the water began to drop steadily. I breathed a sigh of relief.

On the morning of the 12th day I was on my way to the river with the dog, when suddenly a second dog ran towards us in the forest. It was white and huge, approximately twice as large as Tishka. I felt a jerk on the leash. Then I heard a dark growl, more threatening than anything I would ever have expected from Tishka. Please don't, I thought. But it was too late.

When it was over, Tishka lay on his back, whimpering. A few centimetres from his throat gaped the lacerated mouth of the second dog.

The winner yawned, snapped his mouth shut contemptuously and went on his way.

Tishka's back was bleeding. He was trembling all over. When I tried to calm him down, he bit my right hand with all his might. For a second we both stared at each other in shock, as if paralysed, before I tore my hand away. Tishka jumped up, snapped at me once more and got hold of my left hand. He bit it so firmly that it took me a few seconds to pull free. He turned on his heels and ran towards the river.

I only caught up with him at the bank. Trembling, he stood in the shallow shore water and stared at me, panic-stricken. I sat down on a stone and tried to soothe him, while a red puddle gathered under my dripping hands.

In the hospital they washed my wounds out and sprinkled them with an emerald-green liquid. The colour was familiar to me. On my journey through Russia I had often seen it on the faces of battered men, and I had always wondered whether those green spots were some kind of punishment for drinkers, thugs and other evildoers. I have never understood why the disinfectant used in Russia needs to be green of all things. The nurse who bandaged my hands could not solve the puzzle either.

'If it wasn't green,' she said, 'then why would it be called *zelyonka*?'

Zelyonka means something like 'greensy'. This made our whole conversation sound a bit tautological.

'But why is greensy green?" I asked.

'Because it contains green chemicals. Don't tell me that greensy is not green in Germany!'

'It is not green, and it isn't called greensy either.'

Indifferently, she shrugged her shoulders. 'Greensy has always been green.'

After the accident everything suddenly moved very quickly. The next morning Misha called, the boat driver. The river was about to reach the navigable level. Two more days and we could depart.

Depressed, I stared at my bandaged hands. A few of the fingers were so badly swollen that I could hardly move them. I forced myself to think of something else. I had waited too long to postpone the journey any further – and who knew if the river level would not rise again in a few days?

The day before the departure San Sanych confronted me with an earnest face.

'Misha said we should buy *spirt*.'

'*Spirt*? What is that?'

'Industrial alcohol. 100 per cent pure. When you dilute it, you can drink it.'

'Why do we need that?'

'As currency. With *spirt* you can buy anything in the Taiga. If we have to stay in a hunting lodge along the way, we need *spirt* for the hunters. Or we may have to pay at the border of the nature reserve.'

Startled, I looked at him. 'What nature reserve?'

It turned out that the entire Taiga south of Abaza was a protected nature reserve. To enter the area you needed a permit. We did not have one.

'Didn't I mention that?' San Sanych asked, grinning.

It took me a few seconds to control my anger. When San Sanych noticed it, he put a hand on my shoulder. 'Don't worry. There is a guard post at the entrance to the nature reserve, but it is unmanned as long as the river is not navigable. If we run into the reserve guards, it will only be on the way back. And in that case we just give them a bottle of *spirt*. You know how these things work in Russia.'

I did know, but as a foreigner I had made it my rule to steer clear of the ubiquitous bribery. Although I did not understand why we had not simply requested a permit, I nodded in silence. It was too late for discussions about principles.

We bought the *spirt* from a neighbour. The man was very taciturn. He handed three large, unlabelled plastic canisters over the garden fence and murmured a frighteningly low price. We went home with six litres of pure alcohol.

It was a short night. Only now, after we had been waiting for two weeks, did San Sanych suddenly think of all kinds of urgent travel preparations. While we packed, he explained to me in detail why we needed every single item, how it was used and how much we would be in a fix if we did not take it with us. 'Here. Do you know what this is? An axe. Have you seen an axe before? I tell you, we would be lost without it. How would we chop firewood without an axe? With our teeth? A man is not a beaver, Jens, a man needs an axe. This is the handle. You hold it with both hands. You need to watch out not to hack yourself in the legs ...'

My private lesson in 'Fundamentals of Safe Living' lasted well into the early morning hours. When the sun rose, it jolted me out of a short, confused sleep. We ate breakfast, but I was not properly awake until we arrived at the bank of the river. It was a clear, radiant day. Reflections of light danced in the current. My gaze wandered along the river, which disappeared in the distance between pine trees and mountainsides. A sudden wave of euphoria flooded my body, dispelling all the tension of the past two weeks.

Misha appeared in a jeep shortly after us. He rolled the window down and screamed: 'What a morning, *ПИЗДЕЦ*! What *ОХУИТЕЛЬНАЯ* weather!' Then he backed the car down the river bank and let the boat trailer roll into the shallow shore water. San Sanych and I waded into the river in rubber boots. When the water lifted the boat from the trailer, we grabbed it and pulled it onto the sandy shore together. It was a broad, squat motorboat with no canopy. When we had heaved our luggage and fuel supplies on board, there was just enough space left for three people.

We squeezed in. Misha reached under the passenger seat. Grinning, he pulled out a bottle of vodka. It was eight o'clock in the morning.

'No,' I said.

'Yes.'

'No.'

'*ТВОЮМАТЬ!*'

He filled up three plastic cups. In hindsight, I was happy about the greasy eggs that San Sanych had fried for breakfast. The bottle was half empty when Misha finally fired up the motor. A brutal roar broke the morning silence, louder than anything I had expected. The boat swung into the current. For a moment it hovered almost without motion, before Misha pressed the throttle. The pine trees along the edge of the river were set in motion. Slowly, then faster and faster, they glided past the boat.

Shortly before the city limits we overtook a long, narrow wooden boat. There were three men on board; our glances met as we were passing them. San Sanych leaned toward me and shouted over the engine noise. 'Look, those are the wardens of the nature reserve,' he said. 'You see, we will have no trouble with them. Our boat is much faster.'

The city ended abruptly. We passed the decommissioned steel mill, then a concrete bridge, then nothing else. Steep cliffs bordered the river, with scattered pine trees clinging to their slopes. Above was the sky, below us the water, stone walls to the left and the right, while straight ahead there was nothing but the endless green of the Taiga. A giddy happiness overcame me, I wasn't sure why. Maybe it was the inevitability with which the goal was now drawing closer. Maybe it was just the alcohol.

I did not think anything of the first few cups. Even when Misha continued to drink at the helm, I was not worried – the bottle would not last forever. When it was empty after half an hour, he threw it over board, cursing. Tired and tipsy I leaned against my backpack. I covered myself with my jacket to protect myself from the icy headwind, and shortly after that I must have dozed off.

Someone shook my shoulder. I opened my eyes. It was San Sanych. He held a filled plastic cup in front of my face. Dazed, I shook my head.

'*ПОШЁЛНАХУЙ!*' Misha roared over his shoulder. 'Drink!'

I took the plastic cup out of San Sanych's hand. 'What is that?'

'*Spirt*,' he said. 'Diluted. With lemon.'

Out of pure curiosity I took a sip. It was more a feeling than a flavour: a metallic burning, followed by a pungent chemical aftertaste. Disgusted, I gave the cup back to San Sanych.

For a while I watched on in disbelief as they drank. A dented plastic bottle was jammed between San Sanych's knees, which he used to dilute the *spirt* with river water. A slice of shredded lemon swam in the liquid. Misha clasped the rudder with one hand and his cup with the other. In regular intervals he turned to San Sanych and yelled, 'Fill it up!'

The fear did not come immediately; it came slowly. I saw the rocks that shimmered just below the surface of the water and the drifting branches that regularly forced Misha into abrupt evasive manoeuvres. The slightest mistake would cause the boat to capsize. We were far away from any settlement. The signal indicator of my mobile had jumped to zero just outside of Abaza. No one would save us in this wilderness.

I leaned toward San Sanych and shouted over the engine noise. 'I thought you didn't drink!'

He looked at me, glassy-eyed. With an apologetic shrug he pointed to Misha.

I climbed over the luggage and crouched next to the driver's seat. 'Misha,' I shouted. 'You are the driver. Stop drinking.'

When he turned to face me, his eyes were full of hatred. 'You have no idea!' he shouted. 'Look at the river, *НАХУЙ*, do you even get how dangerous it is? If I were sober, I would not be able to drive a metre here, *БЛЯДЬ*! I would be too scared!'

In hindsight I have often asked myself whether the story might have taken a different turn if I had behaved in a different way. Many Russian friends later gave me smart advice about what I should have done.

'If I had been in your shoes I would have thrown the booze overboard.'

'You should have punched them in the face!'

'Why didn't you forbid them from drinking?'

'You should have called off the trip.'

All of these options went through my head while I watched my fellow travellers in shocked amazement. In the end I rejected them all. I was at their mercy. If there was conflict, I would lose. There was no choice. All I could do was wait and hope that everything would go well.

Resigned, I rested my head on my backpack and tried to concentrate on the landscape. Birds of prey circled above the pine trees. Toppled trees lined the banks of the river, their roots desperately grasping into the void. In many places the flood had gnawed deep notches into the mountainsides, lined by promontories of rock and eroded earth that jutted into the river. The riverbed of the Abakan seemed to have no fixed shape; it looked as if during each spring flood the water sought a new path through the mountains. At times the river suddenly divided into dozens of thinner tributaries, which a few kilometres further along converged again. At times the riverbed expanded to the width of an entire valley in which the water flowed slowly, almost imperceptibly, only to pick up speed the next moment and to hurl up foam while it shot through narrow canyons.

We travelled all day, interrupted only by short breaks in which we ate in silence. As soon as we moored the boat on shore, the mosquitoes descended upon us. I was in luck given the circumstances: the penetrating reek of alcohol coming from Misha and San Sanych seemed to attract the insects. They largely ignored me.

During the ride I silently kept my eyes on my two companions. San Sanych frequently nodded off, and when he came to half an hour later he seemed reasonably sober. The alcohol had hardly any apparent effect on Misha; it seemed to seep away in his massive body without a trace. Only his swearing gave away the fact that he was drinking. By the afternoon the alcohol had reduced his command of language to an interminable stream of aggressive curses.

When the sun disappeared behind the mountaintops, it grew dark surprisingly fast. As dusk descended, Misha turned on the headlights. They cast two dim strips of light into the current. With horror I thought of the rocks beneath the reflecting surface.

I leaned toward San Sanych. 'What's going on? It's getting dark. Why aren't we stopping?'

I only understood how drunk he was when he opened his mouth. 'You know,' he slurred, 'Misha is just getting in the mood. He'll drive all night long.'

It was at this point I realised they no longer knew what they were doing. I climbed over the luggage and put a hand on Misha's shoulder. 'Listen,' I shouted. 'Drive ashore. We're spending the night here.'

Misha looked at me as if he was waking from a dream. Apparently I had hit the right note. 'Sure,' he said.

We moored the boat on shore and dragged our luggage to a marshy meadow. The last of the sunlight had disappeared, and the moon had not yet come out. The stars shimmered dimly, as if through a veil of mist. Beyond the beams that our flashlights threw into the night there was nothing but utter, seamless darkness. Although the boat engine was mute now, its deafening noise kept echoing in my head, making the silence of the Taiga sound eerie. Every time I heard something crack somewhere, I nervously waved my flashlight. Its glow ebbed into nothingness after a few metres.

San Sanych crouched beside me. He held a tarpaulin in his hand. The didactic expression on his face told me what was coming. 'First,' he stammered, 'you have to find the base of the tent. Pay attention, this is very important ... You have to find the base ... The base ... Hell, where is that goddamn base?' Frantically, he turned the tent inside out and outside in again. In the end he dropped himself onto the tarpaulin, laughing hysterically. 'Damn it,' he spluttered. 'I teach Fundamentals of Safe Living and I can't even put up a goddamn tent!'

I sent him away and put up the tent by myself. When it was up, I realised that it was a two-man tent.

Misha and San Sanych dropped themselves onto the tarpaulin. For a while I heard them fighting over space, until only snoring came through the tent wall. I put my mat on the forest floor a few metres away, crawled into my sleeping bag and zipped it up until only a narrow slit was left for my eyes. The bandages on my hands were completely drenched. The moisture crept into the wounds, a throbbing pain kept me awake. For hours I stared desperately into the darkness and wondered if ever a night had been so long.

When the sun rose, San Sanych came crawling out of the tent. He cast a sheepish glance at me, stumbled to the river and ran cold water over his head. Silently we unpacked what we needed for breakfast. San Sanych made a fire. When the kettle boiled, I went to wake Misha. I had to kick him in the side twice before he moved.

After the breakfast Misha walked over to the boat. When he came back I could tell that something was wrong. With an indefinable expression he scratched his head.

'We brought too much luggage,' he said. 'Or the current has got stronger, I've no idea.'

I looked at him in alarm. 'What does that mean? What is going on?'

'We … We used too much gasoline.'

'Why? What does that mean? How much do we have left?'

He avoided my gaze. 'Enough to get back to Abaza. I think.'

I could feel the anger taking away my breath and my voice. When Misha realised it, he immediately went on the counter-attack. '*ТВОЮМАТЬ*! Don't work yourself up! There's not enough gasoline, so what? What can I do about it? Continue on foot, *БЛЯДЬ*! If you hurry, you'll be there in a week.'

I looked at San Sanych. San Sanych looked at the forest. His red-veined eyes showed blind panic. I realised that he had no idea where we were.

In desperation I turned my back on them. After a few aimless steps I stopped at the riverbank, as if paralysed. While I listened to the murmur of the water, it slowly dawned on me that my journey ended here. I had travelled 5,000 kilometres, only to fail a stone's throw away from my goal.

The rest was a retreat. On the way downstream, nobody said a word.

We reached Abaza shortly before nightfall, with the last drops of gasoline. I took a bus to Askis, then a night train to Novokuznetsk and from there the first available plane to the west. It was not until Siberia disappeared under dense clouds that I breathed a sigh of relief.

GRASS (The Steppes)

The black earth beneath the hooves
Was sown with bones, and was watered with blood;
On Russian soil these sprang up as grief.
The grass bows down with woe.

Lay of the Host of Igor, 12th century

While Yegorushka was watching their sleeping faces he suddenly heard
a soft singing. The song was subdued, dreary and melancholy, like a
dirge, and hardly audible, and seemed to come first from the right, then
from the left, then from above, and then from underground, as though
an unseen spirit were hovering over the steppe and singing. Yegorushka
looked about him, and could not make out where the strange song came
from. Then as he listened he began to fancy that the grass was singing.

Anton Chekhov, 1888

You're lying, Bryokhovich! They didn't call your father 'lie-
mouth' for nothing! There are no Cossacks among the saints!

Mikhail Sholokhov, 1930

Wood People and Grass People

The coat of arms of the industrial city of Chelyabinsk, located in the southern foothills of the Urals, depicts a camel. Nobody could tell me why. A few people murmured something about old trade routes, but they did not sound convinced themselves. The Silk Road was far away. Even its northernmost branches had given the Urals a wide berth. The camel of Chelyabinsk is a historical Fata Morgana.

It was basically a coincidence that I ended up in the Urals. When I think about it in retrospect, I have the feeling that it was the steppe that attracted me. The wide, treeless plains of the Russian south were the antidote that I needed after the disaster in the Taiga.

In a cheap hotel room I showered the crushed mosquitoes off my body and got a sound night's sleep. The next morning I looked at a map. I found that I was not far from Arkaim, the legendary steppe town I had only seen as a model so far, in the pagan village of Popovka. I remembered the disappointed looks of the pagan priests who could not understand why the magic of their recreated sanctuary had failed to cast its spell on me. In the hope that maybe it would work better with the original, I bought a train ticket to the south.

During the journey I saw the sun sink into the steppe, a red coral in a sea of grass. When it rose again, the train stopped in a sleepy settlement near the Kazakh border. I continued by bus. I had not slept much, but the landscape kept me awake. Between me and the horizon there was absolutely nothing, only the gaping emptiness of the steppe, covered by a sky without beginning or end. The low morning sun was shining through the rear window while we drove west. Ahead, the bus cast a shadow that stretched to the horizon. I watched it grow shorter and shorter, until at noon, when the bus stopped in Arkaim, it had completely disappeared under the bus.

Gennady Zdanovich had spent a third of his life under the steppe sun. His hair was white, his skin the colour of bronze, his eyes hidden behind squinted lids. Arkaim had changed the archaeologist's face. And his life.

While he led me over the grounds, Zdanovich told me the story that had preoccupied him for the last two decades. In 1987, as a young archaeologist at the University of Chelyabinsk, he had been commissioned to survey a valley in the Ural steppes. It was a routine examination, no one expected any significant archaeological discoveries. More specifically, discoveries were not desired. The valley was to be flooded; a reservoir was planned. The archaeologists realised that their task was to find nothing.

They failed utterly. The exploration of the site had hardly started when two schoolboys pointed out a ring-shaped chain of earthworks to the researchers. Zdanovich took a good long look at the protrusions. They looked like the outlines of a city. A steppe city.

That evening the archaeologists celebrated until long after midnight. Although it was difficult to foresee what lay hidden under the earthworks, it was clear to everyone that there had never been a comparable discovery in the Ural steppes. The two schoolboys were rewarded with a can of condensed milk – no miserly gift in the Soviet era.

Twenty-three years later you could still tell how very much the discovery moved Zdanovich. When we arrived at the excavation site, he stopped solemnly. For a moment we contemplated his life's work in silence. Zdanovich made a sweeping gesture with his right arm. 'A city,' he said, 'built 4,000 years ago, in the middle of the steppe. Who would have thought it possible?'

What Zdanovich showed me did not look spectacular at first glance. The traces of vanished buildings could be distinguished in the soil discolorations at the bottom of a shallow pit. At its front end stood the reconstructed fragments of a wooden city wall. That was all. But it had been enough to change Russia's view of the steppe forever.

For a long time this view had been shaped by fear. The continuous grass belt of the steppe, ranging from northern China through Siberia and half of Europe to the Black Sea coast, had separated two worlds for centuries. North of it, in the cooler woodlands, lived sedentary peoples like the Slavs; south, in the steppes, lived nomads. For a long time the border between these two vegetation zones coincided with the southern boundary of the Muscovite tsarist empire: where the forest ended, the grass began, and where the grass began, Russia ended.

Only with the conquest of Siberia in the 17th century, and more decisively with Russia's southern expansion under Catherine the Great, did the national frontier overcome its vegetative limitations. Still, the steppe remained a danger zone in the historical consciousness of the Russians, a place of strangeness, of barbarism. Unforgotten was Russia's humiliating subjection by the Mongols, unforgotten were the raids by Turkic-speaking Tatar tribes, who had terrorised Russia's southernmost settlements for centuries. Out of nowhere these nomadic horsemen attacked the sedentary, less mobile Russians, only to disappear just as suddenly, and without a trace into the steppe. It was said that you could smell them before you could hear them, and that you could hear them before you could see them.

Later, when the nomads of the south became subjects of the Tsar, the Russians turned fear into contempt. The steppe dwellers, once dreaded opponents, were now perceived as backward barbarians who had to be converted, first to Christianity, later to socialism, but above all to a sedentary lifestyle. Unperturbed, their most stubborn representatives chose to live in yurts until well into the 20th century, which offended the Russians in their self-perception. The nomadism of the steppes was an outmoded aberration. It was the wood people's historical duty to make the people of the grasslands grow roots.

The discovery of Arkaim turned this conception of history completely upside down. Zdanovich and his colleagues discovered the legacies of a steppe people that had not lived nomadically, but in cities, during the Bronze Age, almost three millennia before the Slavs made their first historical appearance. What was more, the discoveries pointed to a highly complex civilisation. The archaeologists came across traces of about 70 houses, arranged in two concentric rings and surrounded by a double row of wooden fortifications. Each house had its own oven, a well and a sewer. The residents had practiced agriculture and animal husbandry; they had mined ore, gold and copper. In their burial chambers the archaeologists found not only forged sickles, axes, arrowheads and spearheads, but also the first battle chariots in world history, which had until then been attributed to Egypt.

As Zdanovich and his colleagues surveyed the surrounding area, they encountered remains of other settlements, less well preserved than Arkaim, but discernibly associated with the same culture. At least 20 fortified cities had once stood within a radius of 250 kilometres. Soil scientists and biologists participated in the investigations, geologists and anthropologists, linguists and historians. They found answers to many questions. But not to the central one. No one had the slightest idea what kind of people had lived here.

Zdanovich had his theories. But they were wobbly. From the skulls of the skeletons in the burial chambers he concluded that he was dealing with a Europoid, not an Asian people. Possibly, Arkaim had been an intermediate station of the Indo-European migrations. Possibly, it had even been the crucial station, the one that could explain how the Indo-Europeans had ended up in Asia, in Persia, in India.

Immediately after the discovery of Arkaim, Zdanovich had made these uncertain theses public – perhaps a little louder than archaeologists usually do. He had his reasons. The valley was still in danger of flooding. Zdanovich had to put a stop to a reservoir.

He succeeded. Word quickly spread that in the Ural steppes something extraordinary had been discovered, even if for the time being no one knew exactly what it was. People whispered about the discovery of the century, about an eighth Wonder of the World, a Russian Stonehenge. In the end the authorities caved in. The flooding of the valley was abandoned.

Around the same time, the Soviet Union collapsed, and Russia set out to find a new self-image. What the immediate past no longer offered, some now hoped to find in the remote past. Before Zdanovich knew it, his theories about Arkaim developed a bizarre life of their own.

I saw the result of this historical coincidence when Zdanovich led me back from the excavation site to the archaeologists' camp. While we had been talking, something strange had happened. The empty steppe had filled up. Cars and tents had emerged, and people. They were pilgrims. What they were seeking in Arkaim was hard to put into words, even for Zdanovich, who was used to the sight. 'They appear here all the time,' he said. 'Most of them come around this time of year, on midsummer's night. Something draws them to Arkaim.'

By evening the valley was filled with thousands of truth-seekers. A huge tent city arose, inhabited by Slavic hobby nomads who had come here, paradoxically, to pay homage to a sedentary steppe people. Each of them had his own theory about the inhabitants of Arkaim. 'They were Slavs,' I was assured by a young Belarusian who had driven all the way from Minsk to the Urals with a car trunk full of books. His sales table was piled with the most fantastic conspiracy theories. 'Here! Great book! *The Slavic Antiquity*. It describes how our ancestors migrated from Europe through Arkaim to India before they settled in Russia.'

'But how can that be?' I asked in amazement. 'When Arkaim was built, there were no Slavs yet.'

With a knowing smile he shook his head. 'All lies.' To prove it he showed me another book, a weighty tome full of enigmatic drawings. They were Russian folklore motifs, ornaments of the type I had often seen on peasant blouses or in the window carvings of old wooden houses. In the book's drawings, however, a clearly recognisable swastika was at the centre of each flower and bird pattern. The ancient Indian sun wheel, the man from Minsk explained to me, had formerly been one of the standard motifs of Russian folk art. 'But the Bolsheviks did not like the swastika. It was too similar to the fascists' *Hakenkreuz*. After the war they eradicated every single swastika in the whole country.'

Before we said goodbye I bought an edition of the *Slavic-Aryan Vedas* from him, allegedly 3000 years old and handed down through oral tradition for a long time, but now recorded in four volumes, and fortunately also available on CD-ROM. When I tried to read it months later, my computer displayed nothing but confused control characters.

As the steppe sank into darkness, I got to hear many other theories. Two Russian teachers from Volgograd declared that Arkaim was the electromagnetic navel of the earth. A chemist from Saint Petersburg whispered that the Ural steppes were the cradle of humanity. A Muscovite with flaming red hair revealed herself as a disciple of the fire prophet Zarathustra, who, she assured me, had been born in Arkaim.

I spoke with pagans and Christians, Muslims and shamans, new age priests and ufologists. Drums echoed through the pitch-black steppe, fire artists juggled with torches. A guru in orange clothes moved through the tent city, followed by dancing disciples whose continuous mantra could be heard everywhere: 'Hare Krishna, Hare Krishna, Krishna Krishna, Hare Hare ...'

As the shortest night of the year approached its end, the pilgrims gathered on a hill to await the sunrise. The drums fell silent, the songs, the mantras, finally the conversations. As the first red glow appeared above the horizon, the steppe lay in complete silence. Many pilgrims closed their eyes, their faces turned to the east. Others lifted their hands to the heavens and turned into cosmic antennas. Amazed, my gaze wandered from one enlightened face to the other. On each a different question was written, everyone here was alone in their search for answers. When the sun came up, I for my part felt none the wiser.

The Morgue of Yekaterinburg

From Arkaim I took a bus going north. After a few kilometres an old man boarded, his arms were wrapped in bandages from elbow to fingertip. He walked shakily through the bus, his arms balanced in front of him like a bulky piece of luggage. As chance would have it, he sat down in the free seat next to me. Despondently he stared at his bandaged hands. On a sudden dark impulse, I addressed him: 'A dog?'

Only when he turned to me did I see the tears in his eyes. 'I didn't do anything to him,' he sobbed. 'He just came at me!'

To comfort him I showed him my own hands, which had mostly healed. I had taken off the bandages in Arkaim, and now only a few scabbed areas and green *zelyonka* spots recalled the accident.

The road snaked along the edge of the Urals. Along the way we repeatedly passed signs marking the junction between Europe and Asia – the bus zigzagged between the continents. It fit my mood. Since my escape from Siberia I had avoided all thoughts of the Taiga. I knew that the goal of my journey lay east, but I was still so worked up about the failed boat trip that I felt instinctively drawn to the west.

I decided to occupy myself with other things for a while, to gather up strength for a second attempt. Even though for the time being I had no idea what this second attempt was supposed to be.

After a restless night's ride I reached Yekaterinburg. I walked through the city in amazement. I had expected a faceless industrial metropolis, like the dozens I had seen in recent weeks. Instead, I discovered a provincial beauty. Town villas with classicist facades lined the eastern edge of the Urals, as if Russia was remembering the European part of its soul here for one last time before Asia took the helm. Founded in 1723, shortly before the death of Peter the Great, the city seemed in places like a Siberian reflection of Saint Petersburg. But it is no 'Window to Europe'. It is the gauntlet on Asia's cheek.

Yekaterinburg's most famous villa is no longer there. The Ipatiev House, in whose cellar the Tsar's family was murdered in 1918, disappeared one July night in 1977. The demolition order was issued by the local Party secretary, a certain Boris Yeltsin, who later characterised his decision as 'shameful barbarism'. Today a cathedral stands on the site, the 'Church on Blood of All Saints Resplendent in the Russian Land'. It was consecrated in 2003, shortly after the exhumed remains of the Tsar's family were buried in Saint Petersburg, in the presence of a contrite Boris Yeltsin.

Inside the cathedral, dimly lit by candles, I saw pilgrims praying in front of the icons of the canonised imperial family. Whispering lips touched the painted contours of Tsar Nicholas and Tsarina Alexandra, the slender young bodies of the princesses, the face of the infant heir to the throne, as if kisses might bring them back to life.

Eight days after the Tsar's murder, in July of the civil war year of 1918, the Red Army abandoned Yekaterinburg. The city was occupied by White forces, who along with hundreds of volunteers searched for the remains of the imperial family. A soldier who had deserted the Red Army finally led them to an abandoned pit on the outskirts of the city. Inside they discovered the dentures of the imperial court physician, the Rasputin amulets of the Tsar's daughters and a severed finger. The latter belonged, as it later turned out, to the Tsarina. Her murderers had severed it because one of her rings was so tightly in place that they could not get it off.

Traces of fire and remains of sulphuric acid were found in the pit. A White Army commission of inquiry came to the conclusion that the corpses had been completely destroyed. Only in 1991, when their mutilated remains were dug up a few kilometres away, did it transpire that the pit had only been an intermediate station.

Nevertheless, a newly built monastery stands next to the pit today. It was built here because the Orthodox Church still abides by the findings of the 1918 investigation: the tunnel is the last resting place of the royal family; there are no remains. Vladimir, a young seminarian who showed me the monastery grounds, spoke with noticeable reluctance about the bones interred in Saint Petersburg. 'They are not authentic,' he said. 'I don't know whose bones they are, but they have nothing to do with the Tsar's family.' He thought that the state burial ceremony of 1998, which the Church boycotted, was a political staging. 'Yeltsin wanted to atone for his guilt, nothing more.'

I nodded, without understanding him. I had seen the icons of the Tsar's family all over Russia. They were worshiped as martyrs, but still the Church did not want to recognise their relics – I did not grasp it.

'What is so difficult to understand?' Vladimir asked when he noticed my doubt. 'Relics work wonders. People pray to them. The Church cannot allow heretical relics to be worshiped in their name. No one is sure whether these bones are authentic. Even the scientists cannot prove it.'

The Yekaterinburg District Hospital Number 1 is located in the southeast of the city. Birdsong pervaded the hospital grounds, it was a sunny morning. Patients pushed squeaky infusion stands over the asphalt. A doctor studied radiographs while smoking a cigarette. Nothing indicated that an incurable wound gaped in the middle of this hospital.

It took me a while to find the morgue. When I finally stood in front of it, I was suddenly no longer sure what I was actually looking for. As far as I knew, the exhumed remains of the Tsar's family had been examined inside the building in the Nineties. To the present day two of the children have not yet been buried – in Saint Petersburg I had seen their empty burial niches. No one had been able to tell me where the missing bodies were. Presumably they were still here, in the morgue.

On the narrow side of the concrete structure I found a closed steel door. When I rang, it was opened just a crack. A white-smocked woman gave me a questioning look.

'Pardon me,' I said as innocuously as possible. 'Is this where the Tsar's bones are kept?'

The woman lifted an eyebrow suspiciously. 'Who are you?'

I explained myself. The door slammed shut with a thundering crash. Well, I thought, it was worth a try.

But then the door opened again. The woman pushed one arm through the gap and pointed to an adjacent building. 'Speak to my boss. Third floor.' The door slammed shut, this time for good.

The white-smocked woman's boss was Vladimir Gromov. He was a pathologist – by virtue of his office he brought order into the chaos of death. For almost 20 years now he had occupied himself with the murder of the Tsar's family. As the photos on his desk proved, his goatee had turned grey over this occupation. Grey, and a bit more pointed – it had turned tsarist, in a word. When I said this, Gromov laughed. He liked to laugh. Especially when he said serious sentences.

'If my life has any meaning,' he said, 'then it is the resolution of this case.'

Nearly two decades ago a pile of bones had been heaped onto his autopsy table. The juridical covering note supplied by the Russian Prosecutor General basically boiled down to a simple instruction: figure out whose remains these are! Gromov and his colleagues began to sort through the heap. They assembled the individual bones into nine skeletons. They conducted skull studies and genetic analyses, pored over tsarist medical records and dentist diagnoses, compared historical photographs, took blood samples from descendants of the Romanov dynasty. In the end they submitted a list to the prosecutor's office.

Skeleton 1: Chambermaid Anna Demidova
Skeleton 2: Imperial Physician Yevgeny Botkin
Skeleton 3: Princess Olga Romanova
Skeleton 4: Tsar Nicholas II Romanov
Skeleton 5: Princess Anastasiya Romanova
Skeleton 6: Princess Tatyana Romanova
Skeleton 7: Tsarina Alexandra Romanova
Skeleton 8: Imperial Chef Ivan Kharitonov
Skeleton 9: Valet Aloisi Trupp

The prosecutor was baffled. The list was too short. Two people were missing. They had found the Tsar, his wife and four servants, but only three of the four daughters and no son. This, however, was purely a prosecution problem, not a pathological one. For Gromov the job was completed, the heap of bones cleared away.

But then, 16 years later, in the summer of 2007, another pile of bones landed on his table. Additional remains had been unearthed, only a few hundred metres away from the first discovery site. This time the heap of bones was considerably smaller. It consisted of skeletal parts that had been much more thoroughly broken, burned and etched than the first load. Through DNA analyses, Gromov and his colleagues established that the fragments belonged to two different individuals, one male and one female, both closely related to Tsar Nicholas.

Gromov smiled. 'With a probability of 98 per cent, they are Alexei and Maria. If we had money for further investigations, we could increase the probability to 99 per cent, maybe even to 99.9 per cent – but never to 100 per cent.'

He pulled a small, silver cross pendant from his lab coat. 'I am a Christian. I know that it is impossible to be a 98 per cent believer – you either believe or you don't. But as a pathologist, I cannot provide 100 percent results. That is why the Church will never recognise the bone fragments. The whole difference between science and faith is in these two missing percentage points.'

This, however, was purely a theological problem, not a pathological one. When Gromov had completed his examination of the bones, he submitted his findings to the prosecutor's office, which completed its investigation in the spring of 2008. The case was solved.

But then something strange happened. Here is what happened: nothing at all.

In a metal cabinet in the morgue of Yekaterinburg 44 plastic bags are stored, marked with hand-numbered slips of paper. They contain shattered, charred, acid-disfigured bone fragments, the largest about 20 centimetres in diameter, the smallest just barely discernible with the naked eye. For two years there has been no reason to store the bones here anymore. But nobody comes to pick them up. Two imperial children are waiting for their funeral. The graves are ready, and people are praying to them. But a gravedigger is nowhere to be found. Gromov is stuck with the bones. He cannot get rid of them.

I looked at him questioningly. 'You mean the state is hesitating, because it does not want to offend the Church a second time?'

The pathologist shrugged his shoulders. 'Could be. And maybe not. No one knows.' He sighed. 'I think it is the same as always in Russia. Nobody moves as long as there is no order from the very top.' For the first time his sentences were not followed by laughter.

'It is strange,' Gromov said as we parted. 'The Tsar is dead. We killed him. But we behave as if he were still around.'

The Cossacks' Last Battle

From the Urals I drifted west across the steppe, for 2000 kilometres, until the green sea was abruptly stopped by the Black Sea. A thundery midsummer sky hung over the Bay of Azov. The wind curled the water, the grass and the moustache of a merchant who was selling souvenirs on the waterfront. On his table were sabres and whips, saddles and spurs, medals and uniform caps. When I saw the assortment of goods, I knew that I had reached the land of the Cossacks.

On my journey through Siberia I had often wondered what was left of the conquering spirit of this warrior people, to whom Russia owes a good three-quarters of its territory. To find out, I had travelled to the mouth of the Don, the historical homeland of the Cossacks. Here they had emerged in the 15th century, as a curious hybrid between the sedentary forest peoples of the North and the nomadic grass peoples of the South: the Cossacks were Russian, but they lived in the steppe, and their preferred means of transportation was the horse.

Most of them were runaway serfs and criminals, who banded together in mounted groups at the country's southern edge. Initially they lived as professional crooks, as freebooters, whose raids were feared by the Russian settlements in the north, just as much as by the nomadic tribes in the south. It was the latter who gave the steppe desperados the Turkic name *Qazaq*: 'Free warriors'.

The disputed border area between the forest and the steppe became the dominion of the Cossacks. They were not the most pleasant neighbours, but what spoke in their favour, at least from the Tsar's perspective, was that they kept the southern nomads at bay. Soon the Kremlin began to woo the Cossacks. Their criminal past was generously overlooked, in return they would henceforth be the guardians of Russia's southern border.

The conquest of Siberia – begun as a private raid before the steppe warriors were given a government mandate – finally made the Cossacks auxiliary troops of the Tsar. Their units were officially integrated into the imperial army, and soon they were seen riding through Saint Petersburg in their exotic uniforms. As palace guards they kept watch over royal residences, as a mounted elite force they subdued popular uprisings on behalf of the Tsar. The outlaws of yore became guardians of the law.

Their never entirely reliable, but always loudly invoked loyalty to the Tsar was what brought about their downfall after the Revolution. Although they fought on both sides of the barricades in the civil war, the Bolsheviks trusted neither the White nor the Red Cossacks. A wave of terror swept through their settlements in the Twenties and Thirties – those who did not perish in Stalin's camps starved to death in their own houses as the farmland of the steppe was forcibly nationalised. Stalin destroyed the Cossacks by depriving them of their livelihood: their farms, their pastures, their cattle.

Finally their horses disappeared from the steppe. The Bolsheviks preferred a different means of transportation: the tractor, the plough-dragger of socialism, the horse of the future. A gigantic tractor factory sprang up in the old Don metropolis of Rostov, whose remaining Cossack population was re-educated to be tractor engineers and tractor drivers. Even the new theatre that the Bolsheviks opened in Rostov was built in the shape of a combine harvester – with facades and windows that looked like rubber tracks and ventilation grids. For 70 years the stage of the combine theatre was one of the few places where the Cossacks were still allowed to be Cossacks – if only the cheerful Cossacks of folklore, uniformed, but unarmed.

Only after the Soviet demise did they don their sabres and whips once more. In Rostov and the surrounding Don cities I spoke to a few representatives of the reborn Cossack movement, whose uniforms were as fanciful as the titles on their business cards. Some of them were cordial, fundamentally likeable braggarts. Others told me with deeply moved voices how bravely the Cossacks had once fought for the fatherland, and how much they still loved the fatherland, and what they would do to defend the fatherland, and …

'So what exactly *would* you do?' I interrupted.

'Kick out the Chechens! And the Tajiks! And the Turks! And the Chinese! And first of all the Jews!'

When I was just about to resign myself to the fact that nothing remained of the Cossacks but kitschy souvenirs and pompous moustaches and rehashed resentment, I met Vasily Pivovarov.

I barely noticed him at first. One of the business card cavalrymen from Rostov had invited me to a birthday party. We sat in a garden in the old Cossack capital of Starocherkassk, on the banks of the Don, a few kilometres upstream from Rostov. The Cossacks had put on their finest caps and drank to the welfare of the fatherland with tears in their eyes. Between them sat a very old man in a threadbare field uniform. He told World War stories that no one was listening to except me. Only after a while did it occur to me that something was wrong with his veteran's monologue.

'… the sun was just rising when we realised that they had surrounded us. "Damn Bolsheviks," cried Petya, "we'll show them what a real Cossack is …"'

'Bolsheviks?' I interrupted him. 'Which side did you fight for?'

With a challenging grin he turned to me. 'For none, young man. We fought for a free Don – a Don without Stalin.'

I looked at him in surprise. I knew that a number of Cossacks had defected to the German Wehrmacht during the war, but I was sure that none of them had survived – they had later been extradited to the Soviet Union.

'I thought the defectors had all been executed!' I blurted out.

The old man laughed a dry laugh. 'Come visit me,' he said. 'I'll show you my death sentence.'

A day later I drove to Krivyanskaya, a small settlement east of Rostov. Vasily Pivovarov lived in a tiny stone house. In its two rooms he had raised five children. Vasska, Fedya and Seryozhka were dead; Lenka and Antoshka had long since left home. Pivovarov's wife had died only a few months ago. Sometimes the small house seemed very large to him now.

He cracked eight eggs into a cast iron pan. When he scraped them out, they were burnt on the bottom and raw on the top. We ate them with white lard and black bread.

The field uniform hung on a hook above the bed. It was a hot summer day and Pivovarov was wearing boxer shorts. His legs were very thin. Although he ate his four eggs every day, he had become severely emaciated with old age. Pivovarov's right knee was stiff, he could not bend it. For 65 years now he had dragged this unbending leg around with him, and he had learned to come to terms with it. When he dropped himself into his armchair, the leg jutted out horizontally from the cushions. The horizontal leg was even thinner than the vertical one.

He poured a crate full of papers and photos onto his bed. After rummaging around for a while he pulled a yellowed slip of paper from the heap. The typewriting was faded and hardly readable. I recognised only the year 1947 and the word 'Shoot.'

Pivovarov wiped the eggs from his walrus moustache and started his narrative.

'I was born in the Novocherkassk city prison, in the year 1925.'

On the Don the civil war had just ended. Pivovarov's parents, Cossacks from Krivyanskaya, had fought on the wrong side – or on the right, depending on one's perspective. They ended up in prison. The Bolsheviks shot the father before his son was born, and the mother immediately after the birth. Two prison guards brought the screaming infant to Krivyanskaya and put him under the care of a Cossack family.

Only when he was eight years old did Pivovarov learn that his foster parents were not his real parents. The school principal summoned him to his office. 'White Guard bastard!' the director cried, 'did you really think we would not recognise you?' He ripped the red star with the portrait of Lenin from Pivovarov's breast, the badge of the October Children. Then he chased him out of school.

Weeping, Pivovarov ran home. 'Mama,' he howled, 'am I a White Guard bastard?'

He could not return to school. Instead he became a shepherd boy. When he was a bit older he learned how to drive a tractor. He helped out in the collective farm until the war began.

When the Germans occupied the Don, Pivovarov's foster mother went into the garden shed. She plied a plank from the floor, revealing a pit hidden underneath. The foster mother removed a Cossack sabre from the pit, then a saddle, a revolver and a carbine. In the courtyard she untied a horse, a young mare, and pressed the reins into Pivovarov's hands. 'The Cossacks are regrouping,' she said. 'Go and enlist.'

So it happened that Vasily Pivovarov defected to the Wehrmacht, along with 250 other volunteers from Krivyanskaya.

'You knew about the Jews?'

'The Germans made no secret of it.'

'And still you wanted to fight on their side?'

'Whose side should we have fought on otherwise?'

'Weren't you afraid of the Germans? Hitler was not exactly a friend of the Russians.'

'Hitler promised us a free Don.'

'He promised a lot.'

Pivovarov shrugged his shoulders. 'If he had broken his word, we would have kept on fighting. Against the Germans.'

The Cossacks' war did not last long. Shortly after they had defected, the Germans began to withdraw. In January 1943, when the battle of Stalingrad had not yet ended, the Wehrmacht abandoned the Don. Kilometre by kilometre, the Red Army pushed the Germans out of the country, and with them the Cossack regiments who had gone over to the other side. Pivovarov, who had never left his village before, marched all across Ukraine with the retreating Wehrmacht. A few times he was slightly wounded in rearguard battles. It was not difficult for him to fire back, although he knew that the people on the other side of the front were his compatriots. But had it been any different in the civil war? The front did not divide Germans and Russians – it divided Pivovarov from the Bolsheviks.

Once, in western Ukraine, he watched a German officer die. A bullet had torn open the man's abdomen, he was sitting in his own blood. Before he died, the officer slipped off his watch and gave it to Pivovarov. '*Danke*,' Pivovarov had said, in German, but the man could no longer hear him.

In Poland a bomb lacerated his knee. They evacuated him to Glogau, to a German military hospital. He was discharged with a stiff leg. As he was no longer of any use on the front, they sent him to northern Italy, to a reception camp. Almost all Cossacks ended up here at the end of the war, not only soldiers, also fugitive families with their children. Those who were still fit for use were sent on to Yugoslavia to fight against Tito's partisans. The rest waited. For their return to a free Don.

The months passed, but the Don did not become any freer. When the German defeat was imminent, the Cossacks battled their way over the Alps to Austria, in order to surrender to the British. They knew that the Englishmen did not like the Bolsheviks any more than they did. Who knew, the Cossacks thought – maybe one day they would liberate the Don on the side of the British.

When they reached the Austrian city of Lienz, they were taken to a British prisoner of war camp. The Cossacks made advances to the Englishmen. The Englishmen smiled their polite English smile. They did not tell the Cossacks that their fate had already been sealed: at the Yalta Conference, the Allies had promised Stalin to extradite all interned Soviet citizens.

When the British announced one day that the Cossacks would be relocated to another camp, they finally understood what was in store for them. Panic broke out. The next morning, as trucks pulled up outside the camp, the Cossacks hung themselves on the camp fence by the dozen. Mothers strangled their children and threw themselves on the Englishmen's bayonets. Only by force did the British finally succeed in cramming the remainder of the 2000 prisoners into the trucks and handing them over to the Red Army.

The officers were executed; the soldiers, including Pivovarov, were sent to prison camps for ten years. In cattle cars they were transported to Siberia. Pivovarov ended up in a coal mine, where something strange happened. A foreman saw his stiff leg and said: 'What are you doing here? We can't use cripples. Clear out and go home.'

Limping, Pivovarov traversed half of Russia. Along the way he swapped the wristwatch the German officer had given him for a revolver. He knew his release was a mistake, he knew they would soon be looking for him. With the revolver in his pocket he made his way to Krivyanskaya. All that he wanted was to see the Don one last time. He decided to shoot himself if they tried to arrest him.

For an entire year he lived in Krivyanskaya unhindered. He returned to his job as a tractor driver on the collective farm. When people asked him where he had been he simply said: 'In the war.'

One summer day he sat dozing in the steppe, his head leaning against his tractor. From the horizon, the shadow of a second tractor slowly approached. At the wheel, Pivovarov recognised the chairman of the collective farm. Beside him sat a stranger in uniform. When Pivovarov realised that it was time to die, he jumped up and ran limping through the steppe, to his foster parents' house, where the revolver was hidden. The uniformed man jumped from the tractor and ran after Pivovarov. He was faster.

He ended up in a Siberian coal mine once again. This time no one minded his crippled leg. After one year a fellow prisoner told the guards that Pivovarov had not been a common soldier in the Wehrmacht, but had temporarily served as an officer. They sent him back to court. At the end of the short trial the court clerk inserted a strip of paper into his typewriter and typed: 'Shoot.'

For 90 days Pivovarov awaited his execution. Then a public prosecutor visited him in his cell. The man was a Jew, but he liked Pivovarov. He announced that there would be a second hearing, he gave him advice on how to behave, on what to say. At the end of the hearing the court clerk inserted a new strip of paper. This time he typed: '25 years.'

Pivovarov dragged his stiff leg through iron mines and steel combines; he laid train tracks and cleared forests. He came to know the frost and the famine, and the blows from the guards. While constructing a road near the Chinese border, he met his future wife, a Cossack from the Don – Pivovarov knew it immediately when he saw her.

Shortly after Stalin's death they were both prematurely released from prison. They married in Krivyanskaya. Of the 250 Cossacks who had joined the Wehrmacht, Pivovarov was the only one who returned to his native village. 'Here comes the fascist,' the villagers said when Pivovarov walked past them. 'How are you doing, fascist?' Pivovarov learned to deal with the remarks, just as he had learned to deal with his unbending leg. He raised five children and worked as a tractor driver, and ate four eggs every day.

'Have you ever regretted it?'

Pivovarov looked me hard in the eyes. A defiant answer seemed to be on the tip of his tongue, but before it reached his lips he thought better of it. Thoughtfully his gaze turned inward. 'I am sorry, sometimes, about my first-born,' he said. 'Seryozhka.'

His eldest son had been known for having a good head on his shoulders. He excelled in his classes and was liked by all his teachers. After school he had applied to a technical college. They turned him down. He was the 'son of an enemy of the people'. Seryozhka could not cope with the rejection. He began to drink. He picked fights, came home with stab wounds, kept drinking. Seryozhka did not live to grow old.

'Did you enter the village along the country road?' Pivovarov asked.

I nodded.

'Did you see how tall the grass stands on the steppe? In the olden days the horses used to eat it. But there are none of them left. Not one in the entire village.'

Before I left Pivovarov showed me his garden. A huge greenhouse stood in the middle, which did not belong to him, but to a vegetable wholesaler who had leased several plots of land in Krivyanskaya. In the past the town had been famous for its horses. Now it was famous for its tomatoes.

Pivovarov looked around in all directions. There was no one to be seen in the neighbouring gardens. Quietly he opened the door to the greenhouse. Inside, he untucked his undershirt and filled it with tomatoes. His movements were quick and practiced, apparently it was not the first time he stole from his leaseholder.

'Here. For the road.'

Grinning, he poured the tomatoes into my bag. After all, this soil was still his.

A Trunk Full of Icons

From Krivyanskaya I travelled back to Rostov. As the bus crossed the centre of the old Don metropolis, I suddenly saw the bizarre silhouette of the theatre pass by the windows, a combine harvester made of glass and concrete, parked between the houses like the toy car of a giant October Child.

A friend from Moscow had given me the address of a family from Rostov. They lived in the suburbs, in a newly built row house. When I arrived, I burst in on a birthday party. Grandfather Viktor was turning 60. He liked my gift. 'Tomatoes from Krivyanskaya! The best in the entire Don region!'

Till the early morning hours we drank home-distilled vodka that Grandfather Viktor produced in the cellar of his house. 'Purely natural,' he assured me. 'No chemical additives. You'll never get a hangover, guaranteed.'

Nevertheless, I was not quite myself when I woke up the next morning. Half of the house was still asleep, only Grandfather Viktor's grandchildren, Nastya and Vanya, both primary school age, were up; they sat at the kitchen table in swimsuits. 'Uncle Jens!' they cried. 'Are you coming to the lake with us?'

The water was muddy, but it chased away the hangover. Nastya and Vanya were joined by a friend, a boy from the neighbourhood. The boy was a bit younger than the two of them. He was not yet allowed to go to the lake alone, so his grandfather had come along to keep an eye on him. While we swam, the grandfather sat silently on the shore, taking a sip from a bottle every now and then.

When we packed up the towels around noon to walk back to the settlement, the old man was so drunk that his legs would no longer carry him. I put his left arm around my shoulder and dragged him home. His

wife opened the front door. With a sigh, she pointed to the floor: 'There.'
I set the grandfather down carefully. He fell asleep immediately.

Oleg and Katya, the parents of Nastya and Vanya, were my age. They
earned their living as icon dealers. Every few weeks they went around
the local Orthodox parishes to supply them with the small, cheap images
of saints sold in Russian church kiosks. In the afternoon I helped them
load their van. We hoisted cases full of Saviours and Virgin Mothers into
the cargo space. The next morning Oleg and Katya were to head out on
a two-week sales tour, southbound along the Black Sea coast, all the way
down to Sochi. They took me along.

The journey has blurred in my memory into one long, dusty street, its
edges lined at irregular intervals with Lenin monuments and churches.
We drove past the Lenin monuments; we stopped at the churches.
Usually, Oleg would conduct the sales talks with the priests.

'Here, Father, a new product line: self-adhesive Virgin Mothers for
the dashboard, eight roubles a piece. What do you say?'

'Give me five.'

'Take ten, Father. Ten for the price of nine, okay?'

'Five is enough. Better give me Saint Pantaleon icons. Don't tell me
you showed up here again without Pantaleon.'

'Delivery problems, Father. Take Saint Nicholas. He always sells.'

'But don't fob this Ukrainian plastic stuff off on me, you hear?'

'Made in Russia, Father. It's all made in Russia.'

Oleg was a man with two faces. In his conversations with the priests
he was amiable, wheedling, almost subservient. As soon as the car door
slammed shut, his honey voice changed pitch abruptly. 'Son of a bitch!
Haggles over every rouble. Have you seen his car? No haggling there,
that's for sure! You know where the money comes from? Do you think
a priest earns enough for that? He's plundering off his community, the
son of a bitch.'

Oleg hated Russia. He hated Russia's roads, Russia's gas stations and
Russia's traffic police; he hated Russian cars and the Russian driving
style of their Russian owners. He complained about the hotels where
we stayed; he mistrusted the canteens where we ate along the way. But
most of all, Oleg hated the Russian Church. 'It is an absolute mafia!
The priests enrich themselves through their communities, the bishops

through the priests, the metropolitans through the bishops and the patriarch through the metropolitans.'

A long time ago Oleg himself had toyed with the idea of becoming a cleric. He had studied at a seminary in Saint Petersburg. It was the Nineties, and like every other part of Russian society, the reborn Church went through internal power struggles about its future course. Frustrated by hierarchical intrigues, Oleg had abandoned his studies after a few semesters. What bothered him about the Church soon bothered him about the whole country – everywhere he sensed hypocrisy, corruption and slave mentality.

By the time I met him, Oleg's hatred had become almost obsessive. He blamed his homeland for everything that was wrong with his life. Russia tore at him, infiltrated him and poisoned him. 'Are you insane?' he shouted one afternoon as I was about to unwrap a bar of Alyonka chocolate in the car. 'Do you know what kind of shit that stuff contains? Russian chocolate is pure poison! Are you trying to kill yourself?' He snatched the unopened bar from my hand and hurled it out the window. At the next petrol station he bought me a box of Austrian chocolates. 'I just hope they are really from Austria. The Russian shops are full of fake imports – Western on the outside, Russian on the inside.'

Katya, Oleg's wife, sometimes smiled about her husband's paranoia. But at heart she shared his dissatisfaction. Both of them had long been dreaming of emigration – to Canada, to England, to Australia, to some place where the roads had no potholes and the people no cracks in their souls, where the traffic police were incorruptible and the sweets unpoisoned. For years they had been studying English. During the journey they sometimes quizzed each other on vocabulary or asked me to translate complicated words for them, which regularly left me at a loss: 'sophisticated', 'face value', 'gentrification'. After every sales tour they laid a bit of money aside, in the hope they would one day be able to finance their departure with the savings. The icon trade was their escape route. They sold Russia's faith because they no longer had faith in Russia.

It was not the most far-fetched business model. Icons were popular. In almost every small town that we crossed on our way south there was a brand new church, or one was just being built. Oleg knew stories of corruption for each and every one of them, but that was not the reason why I kept staring at them in disbelief. For 70 years this country had done everything to get rid of its churches. Now new ones could not be built fast enough.

Almost all the workers climbing through the scaffolded construction sites were from the former Soviet republics in Central Asia. In a small town near Krasnodar I got into a conversation with a few Tajiks who had not seen their families for two years. They lived in a trailer beside the church and sent most of their wages back home.

'Tajikistan, beautiful country,' they told me in broken Russian. 'Everything beautiful. But no work.'

'Aren't there any churches to build?'

'No churches. Mosques.'

'And who builds the mosques?'

They laughed. 'Chinese.'

Halfway through our journey I began to count the churches and the Lenin monuments. My calculations were incomplete, because we rarely stayed long enough in one place to walk around the entire city. According to my rough estimates, the Lenin monuments were still in the lead, but if things kept going this way, they would certainly lose the race.

I often wondered whether anyone except me even noticed the Lenin statues anymore. People walked past them much the same way they walked past trees or lamp posts. Lonely and ignored, this small, yet larger-than-life man stood on every third village square, his hand clenched into a fist or buried in a pocket or pointing into the distance. Sometimes Lenin's index finger was aimed directly at one of the newly built churches. God punished him for his sins by mocking his poses.

At some point in the distant future, I imagined, the monuments would slowly crumble, the frost would crack off their limbs, the rain smooth down their features, until at some point there would be nothing left of them but shapeless stone steles, indistinguishable from the tombs of the ancient nomad peoples. Lenin would become one with the steppe, a forgotten warrior, one deity among many.

As we drove southward, pursued by Lenin, with a trunk full of icons, I wondered whether this country would ever be able to get by without a faith. Painted gods had displaced the wooden ones, marble statues the icons, now the churches were returning. An eternal longing for redemption drove Russia forward, a suffering in the mortal world that could only be soothed by an afterlife. Even Oleg and Katya were not free of this. I sensed it when they told me about the distant lands where they would spend their future. The West that they described had little to do with the West that I knew. It was not a geographical direction; it was paradise.

Only towards the end of our trip did I begin to realise that Oleg and Katya would probably never leave Russia. Their dream about emigration was a dream, nothing more and nothing less. It alleviated their suffering, it raised their spirits, it bound them together – and they passed it on to their children. They sent Nastya and Vanya to a language school twice a week. During the journey they often called the children and asked them to recite English vocabulary. During one of these phone calls they found out that Vanya had skipped lessons. Instead of learning English, he had spent the afternoon at the lake.

'Vanya,' I heard Katya say on the phone. 'Why are you doing that? You promised to go to school.'

Oleg snatched the phone from her hand. 'How often have I told you that you have to learn English? Do you think people in Canada will speak Russian with you? Do you want to spend the rest of your life in Russia? Do you want to be stuck in this shit forever?'

On the last few kilometres the road snaked along the Black Sea coast in hairpin bends, through the northern foothills of the Caucasus. As the first cypress trees and Mandarin shrubs appeared, the scent of the south drifted through the open car windows. Before us lay Sochi, Russia's subtropical bathing paradise.

After we had supplied the last church with icons, Oleg and Katya dropped me off in the city centre and drove back to Rostov. I rented a hotel room and walked through the completely overcrowded city, on whose beaches half of Russia holidays in summer. Girls in bikinis and high-heeled sandals sat in the coastal cafes, courted by Slavic men whom the sun had transformed into negative images of themselves: their hair bleached, their skin darkened. Even Lenin had grown discoloured in the south: a huge mosaic in the city park displayed his face in bright orange shades.

In the park I got into a conversation with an old man, an Abkhazian named Guri, who had ended up in Russia during the Georgian Civil War. On his shoulder sat a red parrot who constantly interfered in our conversation with a cawing word I did not understand at first:

'*Pr-r-robki*! *Pr-r-robki*!' Guri rented the parrot out to tourists for holiday snapshots. I was intrigued when he told me that he had been in this business since Soviet times, that he had stood on the coastal promenade of his Abkhazian hometown with a parrot on his shoulder.

'You mean you were a private entrepreneur?'

'What on earth makes you think that? I was an employee of the Tourism Bureau! My parrot was part of the five-year plan!'

'*Pr-r-robki*! *Pr-r-robki*!'

I pointed to the parrot. 'Was it this one?'

'No.' Guri sighed. 'This one is new. At that time I had a good bird, the best one on the entire coast. He could repeat everything. Everything! His favourite phrase was: "Workers of all countries, unite!"'

Depressed, Guri pointed to the proletarian parrot's successor. 'I cannot teach this one here anything. He just parrots back what he picks up on the radio.'

'*Pr-r-robki*! *Pr-r-robki*!'

Finally I understood. The cawing was a traffic announcement: 'Congestion! Congestion!'

'I lost the old parrot in the war. I don't know what became of him. Maybe he is still alive. Parrots can live to be 300 years old.'

'*Pr-r-robki*!'

Three hundred years! I suddenly imagined a parrot who remembered Lenin, the Revolution, the Tsar. Who knew, maybe somewhere in Sochi there were parrots who could sing Old Believer chorales. But when I asked around among the parrot owners in the park, it turned out that all the birds were post-Soviet immigrants. Only one, a South American macaw, was rumoured to have witnessed perestroika. 'But he doesn't speak much,' his owner said regretfully. The parrot and I stared at each other stupidly – two foreigners who could not find a common language. I blinked first.

In the evening, shortly before the sun went down, I swam out into the Black Sea, as far as my breath would carry me. Panting, I turned on my back and let myself float. The southern light coloured the sky pink and purple. The beach was still black with people, and behind it gleamed the subtropical green of the overgrown hillsides. As my gaze wandered south along the coastline, it suddenly dawned on me that Russia ended here. The Abkhaz border was a few kilometres ahead. For weeks I had let myself drift, first to the west, then to the south. Now I could not go any further. From here the way only led back – back to the Taiga.

WOOD (Taiga)

Yesterday in the woods I saw the Russian idea
It walked amongst felled pine trees
With a sling around its neck.

Yuri Shevchuk, 1999

What does a Russian think about, somewhere on the shore
of the Yenisey, or deep in the Amur taiga? Every road that
he takes seems to have no end. He can walk along it for days
and months, and always Russia will surround him.

Ryszard Kapuściński, 1993

'But why to the left?' thought Nicholas. 'Heaven only knows
where we are going, and heaven knows what is happening to
us – but it is very strange and pleasant whatever it is.'

Leo Tolstoy, 1869

Misha and Masha

August had just started when I returned to Siberia. I still had no definite idea what my second Taiga expedition would look like. There was no way I was going back to Abaza – the city was so small that an encounter with San Sanych could hardly be avoided, and just the thought of it made my hair stand on end. Instead I flew to Kemerovo, a neighbouring republic of Khakassia famous for its coal mines. I had heard rumours that there was a second route to Agafya from the southern part of the region; it would mean going through the Taiga on foot. On the map it looked like an alarmingly long march across difficult mountain terrain – but at least there was no danger of falling into the hands of drunken boat drivers.

In the regional capital of Kemerovo an acquaintance put me in contact with a local politician, of whom it was said that he could work miracles. When I visited the man in his office he effusively promised me the moon. 'I'll get you a guide! Better, two guides! You will need a satellite phone! And weapons! I'll pay for everything!'

'I would rather pay myself,' I objected cautiously. As much as I appreciated the man's generosity, I could think of no plausible reason why my expedition should be financed by tax money collected from underpaid pit workers.

The next morning a silver sedan drove up in front of my hotel. The driver jumped out of the car to open the door for me. On the back seat sat a young woman who introduced herself as an ethnologist and employee of the regional administration. 'We have prepared a little excursion for you,' she said, 'to the national park.'

During the two-hour ride my mobile rang. An assistant of the local politician sheepishly informed me that unfortunately nothing could be done about the Taiga expedition. 'We tried to find a guide, but nobody wants to do it. It is too far and too difficult. I'm sorry.'

When we arrived at the national park, I understood that the trip was meant as a kind of compensation, an ersatz expedition through an ersatz Taiga. The gesture was well meant, but I was in a lousy mood. Hiding my irritation, I let the ethnologist show me ancient rock inscriptions and old Slavic wood constructions. My mood sank further when the woman suddenly stopped in the forest to look at the birch trees. 'Look,' she said. 'The first yellow leaves are showing already. Our summer is so short in Siberia.' I could feel my pulse quicken in panic. I was running out of time. Soon the first snow would fall, and then there would be no way to get into the Taiga.

The highlight of the excursion was the feeding of the bears. A large cage stood in the middle of the park. Two brown bears nervously paced back and forth behind the bars. They were huge, fear-inspiring creatures. 'Misha and Masha,' the ethnologist said by way of introduction.

She pressed a plastic bag into my hand, filled with raw chunks of meat. Dutifully I threw one piece after the other into the cage. Masha lunged at the meat and tore it into shreds, her jaws working furiously. Misha looked at me with sad eyes. Listlessly he pushed the meat about on the cage floor, without eating.

'What's wrong with him?' I asked the ethnologist.

Embarrassed, she turned her gaze away. 'Ask the park director. That's his field. I'm an ethnologist.'

The park director was waiting for us in his office, a broadly-built man of about 50. 'We have prepared a small snack for you,' he said as we shook hands. An unfolded camping table groaned under the weight of meat pies, pastries, smoked fish and vodka bottles.

'Thank you, no drinks for me.'

The director filled my glass to the brim.

'Thank you, I really won't.'

He pushed the glass in my direction.

'No!'

'To the fraternity of peoples!'

I pushed the glass away. For some reason I was suddenly determined not to back down this time. But it was pointless. The director acted out the entire coercion routine: jovial, begging, pleading, uncomprehending, disappointed, hurt, offended …

Out of courtesy I took a tiny sip.

'Drink up!'

After a quarter of an hour my resistance was completely broken. Toast after toast, I lost control. I conceded that the day was lost. We emptied one, then another bottle, the director, the ethnologist and I. Only our chauffeur sat silently at the table drinking lemonade, for which I secretly admired him.

When I asked about Misha, the bear, a grin spread across the director's face. 'He's an alcoholic.'

I choked on a piece of smoked fish.

'It's the visitors' fault,' the director said. 'They make a joke of it, pouring vodka into the bear's feeding trough. Masha does not touch the stuff, but Misha gets plastered. On holidays, when half the city drives out to the park, he is staggering around in circles by the time we close.'

I coughed helplessly.

'Sometimes,' the director continued, 'it is so bad that we have to give Misha vodka again the next morning. Because he is so hungover.'

I stared at him in disbelief. 'You are telling me fairy tales.'

He shook his head. 'No.'

'If I put that in my book, no one in Germany will believe me.'

'What book?'

I told him. I told him the entire story. About Agafya, about my journey, about the failed trip to the Taiga. When I got to the part about the drunken boat driver Misha, our chauffeur, who had been following our conversation in silence, suddenly leaned over the table.

'I know about that,' he said. 'I used to drive a truck, for a haulage company. Sometimes we had to cross the Altai Mountains, on unsecured roads. Any mistake and your truck would go over the edge and plummet down the slope. I would not have survived that in a sober state! You have to drink away the fear!'

My admiration for him vanished into thin air.

'To our heroic drivers!' the director crowed.

I went on with my story, telling them about the end of the boat ride, about my second attempt, about the local politician's promises, which had come to nothing. Towards the end I must have sounded pretty desperate – the alcohol fuelling my self-pity.

'You have to file a complaint.' The park director's face was suddenly serious. 'You have to make them stick to their promises. You are not just anybody, you are a foreign citizen. The government must provide you with a helicopter. Call the Ministry of Foreign Affairs! No, better talk directly to the president!'

On the ride back I fell asleep immediately. Shortly before we reached the city limits, the noise of the traffic woke me up. My head was throbbing and my mood had hit rock bottom. I suddenly had the feeling that it was not just time that was working against me, but all of Russia. Never before and never after have I felt such a deep aversion to the Russians as on that hungover afternoon in the car. They were the most unpleasant people in the world. I hated their empty promises, I hated their patronising hospitality, I hated their boozing, I hated their childish belief in the almightiness of their rulers.

The Secrets of Russian Women

In the evening I took a night train to Krasnoyarsk, still feeling hungover. Without knowing exactly what I expected, I had arranged to meet with Galina Alexandrovna, the linguist who had put me in contact with San Sanych. We had not spoken since the fiasco in the Taiga. I did not know whether she had since learned through other channels what had happened, and if so, whether San Sanych had told her the truth.

The next day I visited her in her office in the Literature Museum. I had hardly taken a seat when Galina asked me whether everything had gone 'correctly' in the Taiga. It sounded as if she was reproaching herself. Apparently she had spoken with San Sanych and had drawn her own conclusions.

I explained. At first I expressed myself cautiously, because Galina shared her office with a co-worker. But very soon both women began to interject worried questions, urging me on to go ahead with the story. When I had finally unravelled the whole plot, there was a moment of awkward silence. Disapprovingly Galina shook her head. 'San Sanych has always told me that he does not drink.'

'He told me that too,' I said.

Olga, Galina's colleague, laughed dryly. 'That's what all drinkers say.'

'I should have come with you.' Galina stood up, switched on the kettle and put fresh teabags into our cups. 'In the presence of a woman the two of them would not have got so drunk.'

Olga shook her head. 'It's always the same story. As soon as men are amongst themselves …'

'If San Sanych's wife had been there, he would have pulled himself together.' Galina sighed. She sounded as if she was now preoccupied with something that was only remotely connected with my story. 'You know,' she said, 'in Russia it is always the men who snap. They have more difficulty coping with the hardships of life. I couldn't tell you the reason.'

Olga nodded. 'It is always the men. Always.'

'They start drinking, they let down their families, they give themselves up.'

'The entire burden falls to the women.'

I drank my tea in silence, while Galina and Olga went on talking. Their dialogue moved further and further away from its starting point. They told stories about men who had gone astray, about broken families, about Russian women who had to compensate for their men's weaknesses through their own strength. I listened with the strange feeling that my presence had triggered this dialogue, even though I could not make any further contribution to it. Not for the first time in my life I felt glad not to be a Russian man.

The afternoon passed until a flurry of activity signalled the museum's closing time; footsteps and farewells could be heard outside in the corridor. Galina searched my eyes, as if she had suddenly remembered the reason for my visit. 'You want to try it again, am I right?'

'Yes.'

She nodded silently. When I realised what she was driving at, I tried to meet her halfway. 'Maybe,' I said, 'it would be easier if a woman came along this time.'

Galina smiled. 'So that no one gets drunk.'

Olga smiled too. 'Female company disciplines men.'

'Or two women,' I said.

The next day we contacted the Environment Agency of the Republic of Khakassia. Instead of relying on the miracle currency of *spirit*, we wanted to apply for official permission to enter the nature reserve. We were in luck: an enthusiastic official not only assured us we would be issued with travel permits, he also offered to organise an expedition for us. Exuberantly he promised us a guide and a boat. We thought we were almost at our goal. Then the official responsible for issuing permits fell ill; his deputy was away at his dacha; the guide could not be found; the boat had an engine failure; the replacement part from the Japanese manufacturer was stuck in customs; in short, things went their usual Russian way.

But a good three weeks later an unusual group of travellers gathered in Abaza, on the banks of the Abakan: a forestry inspector from the nature reserve of Khakassia, a boat driver from Abaza, a linguist and a literary scholar from Krasnoyarsk, and a journalist from Germany.

While we heaved our luggage into the boat, I tried to guess what our two guides were thinking about their atypical passengers. Both men were burly, taciturn and unceremonious Siberians. Igor, the boat driver, was in his early forties; Lyonya, the forestry inspector, a bit older. Both smiled uncertainly as Olga, while packing, sang the praises of an experimental documentary about the Russian forest. 'You simply must see it! It shows the real Siberia!'

Once we set off, however, our female battle plan seemed to be working. From the beginning the atmosphere was completely different than on the last trip. No one cursed. Nobody drank. Concentrating on his task, Igor steered the boat upstream. In dangerous places he dropped us off on the shore and continued on his own, carefully manoeuvring the boat through rapids and around rock formations before he took us aboard again. When the sun went down, he immediately started looking for a place to spend the night. He found a hunting lodge which was half-derelict, but more comfortable than any tent. Later, when we gathered around the campfire, he opened a beer can labelled with a big zero. I almost flung my arms around his neck. It was the first time I ever saw a Russian man drinking non-alcoholic beer.

When we continued on the second day, I realised why I had hardly recognised the river the day before. It held only half as much water as the last time – the snow melt was over. Dried mud beds now lined the shore. The receding water had washed away the soil from under the trunks of many trees. They balanced on thin, pale roots, like ballet dancers frozen in mid-movement.

About noon we met a couple of anglers. Their long, narrow wooden boat looked just like ours, but it lay capsized in the water, crosswise to the current, wedged between rocks. Four completely soaked men were tugging at the bow. Igor, Lyonya and I pitched in, but the boat did not budge a millimetre – the force of the surging water pressed it against the rocks. In the end Igor lent the men his axe. They hacked up one of the boat planks. It wasn't until the water flowed through the opening that the pressure let up and the boat could be moved. The anglers dragged it to land. They decided to come back in the spring and replace the hacked plank. In an inflatable dinghy they let themselves drift downstream to Abaza.

'Could have been worse,' Igor said when the men were gone. 'Two people have drowned this year already.'

A few hours later, in the early afternoon, I noticed that something was wrong with Igor. He drove more and more slowly. When I asked him what the matter was he pointed to the river. 'We don't have much water under the keel. The level is lower than usual for this time of year.'

I felt my heart sink – it was clear to me that further upstream the river would conduct even less water. 'Will we get through?' I asked anxiously.

Igor avoided my eyes. 'We'll see.'

During the next few hours we regularly passed places where the river was hardly half a metre deep. Igor slowed the boat down to walking pace and wound his way through the rocks. Sometimes we had to get out, in order to take the weight off the boat and move it forward by hand.

Shortly before sunset Lyonya, the forestry inspector who was sitting next to me, suddenly pointed upstream. 'Do you see that house?'

I nodded. A good distance away a bright timber construction loomed between the trees.

'My kingdom.' Lyonya grinned. The house stood on the border of the nature reserve. He and his colleagues had built it a few years before as a guard post. 'Comfortable. You'll see.' Then his face suddenly grew serious. 'In front of the house the river is extremely shallow. If we get through there, everything will be fine, the water gets deeper further on. If not ...' He did not finish the sentence.

Shortly before we reached the house, the river divided into several branches. Igor moored the boat on the shore and proceeded on foot with Lyonya and me to search for the deepest passage. In most spots the water ran over gravel beds, it was hardly ten centimetres deep. 'That won't work,' Igor murmured, shaking his head as we rejected one branch after the other. 'Too shallow.' Only the last branch looked reasonably navigable, but about halfway through we came across rapids. Between angular rocks, the water shot downhill. Sceptically, Igor examined the incline. 'Let's try it.'

We waited on the shore while he fetched the boat. Slowly he manoeuvred it to the lower end of the rapids, then he pushed the throttle. With a jolt, the bow lifted from the water and the boat shot upstream, only to get stuck just before the crest. The motor fought for a moment, but the current was stronger. With a nasty scratching the boat slipped backwards over the rocks, back into the deeper water.

The second attempt ended the same way. The third time Igor jerked the rudder to the right just before the crest, in the hope of finding a deeper passage. For a moment it looked like it would work. Then the boat suddenly careened sideways into the stream. I saw Igor's eyes widen in panic as the bow drifted further and further to the right. Groaning and squealing it was pushed over the rocks, turning on its axis until there was water under the keel again and the boat glided downstream in the opposite direction.

I only understood how close Igor had come to capsizing when I saw his trembling hands. At the same moment, I realised that it was over. Desperately, I stared at the river. For the second time it had thrown me off the track just before the finish. I had only made it a few kilometres further than during the first attempt.

Silently we dragged our luggage to the hut. It wasn't until we had eaten and were watching the sparks of our camp fire dance through the pitch-black night that we slowly found our voices again.

'How much further is it?' I asked. 'Can we go on foot?'

Lyonya looked at me sceptically. 'Too far. You have never been in the Taiga. You don't know what it's like.'

Galina nodded. She knew. 'You hardly make any progress. There are no paths whatsoever. You crawl through undergrowth, over the mountains, across the river. I almost gave up last time, even though we only had to walk for half a day then. The boat driver dropped us off a lot further upstream.'

'From here it's at least two days,' Lyonya said. 'More likely three.'

'Impossible,' Galina whispered.

Depressed, I hung my head.

'Jens,' Igor suddenly said. He had not spoken a word since the incident with the boat. 'Why is this story so important to you?'

I explained it to him. As the campfire slowly burned down, I told the complete story for the third time in a few weeks, from beginning to end. Igor and Lyonya listened silently. Only now did I tell them about the failed boat tour with San Sanych and Misha, which I had avoided until now, because at the time we had headed into the nature reserve without permits.

'Misha …' Something suddenly seemed to occur to Lyonya. 'A beefy fellow?'

I nodded.

'Green sports boat?'

I nodded again.

'Around the end of June?'

I nodded a third time.

Lyonya grinned. 'I was on the river that day. You overtook me. I remember it specifically – there was a passenger sitting in the boat who did not fit in with the others.'

Perplexed, I looked at him. I only now recalled the boat we had overtaken on that day – I saw San Sanych in front of me, how he had bellowed in my ear that the three men on board were the guards of the nature reserve.

'You should have been travelling with me,' Lyonya said. 'At the time the water was so high I could have brought you right up to Agafya's front door.'

For over an hour we sat around the campfire and watched as the logs gradually burned up. The conversation slowly digressed, jumping from homeland to homeland: Galina and Olga talked about Krasnoyarsk, Igor and Lyonya about the Taiga, I about Germany. From time to time Lyonya and I exchanged glances – we were still marvelling at the strange coincidence that had brought us together on the river that June day, without us being aware of each other.

When the last piece of wood toppled over, Lyonya looked me in the eyes. 'Listen, Jens,' he said. 'The way through the Taiga is difficult, but it's not fatal. If it's so important to you, let's try it.'

The next morning we left early. Galina and Olga rode back to Abaza with Igor, Lyonya and I walked in the opposite direction. When we parted, I felt guilty – the two women had done everything possible to get me here, and now they could not come along.

'Don't think about it,' Galina said. She had spent half the night writing a letter for Agafya which she asked me to take along: four pages, tightly inscribed with Church Slavonic letters.

Lyonya and I stood watching as the boat went its way. When it disappeared behind a bend in the river, the only thing left of it was the noise of the engine. It grew quieter and quieter, before the forest swallowed it.

We walked the entire day. After the first half hour I hardly noticed my surroundings anymore, because my field of vision became restricted to my rubber boots and the small patch of undergrowth directly in front of them. We climbed more than we walked. My feet rarely touched the forest floor, which had to be somewhere deep below me, covered by chaotic layers of decaying wood. Fresh shoots crept from the dead subsoil and stretched towards the light, past dying trees resting in the arms of their living neighbours. The entire forest was in cannibalistic motion, it buried its dead and fed on their humus, it lived because it died.

Stepping out from the undergrowth after the first three hours, we reached the banks of the river again. Lyonya pointed downstream. Not very far away I saw a wooden house standing between the trees. It took me a moment to realise that it was the hut where we had spent the night. We had barely covered one kilometre.

Whenever we could, we walked along the side of the river, grateful that we could cover short stretches of the way on firm gravel beds, before steep cliffs would cut off our path again, or swamps, or barriers of driftwood piled up several metres high, which would force us to dodge back into the woods. A few times we ran into dead ends that compelled us to wade across the Abakan and continue our way on the other shore. The river crossings were nerve-racking. In some places the ice-cold water was almost waist deep. The shore seemed infinitely far away, the backpack threw me off balance and the current angrily tugged at my legs. The knowledge that at the slightest misstep the river would sweep me far downstream was paralysing.

In the early evening a couple of dilapidated wooden huts appeared in front of us. It was the abandoned geologists' settlement, whose inhabitants had left almost two decades ago. Only parts of the walls were left of most of the houses, the rest had become one with the forest floor. Lyonya headed for a tiny hut that he and his forestry co-workers had repaired a few years ago. They used it as a makeshift hunting lodge. Inside there was a small cast iron oven. We gathered up firewood, then we took off our soaking wet clothes and hung them up to dry overnight.

Shortly before sunset Lyonya grabbed a fishing rod and walked to the river. Barely a quarter of an hour later he came back with a thick bundle of graylings. We gutted them, scraped off the scales and roasted them over the campfire. They tasted heavenly. When I told Lyonya, I saw his gold teeth shining in the darkness. He was smiling.

'The best fish are just a bit upstream,' he said. 'Where Agafya lives. She is not stupid, your Agafya, she knows where life is good.'

'Do you know her well?' I asked.

Lyonya nodded vaguely. 'Better than most, I guess. I met her here, when I worked in the geologists' camp – I was a drillmaster. Ever since I've been taking care of the forest, I visit her once a year, after the thaw. To see whether she is still alive.'

Lyonya thoughtfully poked the embers with a branch. 'You should be glad that you didn't show up at her place with those two idiots. Agafya would not have spoken a word to you. She takes a good look at the people who knock on her door.'

'Do you think she will talk to me?'

He laughed. 'Don't worry! She will not stop talking. You will be sitting in her hut from morning till evening, while I go fishing – I know all of her stories by heart.'

The next morning fog lay over the river, coloured red by the rising sun. Endless mountain ranges surrounded us, some of their peaks still covered by snow. I felt the hairs on my arms stand up – there was something terrifying about the infinity of the Taiga. It seemed as if the forest returned my gaze with cold indifference. Whether I was alive or not did not make any difference.

For a second time we walked all day. We crossed swamps and mountains, crawled through undergrowth, waded through the Abakan. At one river bend it took us almost an hour to crawl metre by metre through a field of driftwood. On all fours we balanced our way across uprooted tree trunks, wedged together like sticks in the Mikado game of a giant.

Around noon Lyonya stopped to point at a spot in the sand on the river shore. When I looked closer, I recognised the impression of a bear paw. It was frighteningly large and frighteningly fresh. 'A few hours old,' Lyonya said. Grinning, he looked at me. 'Trust your nose. You can smell bears before you can see them. They smell like vinegar. Like vinegar and pepper.'

As we proceeded, the entire Taiga smelled like vinegar and pepper. I was suddenly glad about the automatic rifle that Lyonya was carrying across his shoulder.

In the evening, shortly before sunset, we fought our way through an agonisingly long stretch of undergrowth. When the trees finally thinned and the shore appeared in front of us, Lyonya suddenly grasped my arm. He pointed to the river. I saw a kind of dam that led from one bank to the other, composed of raw logs and clearly made by human hands. A fish trap, I thought. It must be a fish trap.

Then I noticed the woman. She knelt on the wooden beams in a dark dress near the middle of the river, her back turned to us. With a hatchet she worked on her fish trap. The roar of the river was so loud that she had not noticed us. For a few minutes we stood on the shore without moving and watched her, until she suddenly straightened, turned in our direction, and balanced her way over the wooden beams.

When she noticed us she smiled. Agafya Lykova did not seem a bit surprised.

The Long Walk to Paradise

When I think back on Agafya today, I hear her voice before I see her face. She speaks, but I do not hear any words, only an unmistakable melody. She seems to be singing. It sounds like a faint, unfinished song not intended for an audience.

For five days and four nights I heard her singing voice almost constantly. Each of its melodic variations impressed itself on me, even if I did not always understand the text. Sometimes I was not sure whether Agafya herself knew the text exactly. When she spoke, it often sounded as if her song drifted aimlessly and at random through fragments of memory and verses of scripture, through family tales and the life stories of people she had known.

When Lyonya and I set out to leave on the fifth day, the melody had become so familiar to me that I could not imagine Agafya in silence.

Even today I wonder if her song pauses when there is no listener nearby, or if she continues singing – for the birches, for the bears, for herself.

I no longer remember the beginning of the song. It probably did not have one. It emerged seamlessly from the roar of the river when Agafya stood before me that evening for the first time, a tiny woman with a giant hatchet in her hand.

'… Lyonya has come. He has brought somebody …'

She looked older and at the same time younger than I had imagined her. Her face, framed by two headscarves worn one over the other, was weathered and wrinkled with age, but Agafya smiled like a child. She could hardly have been one and a half metres tall. A floor-length dress, pieced together from dark, coarse woollen fabrics, disguised her figure, but she was clearly not very strong; her shoulders must have been smaller than the tree trunks from which her fish trap was composed. How this tiny woman had heaved the wood into the river was difficult to imagine.

'Karpovna!' Lyonya always addressed Agafya by her patronymic. 'I have brought you a fine guest, Karpovna! You can tell him all of your stories!' He spoke to her the way you speak to very old people: a little louder than necessary, a little more genially than necessary.

For a long time I had thought about how to explain to Agafya where I came from. But when I mentioned the name of my home country, a knowing smile crossed her face.

'Germany …' she repeated. It sounded as if she was trying to remember something. 'There was a king, in Germany. He had a wife, but he wanted to marry another. The Pope would not give him his blessing. That was in Germany.'

I could not place the story – was she talking about Henry VIII, was she confusing Germany with England?

'Who told you that?'

'I read it in a book. I have many books.'

'Show him your books, Karpovna! Why are we standing around here?'

While we walked along the river, the evening sun sank behind the mountains. The valley turned red before it paled. I was in a strange mental state, dead tired and wide awake at the same time, exhausted from the hike, electrified by our arrival. I could hardly feel the weight of my backpack anymore, everything seemed strangely light, as if the world in which I had landed was not quite real. Agafya walked in front of me, so close that I could make out the irregular seams in her dress, the dirt under her fingernails, the notches in her hatchet. I memorised every detail with the nervousness of a dreamer who knows that he may wake up at any moment.

I was only half listening when Lyonya told me the name of a smaller tributary which flowed into the Abakan just behind the fish trap: the Yerinat. We continued walking on its shore, until the dense forest suddenly opened up. A clearing wound its way up the mountainside. Three small wooden houses stood about halfway up. Above them I could make out the furrows of a potato field.

The oldest of the three huts was half-dilapidated. Agafya had lived in it until her father had died. The two other houses, which were visibly newer, had been built by Lyonya and his forestry colleagues. Agafya lived in the one on the left. Lyonya disappeared into the right one to unload our backpacks.

I unpacked the gifts I had brought along with me: the headscarf from Doctor Nazarov, the letter from Agafya's cousins in Kilinsk, the jar with the home-pressed sunflower oil, a woollen blanket that I had bought as a gift and finally the letter from Galina, the linguist. Smiling, Agafya turned all the objects over in her hands, as if she was pondering their religious adequacy. In the end she put the headscarf, the blanket and the sunflower oil on a woodpile in front of her hut. Only the letters remained in her hands as she went inside.

A campfire was smouldering between the houses, with a pan full of fish roasting over the embers. While I was wondering who had put them on the fire, a very small man with a very long beard suddenly stood before me. He reached out his hand. 'Alexei.' The high voice did not fit his beard.

Alexei was a distant relative of Agafya's. He visited her each year around this time. Usually he would stay a few weeks to help her with the winter preparations. He came from one of the Old Believer communities in the Altai Mountains. As it turned out, it was a neighbouring village of Kilinsk, the place where I had met Agafya's cousins.

We could not talk for long. When Lyonya returned, he grabbed me by the arm and pushed me into Agafya's hut. 'Here, Karpovna! Tell him your stories! The man has come all the way from Germany!'

I cannot say in retrospect how long she talked that first night – two hours, three, maybe four? Outside the tiny window of the hut, darkness soon descended. Only the moon cast a trapezium of blue light on the floor, otherwise there was nothing left by which I could have measured the time. Even Agafya half disappeared in the night, I could only make out the left side of her face, the one that was lit by the moon. The narrow plank bed on which she sat was strewn with jumbled household items that I could only vaguely recognise in the dark – pieces of fabric, baskets made of birch bark, a metal tub, books, the barrel of a gun. I wondered where Agafya slept. I wondered if she slept at all.

The chaos sprawled over the edge of the bed, it filled the entire hut. The floor was littered with firewood, work tools and baskets full of germinating potatoes. Piled on a shelf were sewing utensils, and behind them three large icons leaned against the wall, their motifs unrecognisable in the darkness. Herbs were hung out to dry under the low ceiling, battered cookware lay next to a giant clay oven that took up a good third of the hut. I could hear the chewing sounds of two goats that lived in a tiny wooden box next to the stove. Their pungent smell attracted insects. It was the season of the *mozhki*, those tiny Siberian flies whose bites I had been warned about in Abaza. The hut was full of them. They gnawed away at my hands while I was trying to transcribe Agafya's singing sentences into my notebook, without really seeing what I was writing due to the darkness. The only thing I could clearly make out the next morning was the figure 7453, the year of Agafya's birth, counted by the old Byzantine church calendar.

'... Easter fell on 6 May that year, although by your calendar it was 23 April, and you call the year 1945, but 7453 years had passed since the creation of the world ...'

Sometimes she would unexpectedly reach for one of her books while she was speaking. She heaved the centuries-old volumes onto the moonlit window sill, unlocked the iron clasps, opened the worn leather covers and quickly found the passages she was looking for. The first time it took me a few seconds to realise that her chant had changed into actual singing – the shift was minimal. She sang liturgies to me, Orthodox prayers the way they had been sung before the church schism – not one hallelujah too many, not one too few.

Although she was sitting hardly a metre away from me, I sat on the edge of my stool with my body bent forward, my notepad on my knees, trying to follow her singing. That first night my pen often hovered over the paper without moving. I understood little. I had not yet grown accustomed to Agafya's song, to the seemingly aimless drift of her sentences, to the way she stretched her words, words I had never heard, because no one used them anymore but her.

Eventually I put the notepad aside and gave up trying to wring meaning from the words. I simply listened to the sound of her voice. The very fact that she sang, that she was sitting in front of me, that this woman existed at all, was more than I could grasp in one night.

Lyonya and Alexei were already asleep when I entered the second hut. I rolled my sleeping bag out on a plank bed and crawled into it. There was a tiny window right next to my head. I looked out into the night. An almost full moon hung above the mountains, its reflection danced in the river, trembling. The Taiga suddenly seemed as bright as day. With an unreal clarity the outlines of the pine trees stood out against a sky, below which no man was awake but me.

'Karpovna! What have you dragged in here again?'

Lyonya, Alexei and I sat eating breakfast when Agafya entered the hut. Smiling, she put a loaf of bread and a bag of prunes on the table. It was a ritual that would start each morning over the following days. Smiling, Agafya would enter the hut and bring us gifts, a sack of potatoes, a basket of cranberries or a handful of pine nuts. She never ate with us, and I never saw her eat alone; her meal times were a closely guarded secret. When she visited us for breakfast, she spoke to us without sitting down, she just stood beside the table.

Lyonya grabbed the bag with the prunes. It was a sealed plastic package, printed with colourful letters – apparently some visitor had given it to Agafya as a gift.

'Karpovna, what are we supposed to do with this? Keep the vitamins around for the winter.'

Agafya laughed softly, as if Lyonya had made a joke. 'But I do not eat that. It has the barcode on it.'

The word sounded bizarre coming from her mouth, like a sudden flash of colour in a black-and-white film.

'Karpovna, don't be silly. The barcode won't do anything to you.'

Again she laughed. 'John wrote that it is the sign of Satan. Earlier it was a different sign, a red star, father talked about it. Then it was a hammer and a sickle. Now it is the barcode.'

'Agafyushka, you are looking for Satan in the wrong place.' Alexei plucked breadcrumbs out of his beard. 'Satan hides from us, we cannot see him. Do you know where he is hiding? In the television! I'll explain it to you. There are 24 frames per second. But sometimes there are 25 or 26, sometimes even 31! No one can see that fast. Only the devil knows what is being shown to us there.'

For a few more minutes the conversation revolved around Satan's hiding places. When Agafya finally left the hut, I asked Lyonya and Alexei to explain a few of her sentences to me, which I had not quite understood.

'What is there to explain?' Lyonya looked me in the eyes. 'Do you think I understand her? No one can figure her out. She's an old woman. God only knows what is going on in her head.'

Agafya's world is small. Its eastern border is the bank of the river. To the west, the potato patch climbs up the mountainside in steep terraces, for about 100 metres, enclosed by dense Taiga. A narrow footpath leads into the forest on the southern side of the potato field, to a small wooden shed that Agafya uses to smoke fish in the summer. The only direction in which Agafya moves a little bit further away from her hut is to the north, along the river, to the fish trap. Just beyond it, a couple of willows stand by the river. Every morning Agafya cuts off a few branches here, which she feeds to her goats. She rarely goes any further north than where the willows are. All in all, her world is hardly a square kilometre in size.

For five days I was constantly at her side. We emptied the fish trap together in the mornings, cut willow branches, fed the goats. Agafya gutted the fish, I scaled them. We pulled the weeds from the potato field, we stacked firewood, we repaired the roof of the hut and mended the holes in the fish trap. Only for eating and for praying did Agafya withdraw, otherwise she accepted my presence with a naturalness that surprised me until the end. She spoke almost continuously. Her chant began in the morning, when she appeared in the guest hut with her breakfast gifts; in the evening, when we were sitting in her cabin together, she would talk well into the night. It seemed she was happy to have a listener.

Surprisingly soon, I tuned in to the sounds of her language. After the first day spent at her side, I was able to follow her stories to some degree. The outdated phrases which I had not understood at first returned so regularly that I soon guessed their meaning. Still, I regularly lost the thread when Agafya's tales seamlessly jumped from the biographical to the biblical, as if there was no clear boundary between the two. But little by little the fragments of her life story that I got to hear between river bank and forest edge, between potato field and fish trap, began to add up and form a picture.

Her father, Karp Ossipovich Lykov, had been born a good decade before the Revolution, the child of a Siberian family of Old Believers. Agafya's grandparents, whom she never met, raised their nine children in a tiny settlement called Tishi, located on the shores of the Abakan, about 100 kilometres upstream from Abaza. The village consisted of ten or 12 houses, inhabited by large Old Believer families like the Lykovs, who lived in Tishi in almost complete seclusion from the world.

Young Karp Lykov's beard was not yet very long when one day a revolutionary planning squad turned up in Tishi. The Bolsheviks took a good look at the village. In the end they pointed at the Old Believers' fish traps. 'Very good,' they said, 'the state needs fish – from now on, your settlement will be a fishing cooperative.'

The Old Believers did not think too much of that idea. Overnight they gave up their village. Some of them fled into the Altai Mountains. Others, including the newly married Karp Lykov, moved upstream along the Abakan, deeper into the Taiga. They settled down on a tributary called Kair. The Old Believers had hardly built new houses for themselves when the next bunch of uniformed people turned up. This time the Bolsheviks made no effort with the stubborn hermits. Instead of talking about cooperatives, they unceremoniously pointed at the Old Believers' fishing nets: 'Hand them over! The state needs nets!'

The Old Believers did not want to give up their nets. A shot was fired. Karp Lykov's brother collapsed, the bullet had hit him in the stomach. He bled to death while the Bolsheviks packed up the nationalised fishing nets. Before they disappeared, they shouted: 'Your children belong to the state! Send them to school or we will come to pick them up!'

After that the Old Believers split up a second time. The younger families fled to the Altai Mountains. A few old people, including Karp Lykov's parents, stayed on the Kair. Karp Lykov himself, who had two small children, did neither the one nor the other. He knew about the 'godless science' that was taught in the Bolshevik schools. He also knew the Old Believer settlements in the Altai Mountains, and he did not believe that his children would be any safer there. So he moved in the opposite direction: upstream along the Abakan, even deeper into the Taiga.

When the family separated, Karp's mother prayed to God: 'You have taken one son, now take my other children as well, take all nine of them. Do not let them suffer in this world.'

In the years before the war broke out, God took Yevdokim and Stepan, Anastasiya and Alexandra, Feoktista and Fioniya, Anna and Darya. But He did not take Karp Lykov.

A few years later Karp's wife Akulina gave birth to her fourth child in the Taiga. Agafya was born on the shore of the Yerinat, in the same place where she lives today.

Shortly after her birth the Lykovs, who had not encountered any people for years, ran into two stray border guards by the river bank. The men talked about the war against the Germans, which had not yet ended. Then they asked Karp Lykov his age. Agafya's father realised that the soldiers thought him a deserter.

That same night the Lykovs began to build a new house, even deeper in the Taiga. For fear of being discovered from the river, they now cleared a patch of arable land in the middle of the forest, nine kilometres away from the shore.

A few years later, while fishing, Agafya's siblings unexpectedly stumbled into a group of anglers, who casually inquired about the children's age. Apparently they wondered why they grew up so far from the nearest school. After that the Lykovs stopped fishing. They avoided the banks of the river. For three decades they encountered no other humans.

It was the hardest period of their solitary life. The arable land they had cleared in the forest was so high up that no grain would grow on it. Peas no longer flourished either, only potatoes and onions and carrots. Apart from that, the Lykovs ate what the forest had to offer: mushrooms, berries, roots, herbs, fern leaves and birch sap. They dug animal traps in which sometimes an Altai wapiti would get caught, or a wild boar or a wood grouse. They cooked the meat and let it dry in the sun for the winter. They baked bread from potatoes and grated pine nuts, sewed their clothing from hemp and flax, made their shoes from birch bark and animal skins.

When Agafya was 15 years old, the Lykovs woke up one winter morning to find a trail of gnawed grains on the floor of their hut. It ended in front of a gap in the outer wall. A rodent had invaded and destroyed the family's seed supply overnight. In the summer the Lykovs sowed what was left. In the autumn they brought in a meagre harvest. In the winter Agafya's mother died of starvation. On her deathbed she asked her husband to dig six graves, one for each of them. When the end comes, she said, lie down in the graves, die like Christians. After the mother had died, the father and the brothers began to dig. The ground was frozen so hard that they left it at one grave.

The years passed quietly. Five of the Lykovs lived on, they worked and they prayed, they prayed and they worked. Sometimes they would see aeroplanes moving through the sky, without knowing that they were aeroplanes. Sometimes at night they would catch sight of stars that did not stand quietly in one place like all the others, but moved in glowing paths. They were the first satellites, but that too the Lykovs learned only later.

Apart from these celestial phenomena, the world beyond the Taiga remained distant to them. The two older siblings had only vague memories of childhood encounters with other people, while the two younger ones, Dmitry and Agafya, had never seen anything other than their small piece of forest. Their father often told them about the world that he had left behind, but he could not tell them anything about what had become of that world.

'We did not know whether any of our relatives were still alive,' Agafya said. 'We did not know whether the persecutions had ceased, whether there were any Christians in the world besides us.'

The Lykovs said their prayers together, and they split up their work. Savvin, the oldest son, was responsible for the firewood, for tanning animal skins, for making shoes. Dmitry, the younger one, took care of the fishing and later the hunting. Natalya, the eldest sister, cooked and sewed. Agafya handled the vegetable plot.

Keeping the calendar was also one of Agafya's tasks. The years, months and days elapsed in time with the old church calendar. Every morning Agafya would determine which saint, which icon was to be celebrated, what liturgy to be prayed. In the four decades of their isolation the hermits did not lose a single day.

One day, in the year 7486 after the creation of the world, when Easter fell on 30 April, 1978 years after Christ's birth, the sky began to roar. An iron dragonfly swept over the Lykov's hut, large and dark and low. For a while it hovered motionless above the potato field, then it approached the hut. The roar was deafening. When the dragonfly disappeared, the Lykovs knew that they had been discovered.

A few days later Agafya heard strange animal sounds in the forest. She ran home and told her father. The father listened. Dogs, he said, frowning. Agafya had never heard a dog.

As the barking grew closer, it mixed with voices. Then four people stepped out from the forest, three men and a woman. For a few seconds the geologists and the hermits faced each other wordlessly, the former full of curiosity, the latter full of fear, and both confused by the strange clothes the others were wearing.

'Who are you?' the geologists asked.

'True Christians,' Karp Lykov answered.

After a few uncomfortable minutes a conversation began. At first incredulously, then with relief, the Old Believers realised that the unexpected visitors meant them no harm.

The first return visit took place after a few days. With baskets full of potatoes and pine nuts the Lykovs showed up in the geologists' camp. They fought off all attempts to present them with gifts in return, stubbornly shaking their heads in denial – it is not allowed for us, they said. Suspiciously, they eyed the geologists' tools. It was not until the station manager explained the purpose of ore drilling to them that they nodded full of understanding. For 40 years they had been using the same worn-out tools. No one had to explain the importance of iron to them.

A kind of friendship developed. As time drew on, the Lykovs lost their shyness. They still would not take any provisions from the geologists, but they did accept other gifts: fabrics, rubber boots, an axe, two goats. The most important gift, however, was the news that the Old Believers were apparently no longer threatened by persecution – for the first time in three centuries.

Three years after the family had been discovered, Dmitry began to cough. He continued to work – it was autumn, the potatoes had to be harvested. The cough grew worse. For a few days Dmitry lay motionless on his cot. Then he was dead. Two and a half months later Savvin died, and ten days after him Natalya. Agafya also fell sick, she was sure she would not see the end of the week. But after a few days, the cough eased off.

Of the Lykovs, only the old father and his youngest daughter remained. Together they dug three graves. They waited for the end of winter, then they packed their stuff and moved back to the shore of the Yerinat, where life was easier than in the mountains. Agafya was 36 when she returned to the place where she was born. It was the second and last move of her life.

During our hike through the Taiga Lyonya had told me about a second hermit, a neighbour of Agafya's. His hut was a few hundred metres further downstream. It was not until the second day that I got around to visiting him.

When Yerofey opened the door for me, I must have looked pretty dumbfounded, even though Lyonya had prepared me. In front of me stood a broad, bearded man of about 60, whose right leg was missing. He wore a Soviet-made prosthesis that looked more like a relic from the tsarist era – a pirate's wooden leg. Grinning, Yerofey enjoyed the element of surprise. Then he invited me into the hut, where he dropped his massive body into an armchair. He looked like a good-natured, one-legged bear.

Before his accident Yerofey had worked as a drillmaster in the geologists' settlement, just like Lyonya. He still remembered the day when a few of his colleagues had told him they had discovered a potato field in the middle of the Taiga. At first Yerofey thought it was a joke – it was not the first time he heard stories about incredible Taiga discoveries. But a little later the hermits turned up in the geologists' camp in person. Not everyone got along with them right away. They smelled, they talked incoherently, they were afraid of drill bits and diesel generators. But Yerofey liked the Lykovs immediately. He took them into his Siberian bear heart.

Ten years later the geologists' settlement closed. For a few years Yerofey continued to work as a drillmaster, in the oil fields of Siberia.

But soon he felt that he was missing something. At first he did not know what it was. Then he realised that he missed the Taiga. More and more often he reminisced about the Lykovs, those strange people who seemed so happy in their self-chosen solitude. Perhaps, Yerofey thought, it is the solitude that makes them happy.

He gave up his profession. Yerofey became a fur trapper. He spent whole winters alone in the Taiga, camped in tiny hunting lodges, far away from all people, surrounded only by snow and pine trees. It was the happiest time of his life.

It ended in tragedy. One day in the Taiga Yerofey caught frostbite on two of his toes. It was winter, he was stuck in the hunting lodge, unable to get help. By the time a helicopter picked him up in the spring, his entire foot was black.

In the hospital they cut off his toes. The wound did not heal. They amputated his foot. The wound festered. Eventually they removed Yerofey's entire leg, with only a stump of his thigh remaining. The pain did not subside. One day a doctor took Yerofey aside. He explained that the second leg was also in danger.

'What can I do?' Yerofey asked.

'Not much,' the doctor said. 'Avoid sources of infection. It would be best to move to the countryside, to a germ-free environment.'

And so it happened that Yerofey decided to emigrate to the Taiga.

A few years earlier Agafya's father had died. Yerofey knew that the hermit needed help. He also knew that a one-legged man is no great help in the Taiga. But a one-legged man is still better than no man at all.

Yerofey's son brought him to the Taiga. They loaded up the boat with a few belongings and headed out. When they arrived, the son built a small hut for his father on the bank of the river, a few hundred metres away from Agafya. The hermit was glad that her new neighbour was an old acquaintance.

Yerofey made himself at home. Among the belongings he had brought with him was a swarm of bees. All summer long Agafya and Yerofey drank their herbal tea with honey. In the winter the bees died.

The bees had six legs, Yerofey only one. The bees died, Yerofey survived. He survived the next winter in the Taiga, and the next, and today, 15 years later, he was still alive. His leg had never grown inflamed again.

Once a year his son visited him. He brought food, canned meat, canned milk, canned vegetables. Usually the son stayed for a few weeks, to patch up the hut and chop firewood for the winter. There was enough firewood for two, and Agafya was glad that she did not have to chop it herself anymore. In return, she gave Yerofey two sacks of potatoes every month.

Only after the third or fourth day of my stay did I realise that, except firewood and potatoes, there was no longer very much that united Yerofey and Agafya. When the two of them met on the banks of the river, they greeted each other, but I never saw them in conversation. Before I managed to ask Yerofey about it, he brought it up himself. There were religious conflicts between them. Yerofey had never brought himself to follow Agafya's rigid rules. He believed in God, he even had Old Believer roots in his family, but he did not understand what God had against canned food, why barcodes were the devil's, why you were only allowed to re-light the furnace with a pine spill, not with a lighter.

They had drifted apart. Within a radius of 200 kilometres there was nobody except Yerofey and Agafya, but they lived side by side like neighbours in a row of terraced houses. Neither of them seemed particularly unhappy with this state. Yerofey had gone to the Taiga because he sought solitude. Agafya had stayed in the Taiga because she did not need company.

In retrospect, my days on the Yerinat seem like weeks. Time passed slowly; it seemed to obey other laws than those outside the Taiga. When I listened to Agafya, it sometimes seemed to me as if she lived beyond time, as if the events of the previous day were no nearer to her and no further away than the events of past millennia.

She could trace her family history back to the 17th century. Her ancestors had lived far west of the Ural Mountains, on the Kerzhenets River, a tributary of the Volga, near the town of Nizhny Novgorod. I had heard of the region – it was one of the old centres of Russian Orthodoxy, a land full of monasteries and hermitages which the church schism had transformed into a bastion of Old Believer resistance.

The place Agafya's ancestors came from was called Olenevsky Skete: 'the Deer Monastery'. Agafya pulled a folded sheet of paper out of one of the old books. It was brittle and yellowed beyond recognition, the hand-painted letters barely stood out against the surface. 'Chant of the Destruction of the Deer Monastery', Agafya read aloud. She lifted her gaze from the paper and looked me in the eyes. 'We often sang that in the family, when the others were still alive.'

It was more a prayer than a chant. In syllables of unchanging length, without rhythm or meter, Agafya's voice followed a melody which consisted of only five or six recurring tones. The song was long. It began with a description of an earthly paradise:

Once on the Kerzhenets there was a place
That offered all true believers refuge
Daily we celebrated worship
Uninterrupted was our prayer
Our bells echoed like thunder.

While Agafya was singing, I tried to imagine how the song must have sounded with six voices, sung by the entire family, three bearded basses, three bright soprano voices. I saw and heard the Lykovs sing about the lost world of their ancestors, a paradise of Orthodoxy that was abruptly shattered when the drama of the schism began:

They came in, the merciless judges
And read aloud their commands
They broke open the chapels
From the altar they took the doors
And stole the holy icons
To prohibit us from worship.
But we answered with one voice:
We will not break with our faith.

And so it had begun, the long escape that had led the Lykovs to the Taiga. Their ancestors had left the banks of the Kerzhenets behind them and had wandered eastward, from one place of refuge to the next, century after century. The song must have been written along the way, during the flight, and generations of Old Believers must have sung it while they continued to flee. Even on the banks of the Abakan, 3,000 kilometres away from the paradise of their ancestors, the Lykovs still sang of a flight that would never end.

Like our forefather Adam we have become
Whom God drove from paradise
Because he ate the forbidden fruit
So we too live as exiles
For the sake of our sins.

When the song came to an end, Agafya folded the sheet of paper and put it back in the book where it had rested for centuries. Then she talked about the long route that had led her ancestors to the Abakan. Until now I had assumed that the Lykovs had more or less randomly landed in this area. As it turned out, it was anything but a coincidence.

'They wanted to go to Belovodye,' Agafya said.

At first I was not sure whether I had heard her properly, but Agafya repeated the word: Belovodye. The Russian Atlantis. A place not to be found on any map. Paradise on earth.

'They knew that true Christians lived in Belovodye. And that there were churches. And priests. Even bishops. They wanted to live in Belovodye.'

'And … how do you get to Belovodye?'

'Not at all. It is no longer possible. The route is closed.'

'And before?'

'Before, it was very difficult. Our ancestors had directions, but they don't exist anymore. They were lost. Father knew them, he told me about it.'

Amazed, I listened while Agafya tried to reconstruct the route to paradise from her father's stories. I wrote frantically, but when I later read through my notes, they were not much use in terms of directions. All I could gather was that the Lykovs' ancestors had tried twice to emigrate from the world. The first time they went north, to the Arctic coast. The route to Belovodye was supposed to lead through the waves, but only on certain days. Boats and horses were required, in that order. In the end, the Old Believers were very wet and half frozen, without coming one step closer to paradise.

Their second attempt led them far south, to the Chinese border. For a long time they wandered through the Altai Mountains in search of a bishop who was supposed to lead them to Belovodye, but only under a full moon. Unfortunately, the bishop did not show up. It must have been the wrong mountain range. Or the wrong lunar phase.

Disappointed, the Old Believers turned back. A few hundred kilometres north of the Chinese border they discovered a river which came as close to their idea of a secluded paradise as is possible on earth. The river was called Abakan.

'That was under Tsar Alexander,' Agafya said. 'Before Tsar Nicholas.'

She went on to talk about the persecutions which had driven her ancestors from one tributary of the Abakan to the next, ever deeper into the Taiga. I listened, but I could not stop thinking about paradise.

'Agafya,' I said. 'Are you sure that the route to Belovodye is closed today?'

'Father said so. And also my cousins in Kilinsk. It has been a long time since anyone reached Belovodye. No one knows the way anymore, and whoever knows it would no longer find it, because everything is full of fog there now. That is what they said in Kilinsk. You cannot go there. Not even with a helicopter.'

In the evening, as I sat in the hut with Lyonya and Alexei, I told them about my conversation with Agafya. When Alexei heard the word 'Belovodye', he immediately caught fire.

'The old directions still exist. Agafya keeps them safe in her hut, she just doesn't show them to anyone. Her father told me about them, the old Lykov. He said the route to Belovodye is only open every two years. When the time comes, two lights appear on the peaks of two mountains. You must pass between the mountains, and behind them there is a white river, but that is not yet Belovodye ...'

I saw Lyonya grin. He did not think much of Alexei's stories.

'... you must continue to walk until you reach a lake, where a bishop in a white robe will be waiting ...'

Alexei loved stories. Whenever we sat at the campfire, he liked to tell me about mysterious discoveries he had made on his wanderings in the Taiga: an arsenal of weapons from the civil war, hidden in a cave; the roof shingle of a house, even though there was no house around for hundreds of kilometres; the skeleton of an enigmatic animal, too large for a wolf, too small for a bear.

He was a gentle, warm man with childlike eyes that spotted wonder everywhere. I liked him very much, and I did not understand why he had no luck with women. The last two had left him, taking the children with them. Since then, Alexei had avoided people. Only rarely did he leave the Taiga, he lived by hunting. In winter he hunted sable, in summer Altai wapitis. Stories he hunted all year round.

The day before our departure Alexei told me the story of the cave people.

'One day the old Lykov wanted his oldest son to get married …'

Lyonya moaned. 'Are you starting that again?'

It was early in the afternoon, the three of us were in the hut. Alexei and I were sitting at the table drinking tea, while Lyonya lay dozing on the hearth bench.

'To find a bride, the old Lykov took his son to the cave people.'

The cave people were Old Believers, just like the Lykovs, though they did not hide under trees, but in caves. When the old Lykov turned up amongst them with his son, a willing bride was quickly found. Unfortunately, the families could not agree on where the young couple should live. The cave people did not want their bride to go to the forest, while the old Lykov did not want to send his son to the caves. Only the devil, he said, lives under the earth. Without having achieved anything, the father and his son went away.

'Fairytales,' Lyonya growled.

'I have seen the cave people myself,' Alexei said. 'The old Lykov sent me to them shortly before he died.'

The old Lykov had pressed a package into Alexei's hand and had taught him a few long prayers. 'You must pray,' he said. 'As long as you are praying, the cave people will not shoot at you.' Praying, Alexei set out. When he arrived, two cave people came crawling out of the earth and received the package. They asked how things were in the outside world, 'Still bad?' Alexei nodded, 'Still bad.' The cave people sadly shook their heads and crawled back into their caves.

'Hans Christian Andersen,' Lyonya growled.

'It is true! 28 people live there. I only saw two, but they told me everything. In the summer they gather provisions, in the winter they close the caves from inside and do not come out again until spring.'

'Like bears,' I said in wonder.

Abruptly Lyonya jumped up from the hearth bench. It was not until he grew loud that I noticed how upset he was. 'Storyteller! Be careful what you put into Jens' head! If he writes all of that up, everybody in Germany will laugh at you! Cave people!'

'But it's true!' Alexei sounded offended.

Shaking his head, Lyonya looked at him. 'Listen, I know the Taiga just as well as you do. If there were 28 people living here, I would have met them a long time ago. Where are their potato fields? Where do they chop their firewood? Where is the smoke from their campfires? You cannot hide here anymore, Alexei.'

Later in the evening I met Alexei alone by the campfire. 'Lyonya doesn't want to admit it,' he whispered. 'But it's true. There are still Old Believers here that no one has heard about. Agafya knows them, she just doesn't talk about it. Only sometimes something slips out by mistake, you have to listen to her closely to notice it. Sometimes she will point to the mountains and say: 'Over there.' And then she bites her tongue. I always register what she says, I remember where she points to. Someday I will find them all.'

I did not know what to believe anymore. What Alexei said sounded fabulous and unlikely; Lyonya's arguments were plausible. On the other hand, for days I had been lingering in a world so fabulous and unlikely that I was slowly losing the benchmark for credibility. I had to think of Yuri, my friend from Berlin, and his words about Russia: 'a country where the real stories are more incredible than the invented ones.'

On the way to Agafya's hut, I let my gaze wander over the mountains. The Taiga suddenly seemed strangely changed. Before, I had only seen indifferent infinity in it, a frightening absence of human beings. Now I was no longer sure whether there might be someone out there after all, a hermit, or two, or many, who returned my gaze from afar. The Taiga was staring at me.

But when I asked Agafya about other Old Believers, she vehemently shook her head.

'Only a single family survived. Only one, no more. If there have been others, they died a long time ago.'

She seemed restless during this last night. While she talked, she kept going back and forth between her bed and the windowsill, to spread out sheets of paper in the moonlight and cover them with her painted church alphabet. She was answering the letters I had brought her. It was no easy task for her. She contemplated every phrase for a long time, saying the sentences out loud in a whispered voice. The letter to her relatives in Kilinsk was the hardest one. Several times she read to me what her cousins had written: 'Come to us, why will you not live with us, how many times have we offered?'

'I cannot live with them. I cannot bear the water, I was half dead when they brought me back home. We argued. The cousins said: "The earth turns, it circles around the sun." I read to them from the Scriptures: "the earth stands immovable".'

While she continued to talk, I suddenly regretted that I had gone to Kilinsk. The letter, which would never have been written without my intervention, reopened old wounds. Agafya was tormenting herself. Her decision not to leave the Taiga was firm, but she did not want to offend her cousins.

In the end she answered them with a parable from the Bible. I only half understood what it was about: Simon, Jerusalem, a dark warning – the rest slipped away from me as Agafya's chant returned from the biblical past to the present day.

'I will stay here. Where am I supposed to go? I do not know where there are still Christians in this world. There cannot be many anymore.'

A quiet hissing noise accompanied her words, followed by a sharp odour. When I turned to the stove, I saw that one of the goats had pissed on the floor.

Agafya folded the sheet of paper and put it on the table in front of me. Behind her stood the Saviour. The icon rested beside the window, Christ as Ruler of the World, two fingers raised in a gesture of blessing – as if he was making the old sign of the cross that had driven Agafya into the Taiga.

When she noticed my gaze she went to the oven and lighted a pine spill. She held it in front of the Christ icon. Then she showed me the two other images that stood to the Saviour's left and right. The icons were ancient, painted in the time before the church schism. The centuries had almost obliterated their motifs. All that remained of John the Baptist was a shadow in golden brown darkness. The Last Supper was a black piece of wood. For a few minutes I kept looking at these invisible images, spellbound and speechless. No one could see them – no one but Agafya.

The next morning I got up before everyone else. Quietly I walked past

Agafya's hut and climbed uphill along the edge of the potato field until I reached the upper end of the clearing. On the other side of the valley the sun was rising, a reddish fog hung above the river. My gaze wandered along the Yerinat and on to the Abakan, whose tortuous course Lyonya and I would be following in a few hours, this time downstream.

The sky was riddled with tiny clouds. Unconnected, their white silhouettes floated side by side like the pieces of an unsolvable puzzle.

Thanks

This book would never have been written without the help of many friends and supporters. I would like to thank Leonid Astafyev and his family, Aleksey Bobrinsky, Ivan Branovets, Douglas Cowie, Igor Drozhdin, Oleg Filatov, Anatoly Fomenko, Leonid Gorbatov, Kristina Graaff, Vladimir Gromov, Alexander Gurtsev, Eugene Hayworth, Thomas Hölzl, Sergey Ivanov, Yury Yanoshevsky, Irina Yazykova, the Yerofeyev family, Kirill Kaleda, Galina Kazachinova, Yury Klebanov, Igor Knyazkin, Annika Mühling, Igor Nazarov, Roman Pimenov, Vasily Pivovarov, Yelena Polyakova, Ruslan and Lisa, Aleksandr Zakatov, Aleksandr Sheksheyev and his wife, Gennady Zdanovich, Vladimir Semyonov, the Soldatov family, German Sterligov, Sergey Teryayev, Galina Tolstova, Igor Cherbakov, Tatyana Tyukpiyekova, Sasha Voloshin, Tanya Wood and Vladimir Voronin.

I am grateful to the German 'Fachverband der Konfessionellen Presse' for generously funding parts of my research, as well as the editorial staff of 'Der Tagesspiegel' for their patience and support.

Furthermore, I would like to thank all the authors whose works I have used as sources:

Anna Akhmatova, *Complete Poems of Anna Akhmatova*, tr Judith Henschemeyer (Boston 1992).
Neal Ascherson, *Black Sea. The Birthplace of Civilisation and Barbarism* (London 1995).
Avvakum, *The Life of the Archpriest Avvakum, by himself*, tr Jane Harrison and Hope Mirrlees (London 1924).
James H. Billington, *The Icon and the Axe. An Interpretative History of Russian Culture* (New York 1970); *Russia in Search of Itself* (Washington 2004).

Thomas Bremer, *Kreuz und Kreml. Kleine Geschichte der orthodoxen Kirche in Russland* (Freiburg 2007).

Anton Chekhov, *The Tales of Chekhov*, tr Constance Garnett (New York 2006).

Fyodor Dostoyevsky, *A Writer's Diary*, tr Kenneth Lantz (Evanston/ Illinois 1994).

Orlando Figes, *A People's Tragedy. The Russian Revolution 1891–1924* (London 1997); *Natasha's Dance. A Cultural History of Russia* (London 2002).

Oleg Filatov, *Istoriya dushi ili portret epokhi* (St. Petersburg 2000).

Anatoly Fomenko, *Chronology: Science or Fiction?*, 6 volumes (Olympia/Washington 2003–2006).

Ian Frazier, *Travels in Siberia* (New York 2010).

Arkady Gaidar, *Timur and His Squad*, tr Leonard Stocklitsky (Moscow 1973).

Lidiya Golovkova, 'Khudozhniki i butovskiy poligon', *martyr.ru* (2006).

Maxim Gorky, *Selected Short Stories* (Moscow 1955).

Peter Hauptmann, *Russlands Altgläubige* (Göttingen 2005).

Herodotus, *The Histories*, tr George Rawlinson (London 1992).

Felix Philipp Ingold, *Die Faszination des Fremden. Eine andere Kulturgeschichte Russlands* (Munich 2009).

Vasily Kaleda (ed), *Svyashchennomuchenik Vladimir Ambartsumov* (Moscow 2008).

Ryszard Kapuściński, *Imperium*, tr Klara Glowczewska (London 1994).

Igor Knyaskin, *Bolshaya kniga o Rasputine* (St. Petersburg 2007).

Sheiko Konstantin, *Lomonosov's Bastards* (Wollongong 2004).

Tatyana Lagutina, *Lecheniye Vodkoy* (Moscow 2006).

Leonard A. Magnus (ed and tr), *The Tale of the Armament of Igor* (Oxford 1915).

Philip Marsden, *The Spirit-Wrestlers. A Russian Journey* (London 1998).

Robert K. Massie, *Peter the Great. His Life and World* (New York 1981); *The Romanovs. The Final Chapter* (New York 1996).

Maxim Maximov, 'Mozhno li speshit' s kanonizatsiyey', *Tserkovny vestnik*, 1–2 (2004).

Heiner Müller, *A Heiner Müller Reader. Plays, Poetry, Prose*, tr Carl Weber (Baltimore/Maryland 2001).

Igor Nazarov, *Tayozhnye otshelniki* (Krasnoyarsk 2004).

Nestor, *The Primary Chronicle*, tr Samuel Hazzard Cross and Olgerd P. Sherbowitz-Wetzor (Cambridge/Mass. 1953).

Konrad Onasch, *Icons*, tr Marianne von Herzfeld (London 1963).

Shane O'Rourke, *The Cossacks* (Manchester 2007).

Vassily Peskov, *Lost in the Taiga*, tr Marian Schwartz (London 1994).

Vadim Petrov, *The Escape of Alexei, Son of Tsar Nicholas II* (New York 1998).

Alexander Pushkin, *Pushkin's Bronze Horseman*, tr Waclaw Lednicki (Berkeley/California 1955).

Vadim Redkin, 'Posledniy Zavet', *vissarion.ru* (2010).

John Reed, *Ten Days that Shook the World* (London 1977).

Anna Reid, *Borderland. A Journey Through the History of Ukraine* (London 1997).

Nicholas V. Riasanovsky, *A History of Russia* (New York 2005).

Wolfgang Ruge, *Lenin. Vorgänger Stalins* (Berlin 2010).

Karl Schlögel, *Moscow, 1937*, tr Rodney Livingstone (Cambridge 2012).

Robert Service ('Lenin. A Biography', London 2000)

Alexander Shargunov (ed), *Novy muchenik za Khrista voin Yevgeny* (Moscow 1999).

Alexander Sheksheyev, 'Gaydar i krasny banditizm', *Abakan*, 2 (2006).

Yuri Shevchuk, *DDT: Mir nomer nol* (Moscow 1999).

Mikhail Sholokhov, *And Quiet Flows the Don*, tr Stephen Garry (London 1957).

Viktor Shnirelman, 'The Discovery of Arkaim', *Museum International*, 2 (1998).

Vladimir Soloukhin, *Solyonoye Ozero* (Moscow 1994).

Colin Thubron, *Among the Russians* (London 1983); *In Siberia* (London 1999).

Thucydides, *The History of the Peloponnesian War*, tr Richard Crawley (Oxford 1943).

Galina Tolstova, *Drevo Avvakuma* (Krasnoyarsk 2008).

Leo Tolstoy, *War and Peace*, tr Louise and Aylmer Maude (Oxford 1991).

Irina Yazykova, *Hidden and Triumphant. The Underground Struggle to Save Russian Iconography* (Brewster/Mass. 2010).

Gennady Zdanovich, 'Strana gorodov', *Rodina*, 11 (2001).